MAKING HEADLINES

The History Of Bolton Wanderers Football Club
As Seen Through The Pages Of The

Bolton Evening News

An official Bolton Wanderers Football Club Publication
First Published in Great Britain by Bolton Wanderers Football Club, Reebok Stadium, BL6 6JW

Designed and Printed by
Greenpark Publishing, 151-153 Wick Road, Brislington, Bristol, BS4 4HH
Telephone 0117 977 9188 **Website** www.greenparkpublishing.com

ISBN 0-9537444-4-2

Researched and compiled by

LES GENT

With advice, guidance and help from, at the Evening News, Gordon Sharrock, whose reporting on the Wanderers' ups-and-downs spans almost 25 years; Christine Bell and Jackie Sidebottom in the paper's Library; the Picture Desk, because most of the pictures in the book have been taken by the paper's photographers, past and present (some are also taken by Action Images); Frank Booth; and, of course, Editor Steve Hughes and other management for their support.

Much assistance has also been given from the Wanderers', including Danny Reuben, the Communications Manager; Simon Marland, the Club Secretary and historian; Gareth Moores, the Commercial Director; Andrew and Martin Dean and Tom Hall, the Stadium Tours Manager who also looks after the club museum. I would also like to thank Barry Mills of the Archives and Local Studies Department at Bolton Central Library.

Without the encouragement and commitment to the project of those named above, and others, the task of completing this book would have been a much more difficult and arduous task. Thanks to them all.

Introduction

The story of the origins of Bolton Wanderers Football Club is well known, having been set up in 1874 by scholars and teachers at Christ Church, Deane (nearby where Bolton Institute stands today) to participate in outdoor recreation. In 1877, however, the vicar objected to meetings being held in the schools without him being present (he had been made President), so the headquarters were moved at first to the Gladstone Hotel, close to Pikes Lane, then to the Britannia Hotel on Deane Road and the club re-named Bolton Wanderers because of its "wandering from one headquarters to another".

From the result of that lowly meeting grew the world-wide popular Premiership club that we know today, with a history that rivals that of any other club. The Wanderers have never won the top division title, have often see-sawed between the first and second divisions - and once have fallen as low as the Fourth Division - but have won the F.A. Cup four times (as well as being on the losing side) and other minor cups, and have always been a force in English football.

The first ground for the Christ Church team was Bob's Wood (part of where Heaton Cemetery now stands); then they moved to Smith Fields on Plodder Lane, had a spell at Heywood Park (Park Recreation Ground) then on to Bob Cockles Fields (opposite the Cross Guns pub on Deane Road) before, as Bolton Wanderers, moving to Pikes-lane.

In the middle 1890s Burnden Park was built, and from there and the new ground at the Reebok, Bolton Wanderers have carried the name of the town around the globe, providing not only good local players, but many who appeared for their own various international teams. In modern times, communications such as television and the Internet have made it possible for supporters throughout the world to follow the team's games as they happen, something unheard of until a few years ago, so the following continues to grow.

Throughout this long history, the Bolton Evening News - founded in 1867, seven years before the Christ Church team - its associated sports papers the Football Field, The Buff, The Green Final, and daughter paper the Bolton Journal, have reported the fortunes of the Wanderers, and this book follows those reports, printing them as they appeared over the years. We have tried to determine the most important moments from the end of the 19th century until today, painting a broad picture of the club.

In the early days, not much appears to have been said in the paper, because it was then just another local club playing others in the local league. However, as it became more important and overtook with success those other minor clubs, in the process becoming a founder member of the Football League, the paper became more interested and millions of words have since appeared in its columns. Those using the pseudonyms "The Tramp" and "Olympian" told readers of the "Wanderers" stories until about the 1950s, but among the journalists who have reported since then have been the Haydn Berry, J.K. Fletcher, Harold Hodgson, Frank Booth, and the present incumbent for the past 25 years, Gordon Sharrock.

It may be that your favourite moment or match, or mention of your favourite player, does not appear in this book. If so, we apologise; space is of necessity limited. This is not intended to be a detailed record of the club and player achievements, but more of a general and hopefully entertaining read, reporting major events, but also touching on many subjects which will not have seen the light of day since the report or picture first appeared in the paper. For the same reason of space, many of the articles have also had to be condensed.

However, we have tried to give a fair reflection, through the eyes of newspaper articles of the time, of various events which moulded the club over the years.

In the Beginning

It appears that perhaps the name "Wanderers" was incorporated into the title on August 28, 1877, because there was already a Bolton Football Club, and in the column headed "Football", that club took up most of the space, followed, for example, with a report of the Wanderers' match as this one from November 17, 1877: -

"Bolton Wanderers v Edgworth: On Saturday the first match this season between these two teams was played on the ground of the latter. Edgworth winning the toss decided to play with the wind in their favour. The ball being kicked off, both sides worked hard for about twenty minutes, when rain stopped the game for a short time. Play was resumed, and when half time was called neither side had obtained a goal. Ends were now changed, and a very hot contest waged for a considerable time which ended in a goal for the Wanderers. No other points being gained, the game ended in a victory for the Wanderers by one goal to Edgworth nil."

However, within a few years, indications are that the Bolton Football Club must have gone out of existence, because civic leaders in the early 1880s suggested that the word "Wanderers" should be dropped and the club should be called simply "Bolton", a move that was rejected.

It would be remiss not to mention the history of the Wanderers in those early years, which was not necessarily reported at the time. In 1877 Mr Peter Parkinson became a member of the club, and was one of its leading spirits for many years. He was made President in 1881, and the club launched out on more ambitious lines (he was instrumental in the introduction of Scotsmen into the club) fixtures being arranged with Blackburn Rovers and Preston North End among others. In 1882 players were advertised for, and the Wanderers were the first to win the Bolton Charity Clup, beating Astley Bridge 5-1. Next year they entered the English Cup competition "and after playing a couple of draws with the Druids, were thrown out by a bad decision of the referee". The previous year the Wanderers had lost in the second round of the F.A. Cup to Blackburn Rovers. In 1884, memorable cup ties against Notts were played, when, after a draw, the Wanderers were defeated at Pikes-lane in front of a crowd of more than 26,000.

In the early 1880s, Mr J.J. Bentley became secretary of the club, but in 1885-6 internal problems led to Mr Parkinson and other officials resigning. At a stormy annual meeting which followed, the player W. Struthers was elected secretary rather against his will in place of Mr Bentley, but soon resigned in favour of Mr Fitzroy Norris. At the end of the season the players were discharged, most of them going over to the Halliwell club, but in October, 1887, Mr Bentley resumed his post as secretary, and the club continued its progress.

Even before that, however, in 1885, the Wanderers' team had been engrossed in controversy in the F.A. Cup ...

Contents

Bolton's Town Hall Square, 1887.

PRE 1920s

DATE	WORLD EVENTS	BOLTON EVENTS
1873		Town Hall opened by Prince & Princess of Wales (later King Edward V11 & Queen Alexandra).
1879	Thomas A. Edison invents electric light.	
1883		Bolton Royal Infirmary opened.
1889	Eiffel Tower built for the Paris exposition. Boer War (or South African War): conflict between British and Boers (descendants of Dutch settlers of South Africa).	First locomotive built at Horwich Loco Works - by 1907, the 1000th had been built.
1901	Queen Victoria dies, and is succeeded by her son, Edward VII.	
1905		Cotton industry in Bolton provided 58,000 people with jobs in well over 200 mills.
1910		Pretoria Pit disaster, when 344 miners lost their lives.
1912	Titanic sinks on maiden voyage; over 1,500 drown.	
1914	Outbreak of World War I. UK enters hostilities against Germany.	
1918	War ends in November with armistice. The number of UK war dead runs to several hundred thousand.	

In 1885, the FA ruled that a professional player could only compete in the FA Cup if he had been born within a six-mile radius of the Club's headquarters or ground or had lived in that area for at least two years. This had immediate repercussions on the Wanderers. In the third round of the F.A. Cup they were drawn against Preston North End. Both clubs fielded ineligible players and were disqualified from the competition.

2 JANUARY 1886

OUR PROFESSIONAL PLAYERS

From their recent decisions in the protests of the Bolton Wanderers and the Preston North End, it would appear that the F.A. Committee, now that they have legalised professionalism, are determined to show to clubs belonging to the Association that their rules must be carried out to the very letter, and that any infringement will be severely punished. The particulars of the protests are brief: Drummond (Preston) resided in Scotland about three months during the summer of 1884, and worked in Edinburgh during that time. Against Ross (Preston) that he resided in Edinburgh, was the alleged tenant of a house, and had left the North End to join his old love, the Hearts of Midlothian. Powell (Bolton) was charged with residing in Wales during the summer of 1884, and working there in January of last year.

The cases of Drummond and Powell were both proved, and the two clubs consequently thrown out of the competition, though the Committee were unanimous that neither club knew that the professionals had disqualified themselves, and were therefore not to blame for playing them.

Powell made the mistake in hiding from the Wanderers' Executive that he has been paid for working in Wales, and has gained nothing by his deception. If he retains his position in the team he cannot take part in cup-ties until January, 1887, which circumstance, of course, devalues the value of his services.

The recent legislation of the F.A. shows that they are not to be trifled with. Well conducted professionals have, of course, nothing to fear, but those obstreperous individuals who do not know the difference between right and wrong are beginning to find out that the professionals' lot is not altogether a bed of roses.

7 JANUARY   1888

SCOTCHMEN AT PIKE'S LANE

At New Year's time, the Scots fro' over the border delight, after the manner of their ancient precursors in ante-Saxon days, to make incursions southwards, and, like the Romans, to come, to see, and to conquer. And so as soon as ever the year is on the wane, and only the last day or two has to run of the old year, down troop the Scotchmen from "Edinbro' toon" and elsewhere, to take the Englishmen by storm in the matter of football. Sometimes they do and sometimes they don't. This time the don'ts had it, for the Scotchmen had to return to their native heather beaten at many points.

On Saturday the Wanderers received for their visitors the Kilmarnock team, and in the words of classic story "knocked lumps" out of them, not allowing them to score and placing two to their own credit. The day was all that could be desired, crisp, clear, and as bright as can be expected in these regions of almost perpetual cloud and gloom. The weather was cold and yet not of that searching nature which makes you wonder whether you have any marrow left in your bones or whether all has not been congealed into icy freezibility.

The Scotchmen appeared on the turf, tripping it on the frozen heather, as though certain of victory. But the race is not always to those who first appear on the ground, and it soon became patent that the Scotchmen were not be cocks of the walk. The game commenced spiritedly enough, and soon the ground became slippery and decidedly uncomfortable for the players, while for the spectators the spectacle of two or three of the contestants sprawling on the ground because they could not maintain their equilibrium, was entertaining. The game was a fast and lively one, each set of players infusing as much verve into his display as possible. The backs on both sides were in fine form, and it was difficult to get past them. The Wanderers, however, managed to score once in the first half and once in the second, and won by two to none.

Pikes Lane was the home of the Wanderers until the move to Burnden Park, and obviously attracted good crowds. The pictures were taken in the early 1880s, just after the club had gone to play there.

In 1888, the Wanderers were prominent in the formation of the Football League, being one of the 12 clubs selected to take part.

21 APRIL 1888
ANOTHER LEAGUE PROCLAIMED

The Millennium at hand. No more debts. Both ends to meet. Plain sailing. These, we suppose, are the ideas of the promoters of the New Football League. A dozen Association clubs, who style themselves the pick of the talent, have joined hands for their own mutual benefit, apparently without a care for those unhappily out in the cold.

Here are the names of the twelve New Apostles in alphabetical order:- Accrington, Aston Villa, Blackburn Rovers, Bolton Wanderers, Burnley, Derby County, Everton, Notts County, Preston North End, Stoke, West Bromwich Albion, Wolverhampton Wanderers.

Now we wish it to be distinctly understood that we have not the slightest antagonism towards this "new departure"; on the contrary, we wish all and several the heartiest success. No-one can object to the search for the big gates and the strangling of the demon debt. But is it quite fair to the clubs thus coolly barred out and left to shift for themselves? On what principle has the selection been made? Are the clubs chosen absolutely the strongest, or is it a case of cliqueism in the hope of starving out thriving and dangerous rivals? Does the League deserve to flourish by wholly ignoring the claims of those to whom they refuse membership? There are at least 20 other clubs whom could quite hold their own with a good proportion of the New League.

A strange side to the new picture is that of the twelve members, no fewer than six hail from the county of Lancaster, so the others will have to travel to Lancashire on six separate occasions. Will it pay them?

Personally, writes "Olympian", I do not see the slightest objection to the remaining prominent clubs forming a second League. A second League must naturally take a secondary position for, though several clubs in the present League are not first-class, the majority of them are without doubt the pick of English football, and my suggestion would be to work amicably with the second League, and the four best clubs at the end of the season to be put in competition with the four worst of the first League.

This is believed to be the oldest team picture taken of the Wanderers in the 1882-83 season. On the back row, from left, were J. Kennedy, G. Dobson, A Bromley, J McKernan, W. Steele, and umpire J. Parkinson. Front row: T. Howarth, J. Fallon, W. Struthers, J. Gleaves (captain), K. Devonport, J. Scholes. They had just won the Bolton Charity Cup.

The first team had just won the Charity Cup, the Lancashire Cup, and the Derbyshire Cup when this picture was taken in the 1885-86 season, and they are also pictured in the 1889-90 season.

10 SEPTEMBER 1888

THE FOOTBALL FIELD

The prophets of evil and not good have had their innings as regards the Wanderers. Beaten at Newton Heath on Saturday week, their friends consoled themselves with the reflection "Wait till we see them on their own ground", and the opportunity came on Saturday, when the first of the League fixtures was brought off against Derby County. The result came as a regular "Oh, what a surprise", and is difficult of explanation. In all, no less than nine goals were scored, and scored with an ease seldom witnessed. We never saw more feeble back play, and in this both teams were sinners, the exhibition contrasting widely with the display of Newton Heath against the Wanderers the week before.

At the start the Wanderers had very much their own way, and in the first few minutes Davenport and Brogan had scored three goals between them. Then came Derby's turn, and so well did their forwards acquit themselves that the score stood at four-three in their favour at half time. Later on further disasters befell the Wanderers, who finished up in a minority of three goals, the final reading 6-3.

The play of the Wanderers when once collared was very weak. At the start, when scoring freely, they were on good terms with themselves; but the pace set by the County men seemed too much and wore them down long before the end of the first half. It is difficult to find a reasonable excuse for the result. Undoubtedly weak defence had a lot to do with it, for after getting three ahead the back division ought to have contrived to keep out their opponents. As it was, they were feebleness itself. It is unnecessary to individualise, as the play was all round of the "has been" order. Davenport and Brogan were most noteworthy, and more than once did work in the best style. If the Wanderers are to retain their following they will certainly have to improve on the form displayed until the present time.

On February 1, 1890, the Wanderers took on Sheffield United in the second round of the F.A. Cup. The match should have taken place at Sheffield, but because Sheffield Wednesday were playing at home, United agreed to play the tie at Pikes Lane . . . they probably wished they hadn't, because Wanderers won 13-0.

1 FEBRUARY 1890

VICTORY IN THE F.A. CUP

What price the Wanderers' goal record in the English Cup ties? Belfast Distillery 10-2, Sheffield United 13-0. "Who can play on a ground like this?" asked Mr Maiden, of the United. Answer first time: The Wanderers. Seeing that the "Blades" came of their own option, nibbling at the tempting golden bait dangled by the Wanderers, they can scarcely grumble at a little mud - although it certainly was thick.

The Pike's Laners soon had the measure of their visitors, and the ball was popped through the posts with gratifying regularity. By a strict attention to business the Wanderers soon had the issue out of doubt, Cassidly, Brogan, McNee, and Weir rattling them in capitally. Little Rushton, who partnered Brogan, displayed meritorious energy, and when he gains discretion he will be all right. Even Robinson enjoyed the unique pleasure of scoring a goal, and when the 'baker's dozen' was reached a facetious stand member shouted out encouragingly ' You only want seven more' - to make the score.

5 OCTOBER 1894

BOLTON WANDERERS FOOTBALL AND ATHLETIC CLUB

The prospectus of the new company that is to take over the Bolton Wanderers' Football Club is now issued. The capital required is £4,000 in shares of £1 each. The prospectus sets forth that the Bolton Wanderers is one of the oldest Association clubs in the country, having been established over 20 years, and is entitled to rank with and play the best clubs, on account of being in the First Division of the League.

Owing to the tenancy of the Pikes-lane ground expiring May next, a plot of land (150 yards by 150) has been secured at Burnden, off Manchester Road, from the Corporation, on a 14 years' lease on an annual rental of £130, and this will enable the company to provide a football ground equal to any in the country, and to form a cycling track a quarter of a mile in circumference. Shareholders are entitled to season tickets for football purposes, at reduced rates.

The new ground will have tram conveniences, and the L. and Y. station is only five minutes' walk off, whilst there is the possibility of securing a special siding.

A typical front page of the "Cricket and Football Field" in 1890. That Saturday sports paper of the Evening News was launched in 1884 and published until 1915 when the Buff appeared. With interruptions for the Second World War and a few years afterwards (during the war and until 1952, Evening News' Saturday Finals and White Specials were published), the Buff lasted until 1988. For some time in the early 1950s there were also Green Finals. Many people will recall an Evening News' caravan carrying a small printing machine parked in front of Burnden Park on match days, in which the final results of the days matches were printed and sold as the crowds were leaving the ground!

29 OCTOBER 1894

THE WANDERERS' NEW GROUND

The Central Hall, Acresfield, was crowded last evening, despite the inclemency of the weather, when a meeting of shareholders and others interested in the proposed football and athletic company for Bolton was held, Mr Joseph Magee presiding. At the outset the chairman expressed pleasure to see that there were yet some who took an interest in the Wanderers. (Hear, hear.)

He stated that though they required £3,000 before they could go on with the new ground, only shares to the value of half that amount had been taken up, and they felt they could not go on with that. It would cost £2,500 to lay out the ground and provide a track with stands, and they wanted £500 in reserve. They wished to see whether the public wanted the club to go down or not, and he had therefore called that meeting. Mr J.J. Bentley (secretary) said that under 60 individuals had taken up shares in the company, and less than half a dozen had taken £1 shares. They thought the Wanderers club had a better hold on the working man than that, and they wanted them to express their opinion on the question that night.

The athletic and cycling clubs were not altogether satisfied, and had held aloof, but if they did not want the track, the Wanderers could provide a ground for £2000. A discussion took place, in which it appeared that the athletes were prepared to invest if they could have certain privileges, and it was ultimately decided that a meeting of the cycling and harriers' clubs should be held on Monday evening for them to explain their wants, and state how many shares they were prepared to take.

Several rousing speeches were made by old followers of the Wanderers, Mr J.W. Makant, J.P., stating that he knew there were more than 60 people who would help them, and at the invitation of the chairman a large number of persons came forward, and took shares on the spot, with the result that the chairman announced, amid ringing cheers, that the directors had received such additional shares that night as would encourage them to proceed with a ground for football, at least. He trusted that the enthusiastic meeting would have its effect and that during the coming week they would have all the shares taken up.

If working men did not care to go to the bank, they could bring their half-crowns to the Secretary's office, and take £1 shares, or they could also secure them on the Pikes-lane ground, or any of the directors would oblige them.

Burnden Park was not going to be simply a football ground, it was to have a cycling track, and athletics were also to play a major part. In fact, for a number of years athletic meetings were held there, the first on August 17, 1895, the opening of Burnden Park, when 20,000 people attended, and then on August Bank Holiday Monday, with 15,000 in attendance.

Shortly before, the paper had described the venue . . .
With the completion of the new ground of the Bolton Wanderers and Athletic Company - Burnden Park - Bolton will be able to boast of one of the finest athletic enclosures in the country. Too long this town has had to make shift with rough fields and altogether inadequate conveniences for public athletics, and the want of a cycling track has told greatly against the ambitious wheelman of the district, whilst the old Pikes Lane football ground was not clear, if very familiar, to visiting teams, and spectators of two or three years have had to put up with discomforts seldom now experienced on first-class enclosures.

All this is now remedied, and in a few months, the almost desolate regions to the left of Manchester Road have been changed into a magnificently equippped enclosure which is a credit to both the Company and the town for which it is provided. A better situation could scarcely have been obtained.

The total of the new site is close upon six acres. An enormous amount of tipping has been necessary, and the enclosure is well-elevated. The football portion was finished two or three months since and is in splendid condition - much better than we should have expected so early. The laid portion is 118 yards by 80, and the goalposts are at the Bolton and Great Lever ends.
Strong barriers outside the cycling track have been erected, the running track and football portion being thus also protected. The cycle track, measuring 18 inches from the inside, is a dead quarter of a mile round. The Burnden track is the only cement track in Lancashire, and one of the few in the country. Inside the cycle track there is a cinder running track about seven yards wide.

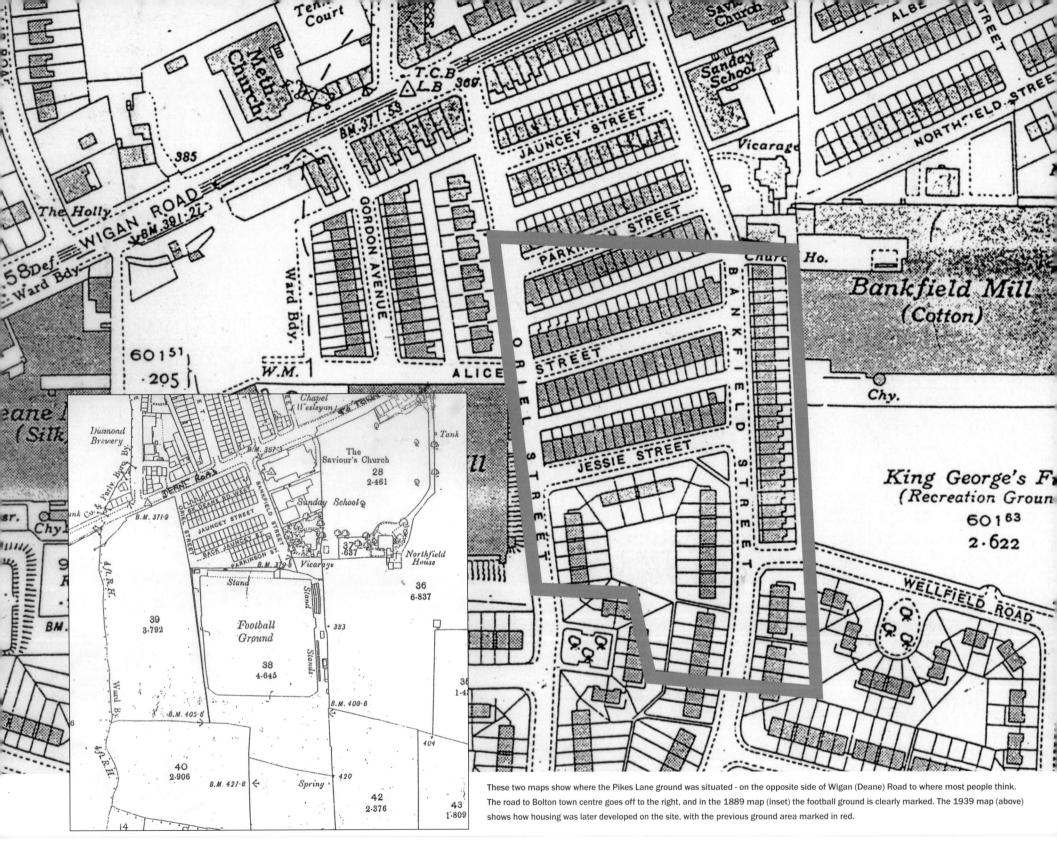

These two maps show where the Pikes Lane ground was situated - on the opposite side of Wigan (Deane) Road to where most people think. The road to Bolton town centre goes off to the right, and in the 1889 map (inset) the football ground is clearly marked. The 1939 map (above) shows how housing was later developed on the site, with the previous ground area marked in red.

OLD BOLTON TALES

FOOTBALL COMES TO PIKES-LANE
(written by Evening News' columnist Quidnunc and published in 1935)

It was a cold day in September, 1881, the sort of Saturday afternoon to tempt people to stay indoors and rest after their week's work rather than encourage them to venture forth. There was a prospect of rain, too.

Thus three men who stood on Deane-rd., near the new Pikes-lane Board School, had the road practically to themselves. It was obvious to anyone who gave them a passing glance that they were brothers. Their features had much in common. Each looked worried.

A man passed. "How do?" he called out. "How do?" said Tom. "Hello" said Bob. Dick merely grinned. The brothers Rawsthorne were much too occupied with their own thoughts to pay much attention to anyone else.

They had hoped for fine weather for the opening match of the new season on the Wanderers' ground at Pikes-lane. And here it was - cold, blowing, and likely to snow. "Not much chance of a big gate," said Tom. "No," replied Dick. Bob didn't bother to make any comment. It seemed so obvious anyway.

Then they walked up Pikes-lane and stopped once more, gazing this time at an expanse of ground on which stood two sets of goal posts. It was a football pitch, but it seemed more like a sea of mud. The prospect only served to make the brothers even more glum. "Looks bad enough," said Dick. "Aye," said Bob, "it does. But perhaps them boards we've put around the edge of the pitch to stand on will help matters somewhat."

As they waited the crowd began to roll in twos and threes, and as they stood stamping their feet the three brothers saw the crowd gradually grow to a few hundreds. The crowd were disussing the last match they had watched - almost the first on the new Pikes-lane ground, when Naylor's team beat Struther's team by 11-7. That was a great game.
Saying that he would go and see if all the team had turned up Tom went over to a small wooden hut that did service as a dressing tent. Shortly afterwards the teams came out and attempted to play football under really shocking conditions. But for all that, play was vigorous, and the crowd was ever urging the home side to even more vigorous tactics. "Kick 'is legs from under 'im," shouted one. "Put thi' feet into 'im," urged another.

The play was rough. But so long as the home side was doing the "rough stuff" the crowd was delighted. When, however, the visiting team - I think it was Eagley - tried the same tactics, the crowd became annoyed and were only appeased when the home side scored. When, after the change of ends, the other side equalized, there was much booing and hissing of the visitors.

When all the crowd had left, the brothers might have been seen crossing Deane-rd. again. Bob and Dick seemed in a happier frame of mind. "It wur a good game," said Dick. "Aye, but they were a rough lot, and that goal should never have been allowed," said Bob. Tom was still sullen. "It was a poor crowd. I don't know what we shall do."

As secretary of the Bolton Wanderers F.C. he could be excused his depression, for it was a big day for the sportsmen - no less than the opening match at the new Pikes-lane ground. And owing to the weather the crowd had not been too good.

He had no visions of the team with a world-wide reputation as League and Cup fighters that was to emerge from that Pikes-lane era in the years to come.

A VETERAN LOOKS BACK TO PIKES LANE
(written by W. Partington, and published first in 1946)

Here we are, shouting for the Wanderers in the F.A. Cup-ties again. My earliest vivid recollections of cup-ties are of thrilling games at Pikes-lane in the early 1880s. I don't know what the charge for lads was in those days, probably 2d, but we didn't always pay it. Oftener, we climbed the boards round the ground and got a good view of the game for nothing, in spite of being driven off from time to time. The Football League was not formed until 1888, but fooball had reached a pitch by 1882 or 1883 to provide exciting times. There was the amazing cup-tie with Notts County when, not only was there a record gate, but all the hillside outside the ground, rising up to Willows-lane, was also crowded. The farmer charged these unofficial spectators 3d each for admission to his fields, but great numbers got through the gaps in the hedges.

Well-known players of those early days I recall were, amongst others, Powell, McKernan, Struthers, Steel, Gleaves, Brogan, Davenport Vaughan, Roberts, and well-known goalkeepers were Parkinson, Tom Hay and Trainor. I also remember seeing F.J.K. Cross, the amateur mile champion runner of his day, play in a Wednesday afternoon match. I saw Jimmy Settle play his first match with the Wanderers. I shall never forget his short red socks hanging over his football boots.

It was also on a Wednesday afternoon that I saw one of the most talked-of players that the Wanderers ever signed. I don't know how they got hold of him. It was rumoured at the time that a Wanderers' representative, up in Scotland looking for talent, saw a player he very much fancied, and having got permission to approach him, promptly signed him up and brought him to Bolton.

We never learned the "how, who and why" of the transaction. But it was a nine day's wonder in Bolton football topics. Docherty was the man, and he was the least like a centre forward that I ever saw in what was supposed to bea good team. He had very large feet enclosed in a new, light coloured, pair of football boots. He bumped and stamped about the football field like - as we used to say in the country - a prancing horse, treading on anyone who stood in his way. It was better than a comic pantomime. He didn't stay long in Bolton. For years his name was a by-word. Any fresh player introduced into the team who did not come up to the expectations of the crowd was put down as another "Docherty."

Little Willie Joyce I remember particularly in a match against Aston Villa. The ground was ankle deep in mud, and didn't Willie revel in it. He was plastered from head to foot. The Wanderers, and the Pikes-lane mud, beat a great Villa side that day.
There was also a lad named Peter Turnbull, who was loaned to the Wanderers by Blackburn Rovers when they were doing very badly, and he played a great part in saving them from relegation. He later became a registered Wanderer.

Many people who knew them at their best still argue that Sutcliffe, Somerville and Jones were the finest defence the club ever had, unmatched in those days.

Some clever footballers who played for the club did not stay long. Men like J. Lyden, clever but unstable. And one of the coolest and cleverest half-backs that the team ever had was McGeachan, who played his first game in company with Lyden. In addition to Mac's skill with the ball, he was very clever in fouling an opponent without the referee seeing him. They used to say that there was only one referee who could catch him, John Lewis - and that was the reason why every time a player stumbled or fell when near Mac, the referee's whistle went.

12 SEPTEMBER 1895

FIRST MATCH AT BURDEN PARK

Bolton Wanderers v Preston North End

The opening match on the new ground at Burnden Park, Bolton, was played yesterday evening for the benefit of 'Di' Jones, the Wanderers' captain and Welsh international full-back.

There were over 3,000 spectators, and as the tickets sold well the benefit was a success.

Teams -
Bolton Wanderers: Sutcliffe, goal; Hamilton and Jones, backs; Paton, McGeachan and Freebairn, half-backs, Martin, Brown, Joyce, Wright and Cassidy, forwards.

Preston North End: Trainer, goal; Tait and Holmes, backs; Sharp, Sanders and Greer, half-backs; Henderson, Eccleston, D. Smith, J. Smith, and Blythe, forwards.

The Wanderers faced a strong wind in the first half. At the onset they attacked sharply, but Trainer saved well, and North End were not long before they troubled Sutcliffe. Play was rather tame, but Blythe, for the visitors, and Martin for the home team, made several good runs. Trainer brought off a great save from Joyce. David Smith shot against the bar. Half time arrived without a score. Resuming, Brown got away and troubled Trainer, but North End retaliated, taking a couple of corners, which were cleared with difficulty. The visitors continued to press, but eventually Cassidy broke away and centred splendidly, Martin tipping over. Play was generally very quiet, the Wanderers doing most of the attack, but David Smith scored at last as darkness was coming on, and North End won by a goal to nil. There was nothing to choose in the play, neither team exerting themselves to any extent, but Martin, at outside right, and Hamilton, right full-back, made creditabled first appearances with the Wanderers' first team.

14 SEPTEMBER 1895

FIRST LEAGUE MATCH AT BURDEN PARK

Wanderers 3 Everton 1

As the Wanderers were Everton's first opponents at Goodison Park, it was therefore only fitting that Everton should furnish the first League match with the Wanderers at Burnden Park, the more so from the fact that they were likely to draw a splendid gate, and from the appearance of the handsomely appointed enclosure long before the time announced for the kick-off these expectations were bound to be fulfilled.

Attracted by an hour's cycle scratch race, in which most of the local cracks were riding, which was brought off before the match, spectators commenced to roll up soon after two o'clock, and by three o'clock - an hour before the kick-off - there would be close upon 10,000 present.

The chances of the teams were freely discussed, the majority leaning to Everton, though there were not a few who had confidence in the Wanderers. Everton had won all the League matches for two or three seasons, besides beating the Wanderers in the final for the Lancashire Cup last season but one.

The cycle race finished about twenty minutes to four, Armour's victory being received with great enthusiasm. Spectators began to roll up, the special trains from Liverpool, Manchester and Bury bringing a big contingent.

A better attraction than a visit of the Everton team could not have been wished for. There are few more popular clubs in the country. For several years they have drawn big crowds at Pikes-lane, and this afternoon they performed in the presence of a gathering that would have practically crowded the old enclosure at the other end of town.

The visitors opened their eyes wide at their first look at the new ground, some of them pronouncing it 'magnificent'. Viewed from the grand stand the sight was certainly very fine, and made one wonder how on earth the Pikes-lane field had been tolerated for so long. The only thing wanting is a Press box, on the Manchester-rd. side of the ground, to facilitate the despatch of messages, the present

arrangement meaning a loss of five minutes to get on the highroad. Until this Press box is supplied, the Wanderers will not be quite up to date.

In October, 1899, a team of black South Africans visited Burnden Park - and the paper reported that the match was somewhat one-sided.

Wanderers V Kaffirs

This Wanderers' home match calls for very little comment. It was farce pure and simple, and the Kaffirs lost by 13 to three, the Wanderers treating their dark-skinned visitors from the Orange Free State with humorous contempt. The visitors have yet a lot to learn in speed, combination and shooting. Even with an open goal, and the Wanderers looking on in amused expectation that the opposition might score, the Kaffirs could not pop the ball through sometimes. Some of them are men of much education, the captain, Twazi, speaking four or five languages, his English being very good.

 There would be about 2,000 spectators, and the recepts were £53. After paying expenses, the Wanderers would have a bigger balance than if they had filled the date with a "guarantee" match somewhere. It was a blank afternoon with the Wanderers, there being no League going, or Cup-tie available, or the directors would not have sacrificed a valuable weekend to an exhibition farce.

Teams -
Wanderers: Sutcliffe, goal; Halley and Lockhart, backs; Fitchett, Brown and Freebairn, half-backs; Bell, Morgan, McAteer, Barlow and Gilligan, forwards..

Kaffirs: Adolph, goal; Daniells and Broffitt, backs; Brown, Kortie, and Appollis, half-backs; Stephen, Abel, Twazi, Nicholas and Soloman, forwards.

4 NOVEMBER `1899`

INTER-LEAGUE MATCH AT BOLTON

The Inter-League match between the English and Irish Leagues, with which Bolton has been favoured, marks another epoch in the history of local football, this being the first occasion on which Burnden Park has been selected for an encounter of this description.

Though the appearance of a local respresentative in Inter-League engagements, however, is not unprecedented, the match will have special local interest, inasmuch as 'Jack' Fitchett, the Wanderers' smart right half-back, has, for the first time, been given the opportunity of displaying his abilities amongst the 'talent' of the country. The youngest player on the English side, and the only one selected from a Second Division club, Fitchett's position will be rather an exceptional one, but throughout he has been somewhat of a wonder, Unfortunately for our readers, who have not had the pleasure of seeing him, Fitchett is no great friend of the photographer, and he was unable to provide us with a photograph for reproduction. A smart-looking, well-developed youth, as much unlike a footballer as possible, John Fitchett first saw the light in the City of Manchester, which has not the reputation of providing many first-class footballers, on February 21st, 1880, so that at the present time he is only 19 years of age, and the position to which he has already been elevated bears eloquent testimony to his ability as a footballer.

In April, 1901, the F.A. Cup Final Replay between Tottenham Hotspur and Sheffield United was held at Burnden Park. The teams had drawn 2-2 at Crystal Palace, and Bolton was chosen as the venue for the replay, when Spurs won 3-1. Previous to the game, though, there were rumours of insufficient accommodation, although with measures taken by the Wanderers it was reckoned that 30,000 could be acommodated with ease. However, the railway companies refused to provide cheap travel facilities, many Lancashire soccer supporters were deterred from attending, and just over 20,000 turned up. Local catering establishments, expecting a huge crowd, had bought in extra pies - and were left with most of them, having to virtually give them away that evening. The day became known as Pie Saturday.
The following week the paper commented . . .

27 APRIL `1901`

FA CUP FINAL AT BOLTON

Never before in the history of the old-established Wanderers F.C. has the town been honoured by being chosen for an English Cup Final tie. During the week many 'alarums and excursions' had gone forth about the defective holding capacity of Burnden Park - that courtesy title to a ground bounded on one side by a railway, and on another by a perfume-emitting works. The Wanderers' officials grasped the situation splendid, but unfortunately their enterprse did not receive its just reward, for the expensive seating provided on the cycle track (a grand place, by the way, to view the proceedings) resembled a beggarly array of empty benches.

This failure is attributed to the alarmist reports circulated for some days previous, whereby thousands of people in Bolton and elsewhere, notably the districts whence came the competing clubs, felt they would be safer at home than incurring the risk of a bad crush or possibly an injury, as the result of being jammed amongst a crowd that was expected to be of dimensions never before seen in this district. The sea of faces on Saturday was an agreeable sight, but one could not resist a feeling of sympathy with the Wanderers as eyes were cast around the track.

The paper then followed a description of the match with . . .
There are other phases to the Cup Final in Bolton which are

not directly connected with the play, yet which have provided copy for the local and general press, and a topic for all circles of the community. The food slump was on Monday and Tuesday the talk of the town. Particularly was the pie slump in the subject of chatter. Tradesmen had invested in these comestibles in extraordinary quantities, forgetful that only a certain proportion of the football spectators would be outsiders in want of hunger-quenchers. 12,000 or so would be able to go home to tea, and it was needless to provide for them.

The result was that many a struggling fellow invested money in pies, in the hope of making a lot of profit whilst the football sun was shining. It was pies, pies, pies everywhere, and Cockneys might well ask if Bolton people lived on nothing else. There were piles of them at street corners, mountains in the restaurants, and thousands elsewhere. They were given away, in many places, on Saturday night, and hungry men fed on them on Monday and Tuesday and a halfpenny and a penny a time. Guttersnipes had a royal time with the morsels.

The Cup Final in Bolton will not be forgotten in a hurry.

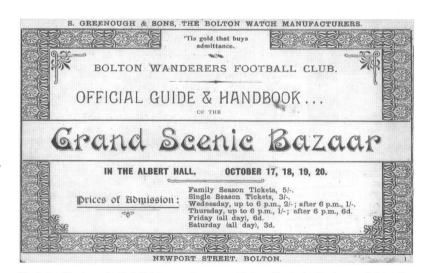

"The Bolton Wanderers Football Club have again recovered their position in the First League Division. If, however, we are to retain this position, much will have to be done by way of placing the club on a sound financial footing. This bazaar will be devoted to relieving the club from debt, and thereby ensuring its continuation as an organisation of the first class." No, that isn't news of a money-raising event in the past decade or so, but the introduction to the programme (more like a book - it was 130 pages!) for a Grand Scenic Bazaar in aid of the Wanderers at the Albert Hall, Bolton, in October, 1900.

When January 17, 1903, arrived, the Wanderers had gained only three points from 22 games, and they had all come from draws. It was not a happy situation, which had been commented on in the Evening News . . .

1 DECEMBER 1902
A DISMAL EXPERIENCE

Three months of the football season have passed away and the Wanderers are still without their first League victory. It was hoped that what is regarded as the unlucky number of thirteen would bring a change of fortunes, but the hope proved vain, the visit to Bury adding one more to the inordinate list of League disasters. Shuffle the cards as they will, the direction of the Bolton club continues to add to their misfortunes.

They have tried innumerable dispositions of the weak forces at their disposal, but all arrive at the same depressing result. Nothing seems to remain but to make the best of the situation, which is surely the gravest in the history of the club. It is a time when their friends ought to stand by them, as we are sure they will. If the Wanderers could really make a move they might still get out of the wood, for other members of the First Division are faring little better.

Both Blackburn Rovers and Grimsby Town were defeated at home on Saturday, and it is worth pointing out that the Blackburn team have actually lost more goals than the Bolton players . . . the real weakness of the Wanderers lies with the forwards and half-backs. They have only twice scored more than a goal, whilst they do not average a goal per match.

But then things improved . . .

17 JANUARY 1903

To the historic possessions of the town has been added a unique form of relic, in the shape of the ball with which the Wanderers won their first match of the season at Trent Bridge, Nottingham, today, the score being Bolton 3, Nottingham 1. It was presented to the club after their victory, and it is safe to say no other organisation in the country possesses such a prize. The occasion was the most memorable in the annals of League football having proceeded so far without securing a victory, and the unenviable distinction is likely to remain with the Wanderers for some time to come. Unfortunately, it is to be feared, the turn in the tide has come too late to save the club from again falling into a lower sphere.

and another victory the following week . . .

24 JANUARY 1903
WANDERERS V DERBY COUNTY

Spectators went away from Burnden feeling happy for the first time this season. They had watched the Wanderers vainly struggle for victory at home on nine occasions, and had this afternoon the satisfaction of seeing them walk round one of the cleverest teams in the kingdom.

On successive Saturdays the Wanderers have defeated clubs that stand in the first half dozen in the League, and it really makes one wonder why they made such a tardy start. However, better late than never, although their wakening up comes too late to keep them in the First Division. There was a splendid crowd - the gate amounted to £270 - and as the home side gave early signs of doing business they grew very enthusiastic.

The stand occupants were especially boisterous, their encouragement of the home talent being very noticeable. There is ground for hoping that the Wanderers will finish an inglorious season with something like credit. A week ago they were the only Lancashire club to win away from home. Today they are the only Lancashire club to win at all in the League.

Final League position: 18th in Divison 1 - relegated.

1 MAY 1903
THE QUESTION OF PLAYERS

At the annual meeting of the Bolton Wanderers' Football and Athletic Club, the Chairman said that the directors were always willing to give local lads a thorough trial, and that when a local lad was dropped it did not mean that he was of no use. Arising out of a question as to who had signed on, Mr Crook asked if the directors were thinking of going through the season with the two goalkeepers they had engaged. - The Chairman: It all depends on circumstances. - Mr Crook: I think you had better get the old one, Sutcliffe is a goalkeeper, and if you can get hold of him get him, and let's get back in the First Division. - Mr Isherwood said he had attended specially in regard to that matter. If the Wanderers wanted Sutcliffe he was in a position to say his services were at their disposal. He (Mr Isherwood) knew a Second Division club were willing to pay £300 for him. - Mr Chadwick: I make a proposition that we have him back again. - This was seconded - The discussion proceeded until, at length, the Chairman quietly but pointedly drew the attention of the meeting to the fact that Sutcliffe was a signed player for Millwall, and so therefore could take absolutely no notice of the resolution which had been made. If he did, the club would suffer materially.

12 MARCH 1904
HE WAS A BOLTON SUPPORTER

The following scene actually occurred in a railway carriage returning from Sheffield:-

Interlocutor (to Gamin, about 14 years old): How much has it cost you today?
Gamin: Why, 2s 1d.
Inter: How's that?
G: I went to Cook's last Friday neet, an axed for hauve a ticket. Chap said I were 15, I said I were only 11. He lowfed, but he gan me one.
I: Well?
G: Well, that were 1s 6s, an' I 'ad to pay a tanner to goo in, and then I 'ad a 1d pie.
I. And have you had no dinner?
G: Neow, I only coom eaut o' t' factory at 12 o'clock.
I: Poor lad:
G: Ah, but look here (dives down into ragged trousers). I've gotten hauve-o-crawn tort semi-final. If t' Wanderers ud laust, I should ha' spent aw this today. When they played United at Clayton, ha only had a tanner, so ha walked it, theer and back.

Moral: Who says the Wanderers lack enthusiastic supporters.

23 APRIL 1904
F.A. CUP FINAL, CRYSTAL PALACE

Manchester City 1, Bolton Wanderers 0

Teams -
Bolton: Davies, Brown, Struthers, Clifford, Greenhalgh, Freebairn, Stokes, Marsh, Yenson, White, Taylor.

Manchester City: Hillman, McMahon, Burgess, Frost, Hynds, Ashworth, Meredith, Livingstone, Gillespie, Turnbull, Booth.

London was truly overrun by Lancashire folk today, writes 'The Tramp'. They had travelled, many of them, through the night to watch the Cup Final, and the Metropolis was favoured with the opportunity of learning what Lancashire enthusiasm means.

On the way to the Palace the roads were simply lined from the noonday hour, and when I found myself within the Sydenham grounds an hour before the start, a sea of faces formed a striking picture, and one not readily to fade from the memory. An hour before kick-off, nearly 40,000 had made sure of the best seats, and fifty thousand soon congregated. Among the distinguished members were the Prime Minister, members of the Cabinet, and various M.P.'s. Club favours were greatly in evidence.

Play had opened at a great pace - too fast to last long. The ball was lively as a cricket, and both keepers were early tested with good efforts. It was a delight to Bolton patrons to note that their half-backs were playing strongly. Davies made one or two great saves but ran risks, and once was knocked over his own goal-line with the ball in hand. This was the City's third corner, but like its predecessors it produced no more than an ugly skirmish. However, as the first quarter of the game drew to a close, City spurted down again, the ball going to Meredith. The Wanderers seemed to hesitate for offside, but the Welsh international took the ball along, controlling it perfectly, and crossing it beyond Davies's reach and into the net.

The jubilee of Mancunians knew no bounds, and an excited fellow running on the field was challenged on the touchline by a policeman, and was escorted off the ground by several constables.

The Wanderers then worked very energetically to protect their goal, meeting the City's raking movements with sterling grit and persistency. As predicted, the game was far more hard nature than scientific. The teams well deserved their breathing interval, and the Wanderers had done admirably not to lose more than one goal.

When play started again, the Wanderers kept the ball in the City quarter, and were contesting every inch of the way in a desperate desire to get within scoring distance. They were cheered to the echo as they swarmed around Hillman, and to stop Stokes, Burgess had again to resort to tactics which deservedly earned for him the disapproval of the onlookers.

'Play up, Bolton' was the cry resounding from all quarters of the ampitheatre, and as the Wanderers attacked with renewed vigour the cheering was deafening. The Wanderers were getting along in irresistible fashion, and the City were constantly in difficulties. As time went on the City were now doing better, play being more evenly divided. As the time was flitting away without an equaliser materialising, I found some consolation in the fact that City had not had an easy triumph as most folks had anticipated. The Wanderers had given them a magnificent game if they had not shown ability.

In being defeated, the Wanderers had extremely hard lines. Nothing could have been finer than their defence throughout the game. In point of real ability, the City had certainly the pull, but they could not have had more worthy foeman.

3 FEBRUARY 1905
WANDERERS TRAIN AT LYTHAM

Since Monday of last week, Bolton Wanderers have been training at Lytham, and one of our staff spent a pleasant day with them this week. The team mustered by ten o'clock at the baths, and there changed into football attire, marched three-quarters of a mile to the football ground where they have obtained permission to train, and had some spirited practice.

Returning for brine baths, the men were fit for lunch, and in the afternoon had a bracing walk by the sandy country that abuts on the Ribble estuary and the Lancashire sea coast. After tea, rest and mild indoor recreation occupied the time, and altogether it seems as if Trainer Lewis is keeping the men thoroughly up to form without, however, overtraining them.

The Wanderers have youth on their side, and all of them except Davies, whose ankle has been a little troublesome, are in the pink of condition.

In 1905, the cycle track was removed from Burnden Park, making more room for spectators.

14 JULY 1905
BOLTON WANDERERS' NEW STAND

Little time has been lost by the Wanderers' directors since the meeting of shareholders gave them permission to proceed with the erection of a new covered stand on the west side of Burnden Park.

Tenders were invited, and considered at the beginning of last week, the result being that the tender of Mr R. Mosley, of Charnock-st. saw mills, was accepted. The structure is being built on the site of the present 9d. uncovered stand on the Manchester-rd. side of the ground, and will be constructed of main steel stanchions at front and back, 25ft. apart, with lattice girders along the front, and rolled steel girders at the back to carry steel roof principals. The total length will be 300ft. The roof will be covered with board and felting. The stand will accommodate 3,960, and in the enclosure and terraces formed on the old cycle track, some 1,970 persons will be able to watch the game. The entrances to the stand are nine in number, and arranged as to enter direct from the street.

When our representative visited Burnden Park on Tuesday, the work was in full swing, and with no little curiosity a number of people put in an appearance to watch the demolition of the uncovered stand. Tons of soil have already been carted away, and several loads are being tipped near the Croft-st. entrance to the old stand, where the trees are threatened with extinction. If these disappear there will go the last semblance of foliage which in some measure justified the name of Park.

In this connection we are reminded of an incident which occurred when Newcastle United came to Bolton to play their English Cup-tie last year. A number of ladies accompanied their husbands from the North. They did not desire to see the match, and would, they thought, content themselves by spending the afternoon in the Park, which they sought in vain.

On inquiry at the office they were sadly informed that the beauties of Burnden Park could only be seen and enjoyed by paying to watch the football match.

4 NOVEMBER 1907
CORRESPONDENCE

Disgraceful language at Burnden Park

Sir:- Will you kindly allow me space in your paper to protest against the disgraceful language which one must hear as a spectator at Burnden Park during a football match? On Saturday last, a gentleman was subjected to immoral, insulting, and filthy language from a half-drunken hooligan, and this in the presence of ladies occupying the new stand.

As one looked at the face of the victim, blushed with shame and humiliation (yet silent) at being made the target of such foul and shameful remarks, and threatened with violence if he retaliated is the least it was plain to see, he could not defend himself against the man who possessed more fist than brains. I appeal to you, who by your presence make the game purer, to raise your voice, or the pen, to stamp out such disgraceful scenes as this, because if we are going to keep this sport a national pastime, something must be done to protect the respectable portion of spectators from the insulting language to which at any time he may become a target. - Yours, etc., PURE SPORT.

OLYMPIAN writes (November 11): - Every lover of football ought to thank the correspondent who has called attention to the bad language that has unfortunately been recently heard at Burnden Park. It always needs courage to advocate reform of any kind, but that reform is necessary was made evident by the publication of other letters following on the same lines. I am glad to know that the directors of the Wanderers F.C. are taking drastic steps to remove any offenders, and I hope they will be backed up by all who can render help, and who have the welfare of the club and of the game at heart.
Persons who misbehave or make themselves a nuisance in any way ought to have short shrift. There is nothing more contemptible than bad language, and when it is used so as to become a grievous annoyance it is intolerable. People pay their money to see the game played, and not to be made the targets of local epithets.

Bowler hats and flat caps were obviously the order of the day for non-players when this photograph was taken of the 1911-12 side at Burnden Park.

1909 saw the first tour abroad by the Wanderers, when they went to Holland.

The Wanderers Return

There was not quite the same display of excited enthusiasm amongst the party of tourists who arrived at Bolton from Holland on Wednesday evening as was exhibited when Trinity-st. was left behind on May 14th, but at all events a deeper shade of colour could be detected. The Wanderers have for three weeks been undergoing a somewhat severe broiling beneath a Continental sun, so it was no surprise to see every man wearing a healthy tan on his countenance.

The tour has been a splendid success, and wherever the Boltonians have gone they have been warmly welcomed. One of the brightest features has been the good impressions the Dutch spectators have received of the tourists' play, and though the Boltonians have found their opponents hot-tempered at times, they have always conducted themselves in the arena with the same gentlemanly control as befitted English sportsmen and Second Division champions.

The net result of five games is five victories, and a margin of goals aggregating 31 to three. Amongst the beaten Dutchmen have been some of the finest sporstmen Holland can produce, and there are bright hopes for Britain's pastime on the Continent.

13 JANUARY 1914
DISTINCTION FOR THE WANDERERS

The spice of football is its variety, and uncertainty, of which we had a remarkable example on Saturday, when not one of the first eight teams in the League gained a victory, and the three who are regarded as the strongest candidates for the championship sustained inglorious defeats. In the circumstances, the Wanderers strengthened their position by forcing a draw at Burnley, whilst had they won they would actually have had the best record in the division.

Certainly they have this season proved one of the most difficult teams to beat, their reverses averaging no more than one per month, and in this they have been equalled by Blackburn Rovers, Bradford City, and West Bromwich Albion. There is, indeed, every prospect of the Wanderers repeating the experience of last season, when at one period they had a rosy

chance of carrying off the championship, but allowed it to escape them, as the result of a bad time in the last month of the season.

Certainly at the present moment, no team has a better prospect than the Wanderers, but with so few capable

reserves to fill first team vacancies when it becomes necessary to rest a regular member of the League eleven, it is almost too much to hope that they will be able to push on one side all the other claimants to the championship. The strain upon the players looks like being increased by the demands of the Football Association Cup competition, and the directors would be wise at this juncture ro reinforce the team with a first-class inside forward and half-back. It would be a pity if by the lack of a little entrerprise the club were to be deprived of its chance of gaining honours that now seem well within reach.

Final League position: 6th in Division One.

17 JANUARY 1914
THE CELTIC CHAMPIONSHIP

Royal Clubs At Turf Moor After 15 Years

It seems years and years since the Wanderers played a first League game at Burnley. Indeed, 15 summer suns have shone since such a contest between the teams, but of today's concourse at Turf Moor one wonders how many folk saw the game watched here by Prince Albert Victor between the same clubs' representatives nearly 30 years ago.

Bolton and Burnley are royal clubs, and are not a little proud of it. There was Will Struthers, Dannie Frial, Trainer, Kenny Davonport, and 18 others, not to mention Harry Brownlow, of Halliwell, as referee, and they gave the Prince and the crowd a rare entertainment when His Majesty visited the town to open their hospital in 1886. It was about the first match of its kind royalty had patronised!

The outbreak of the First World War created difficulties for football clubs, and midweek matches were banned so as not to interfere with the work of making munitions - those difficulties were multiplied when compulsory military service was introduced in 1916. Normal League football did not re-start until 1919. This picture, however, shows the 1914-15 Wanderers team, with: G. Wilson, W. Rowley, J. Thomas, H. Baverstock, E. Sidlow, P. Toone, J. Edmondson, J. Feebury, W. Wallace, G. Eccles (trainer), H. Feebury, T. Heslop, F. Roberts, S. Gimblett, J. Fay, H. Hilton, W. Jennings, T. Hesmondhalgh, C. Hodkinson, J. Seddon, J.T. Walmsley (Assistant Trainer). I. Thomas, R. Glendenning, D. Stokes, T. Donaldson, E. Jones, G. Lillycrop, J. Smith, E.T. Vizard, F.M. Buchan.

A row of shops and houses in the 1920s where the Crescent behind the Town Hall now stands.

1920s

DATE	WORLD EVENTS	BOLTON EVENTS
1921		Prince of Wales (later Edward V111 and Duke of Windsor) visited Bolton.
1922		New local law forbidding charabancs to pick up passengers in Victoria Square came into force after complaints by town centre shopkeepers. Duke of York (later George V1) unveiled memorial in Nelson Square to members of Bolton Artillery who lost their lives in First World War.
1923	The first ever FA Cup Final takes place at Wembley Stadium. Over 127,000 saw Bolton Wanderers defeat West Ham United 2-0.	
1925	John Logie Baird, Scottish inventor, transmits human features by television.	
1927	Charles A. Lindbergh flies first successful solo nonstop flight from New York to Paris.	
1928		War memorial in Victoria Square unveiled.
1929	13 million people become unemployed after the Wall Street stock market crash of 1929 triggers what became known as the Great Depression.	

5 AUGUST 1921

THE SPECTACLE OF SPORT

When the big stand on the Wanderers' ground was built about a dozen years ago, it was considered quite a palatial affair big enough to meet all needs. How mistaken that idea was is proved by the fact that the club are having to spend about £10,000 - or twice the cost of the original stand-on additions.

These improvements are interesting because they show what football has developed into as a pure spectacle. In the old Pikes-lane days we used to be happy if we could stand round the ropes and get so near to the game that we became almost intimately a part of it. One had to be a hardy sportsman to enjoy the game then. But how things have changed!

Folk now roll up in their limousines and Fords, bring their wives and daughters and have nice comfortable reserved seats, and hot coffee at the interval. We haven't got velvet cushions and easy armchairs yet at Burnden, but they have on some grounds. Anyhow, it's still nice and comfortable, like the dress circle at the theatre.

That's what football has become as a spectacle, and that's why the Wanderers are having to put in a couple of thousand or more seats.

"A Board who face a problem" was the headline on this 1921 picture. "Our photograph, taken at Burnden Park recently, is of a group of directors of the Bolton Wanderers F.C. who are anxiously engaged just now in the difficult problem of finding a winning team. Left to right they are (sitting) Messrs S. Jackson, J. Hayward, J.P., W. Hamer (chairman), and J. Sharrock. Standing: Messrs C.E. Foweraker (manager), S. Entwistle, and A. Nicholls. The President, Messrs J.W. Makant, J.P., and Counc. H. Warburton, J.P., complete the directorate."

This photograph shows a mixture of Wanderers' first and second team players from the very early 1920s. It was probably taken at the beginning of the season, when it was customary to play a curtain raiser game of Probables v Possibles. The man between Joe Smith (centre front) and David Jack (third left) is Frank Roberts, who was transferred to Manchester City in 1922 after he insisted on taking over the licence of the Victoria Hotel in Hotel Street, Bolton. On David Jack's right is Tom Buchan, who was transferred to Tranmere in 1924, whilst Hinton, the reserve team goalkeeper in the picture, was transferred to Tottenham the same year.

22 APRIL
LADIES' FOOTBALL AT BURNDEN PARK

30,000 spectators - £2,000 raised for charity

Nearly 30,000 spectators assembled at Burnden Park on Wednesday night to see the football match between a Bolton ladies' team, got together by Mrs Vizard, and the Dick Kerr's team which, formed four years ago, has been instrumental in raising over £35,000 for charitable objects. The proceeds on this occasion were in aid of the Bolton and District Ex-Servicemen's fund, and it is expected that a sum of £2,000 will be raised.

I do not remember a game on the Wanderers' ground that has provoked so much hearty laughter, and yet play was very far removed from being farcical, writes "Olympian". Most of the skill was on the side of the girls who have played together pretty regularly for the past four years, and they displayed not only an intimate understanding of each other's play, but a measure of individual skill and a knowledge of positional strategy which comes only with constant practice.

That was precisely where the Bolton girls were lacking. They often carried the ball into the visitors' half by sheer determination and hard work, but none of their forwards could manoeuvre for shooting positions or round off their attacks, and on not more than two or three occasions was the Dick Kerr's goal assailed. Result: 8-0.

Both teams were entertained to tea by the Mayor and Mayoress at the Town Hall before the match, and afterwards the Wanderers' directors provided refreshments on the ground. A ball, given by Mr J.T. Howcroft, and autographed by the players, was sold by auction, becoming the property of Counc. H. Warburton, one of the Wanderers' directors, who paid five guineas for it.

LADIES' FOOTBALL AT BURNDEN PARK.
30,000 SPECTATORS—£2,000 RAISED FOR CHARITY.

BOLTON WANDERERS Winners of the ENGLISH CUP, 1923
Back Row: Nuttall, Howarth, Rowley, Seddon, Pym, Jennings, Finney.
Front Row: Butler, Jack, J. R. Smith, J. Smith, Vizard.

For Bolton Wanderers, the 1920s was the most successful decade so far - three times in the F.A. Cup Final, in 1923 the first to be held at Wembley, and three times the winners (in all three matches, a total of only 17 Wanderers' players were involved). The town was euphoric with victory, but the 1923 Final was remembered not only because of Bolton's success, but because of the crowds which descended on Wembley, and the police on horses who tried to control them. It is now known as the "White Horse Final". This is how the paper reported on events of that historic day . . .

30 APRIL 1923

THE WANDERERS' MEMORABLE CUP VICTORY AT WEMBLEY

Bolton Wanderers 2, West Ham Utd 0

The Challenge Cup of the Football Association, the most coveted of all trophies offered for competition in connection with the greatest of our national pastime was won on Saturday by the players of the Bolton Wanderers Club and won deservedly. They beat West Ham United pretty much as they pleased on the new Wembley Stadium which was invaded and stampeded by the greatest crowd that has ever assembled in the history of the game. It had been confidently stated that this new amphi-theatre, the home of English sport, was structurally and scientifically perfect, offering comfortable accommodation and an unobstructed view to upwards of 125,000 spectators. Clearly the authorities were totally unprepared for what happened. It is computed that fully 250,000 people made their way to the imposing and spacious ground from all parts of the Empire all anxious to see the blue ribband of the football world decided. About 60,000 people had passed inside the turnstiles when pandemonium broke loose.

One of the main exits was broken down and thousands of people surged inside the enclosure and from that moment the situation showed signs of getting out of hand. People scaled high walls and clambered into seats for which others had paid. Such was the pressure on the ringside fences that they gave way. The crowd rushed across the larger cinder track which encircles the playing pitch and in an incredibly short time the beautiful greensward was occupied by a black uncontrollable mass.

The police, apparently taken by surprise, were for a time powerless to deal with the situation and even more officers, mounted and on foot, had been rushed to the ground. The task of clearing the playing pitch was a tediously slow process. Indeed, when the players came into the arena, there seemed very little prospect of the game being started. Finally, however, when the players added their persuasion to the force resorted to by the constabulary, the crowd was gradually pressed back to the touchline and at 14 minutes to four the referee found it possible to make a start.

VISITORS WHO SAW NO PLAY

The Bolton party made the Russell Hotel their headquarters for the weekend, the players with the manager, Mr C E Foweraker, having spend the last few hours before the match at Harrow, and they made the short journey to the ground in excellent time. But the directors and their friends who journeyed from London in charabancs, had an experience they will never forget.

Dozens of Bolton people saw none of the game. None of the directors, except the Chairman, Mr J W Makant JP, saw the first goal and several of them did not get as much as a glimpse of the game. Scores of people who had paid a guinea for a seat never got to it. Never in the history of the game has there been such a tragedy and for the credit to those who are responsible for the good government of Soccer, the most popular of all pastimes, it is be hoped it will never be repeated.

FEATURES OF THE GAME

But to the game, Joe Smith won the toss from George Kay and set West Ham to face the wind and sun, and before the crowd had settled down to enjoy the game, the Wanderers were well on their way to victory. It was a dramatic start, and the goal which David Jack scored had its influence on the subsequent play. It is easier to play a game fraught with vital issues when you are a goal to the good and it says much for the moral of the West Ham players that they made the contest interesting

The Buff of April 28, 1923, which carried the first report of the Wanderers' win in its Stop Press.

The police had to use horses to clear the pitch so that the match could begin, and the horse which stood out among the crowd was a white one - since then the 1923 Cup game has been known as the White Horse Final.

So many people turned up for the 1923 F.A. Cup Final at Wembley between the Wanderers and West Ham - the first final to be held there - that the 200,000 crowd inside the venue overspilled onto the pitch. It is said that there were another 500,000 people outside trying to get in! Here, police are seen trying to move the fans back to the terraces, with (inset) the teams watching.

and never ceased to try to discover a weakness in the Bolton rearguard. There was a ten minutes stoppage early in the contest in consequence of the crowd again encroaching. The ball control, the method and the craftsmanship of the Wanderers' players were superior to that of their opponents who had plenty of space, swung the ball about with good judgement and never spared themselves.

Twice in the first half, the Wanderers, who kept the ball on the ground with rare discretion, might easily have lost the lead. From a corner placed nicely by Ruffell, Pym and one of his colleagues both failed to get away a high ball, and Watson, in his eagerness to make the most of a gilt-edged chance, propelled the ball over the bar. The other attack which placed the Bolton goal in jeopardy emanated from the right wing, Richards, cutting in towards goal and smartly making his way past Jennings and Finney, shot obliquely when everyone expected him to centre, and Pym, who had advanced, pulled up just in time to thrust out his right foot, and so arrest a ball that would otherwise have gone into the net.

To David Jack fell the honour of scoring the first goal in the quick time of three minutes after the start. Thus he maintained his proud record of having scored in every Cup-tie since the first round. On Saturday he got his chance through Seddon cleverly changing the point of attack by smashing a long pass out to his right-wing when the West Ham defenders obviously expected a pass to the left. Butler had a long race with Young for possession, and the back won by a foot, hooking the ball away, only to find himself challenged by Jack before he could clear. A quick flick of the foot gave the forward possession. Young went down with outstretched leg in a last hope to spoil his opponent, but Jack was away in his full stride, and he shot a high ball on its oblique course into the net before anyone could touch him. Hufton had advanced when he realised that his goal was in peril, and in a last despairing jump to reach the ball, he came down on his shoulder and face, and had to be assisted to his feet again.

The second goal was engineered by four players. Jennings slipped his wing in clever fashion, and slipped a short pass to Joe Smith, who had been lying well behind his forwards as a sort of emergency half-back. The Bolton captain promptly pushed the ball up the centre where John Smith, who was on his toes, held it until he deemed it prudent to send it to Vizard.

Henderson raced across to try and force the Welshman into touch, a policy he exploited fairly successfully in the first half, but this time Vizard evaded his rush, slipped round him, and raced inwards along the goal line with Henderson at his heels. Then we saw the value of two minds with but one thought.

Seeing John Smith coming towards him, Vizard urged the ball gently towards his colleague, and Smith hooked it with his left foot so viciously that the ball rose sharply, went under the bar to hit the netting, which had been pulled tight, and then came out to be scrambled away. But Mr Asson stood pointing to the centre; the ball had been in the net and out again. West Ham had lost the game irretrievably.

KING PRESENTS THE CUP

It was found impossible to get the players through the dense crowds to present them before the match, as had been intended, to the King in the Royal box, and so this part of the ceremony had to be dispensed with. When the final whistle sounded Finney, the young Bolton defender, secured possession of the ball, and the spectators at once surged over the playing pitch like an irresistible wave. All one could see of the Wanderers' players for some time was a white shirt dotted here and there in the black mass of human beings. The police helped them to reach the Royal box where the King presented the Cup to the Wanderers' captain, Joe Smith. Smith briefly thanked the King, and introduced each of his colleagues who shook hands with His Majesty, and received from him the handsome gold medal which goes only to the Cup winners.

Teams -
Bolton: Pym, Haworth, Finney, Nuttall, Seddon, Jennings, Butler, Jack, J.R. Smith, J. Smith, Vizard

West Ham: Hufton, Henderson, Young, Bishop, Kay, Tresardern, Richards, Brown, Watson, Moore, Ruffell

GREAT PANDEMONIUM IN TOWN

The people who stayed at home are beginning to believe that after all they had the best of things and shared in what may be described as the great Pandemonium. So many appear to have journeyed to Wembley without seeing the match! It was impossible to disguise the fact that Bolton was keyed up to an almost unbearable pitch. The thousands who flocked to the town were in the throes of excitement mingled with anxiety to such an extent that it was some kind of relief to jostle one another along Bradshawgate and to seize every possible opportunity of expressing their feelings. In the state of the crowd Dame Rumour had a fairly free hand. She ran riot, and everyone was talking about "game abandoned". But that with hilarity throats gave out great cheers, cat-calls - anything to make a noise - and for the time being Bradshawgate, at any rate, was a rolling thick mass of citizens overwhelmed by the spirit of victory. Everywhere the people strove to do justice to their feelings.

The front cover of the programme for the 1923 match.

The team parade the Cup in Bolton Town Hall square.

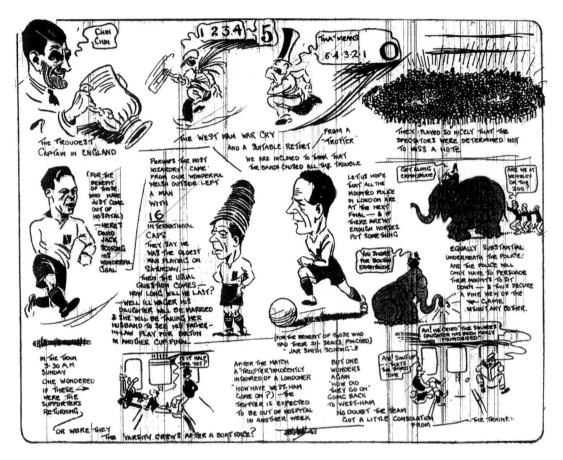

14 APRIL
BOLTON 'TROTTERS'

How the Wanderers and Others Got the Name

Once again the old question has cropped up. "Why are the Wanderers called the "Trotters"? It is asked, this time, in a London contemporary and, it is stated, appeal was made in vain to Mr Foweraker, the Wanderers' secretary, to settle the point.

The name has nothing whatever to do with the real or supposed fondness of Bolton people for a delicacy known by the name of trotter. Years ago, at the beginning of the 18th century, Bolton was famous for the number of practical jokers in the town. These gentlemen looked on strangers and visitors as their natural prey. The practice was known as "trotting", and so widespread was the fame of some of these jokes that the reputation and the name stuck to every Boltonian, who to the outside world became a "trotter".

Perhaps the best-known "trot" took place in the Swan Inn when a stranger rashly accepted a bet that he could put his leg into as hot water as an habitue of the bar. He lost; the Bolton man had a cork leg.

Another and better tale is of a resident of Deansgate who staked a £10 note, with his fellow companions in the Swan, that he could keep silent for 20 minutes. Immediately the trial began, a "trotter" slipped out the back way and informed the wife of the silent one that he had had a stroke and could not speak. The alarmed woman dashed to the hotel and with great wailing besought her husband to "just say one word". When he could stand her noise no longer, "Shut up, woman", he said, "Can't you see they're trotting thee?!

Perhaps some day, when the real reason has been given for the millionth time, the rest of the country will cease to associate the name with tripe shops. It may be that the man who started the story of fondness for the delicacy was "trotting".

Billy Butler played outside right for the Wanderers from 1920 to 1932, and was in all three finals. He was capped for England in 1920 when he and David Jack constituted the right wing against Scotland at Wembley. He left to go to Reading in 1933, and became manager there two years later.

April 24, 1926, saw the second of Bolton's F.A. Cup victories in the 1920s, beating Manchester City 1-0, and this is how the Evening News saw it . . .

24 APRIL　　1926

Bolton Wanderers set the seal on their fame as Cup fighters by winning the Football Association Challenge Cup for the second time in three years at Wembley Stadium, David Jack scoring the all-important goal when the game had only minutes to run. There was not a great deal between the teams in one of the hardest games, the quality of football being a credit. His Majesty the King gave expression to the popular sentiment when, in handing the Cup to Joe Smith at the close of a thrilling struggle, he said he thought the Wanderers just deserved their success. Thus was avenged the defeat inflicted upon the Bolton team by the City in the Final tie of 1904.

For 12 seasons in succession the Football Association Cup has been won by the club to whom the first goal has fallen, and so it was in this case, when the Wanderers vanquished their opponents in the presence of 91,447 people.

On their last appearance there, Bolton opened the scoring within five minutes, and they ought to have repeated the performance here, for a centre by Vizard presented Jack with an easy scoring chance which was not, however, turned to account. As a matter of fact, the game had actually been in progress an hour and 18 minutes when Jack made amends for his previous lapse. Pushed down the centre of the field by Jack, the ball was smartly turned out to the right wing by J.R. Smith as the City backs closed in to prevent him going through himself. The wing forward ran on a few yards, and just as McCoy was about to tackle him, Butler made a fast, low centre, which tore across goal, and eluded everybody but Vizard. The Welshman's coolness and judgment came in useful, for he apparently deceived the City players into the belief that he would shoot. As they moved towards him, Vizard placed the ball all along the ground in front of goal. Cookson touched it, but could not stop it, and with Goodchild thus thrown off his guard, Jack quickly forced the ball under the bar to score a well-got goal.

Teams -

Bolton: Pym, Haworth, Greenhalgh, Nuttall, Seddon, Jennings, Butler, Jack, J.R. Smith, J. Smith, Vizard

Manchester City: Goodchild, Cookson, McCoy, Pringle, Cowan, McMullan, Austin, Browell, Roberts, Johnson, Hicks

PROFITEERING IN TICKETS

Thousands of provincial visitors who had gone unprovided with tickets waited outside the entrances in the vain hope of gaining admission. Several who had purchased tickets for themselves thought to take advantage of the opportunity thus provided of making a profit by selling their tickets to the highest bidders. These tickets were mostly 5s ones, for which as much as 15s was demanded, Earlier in the day a man who said he had twenty 2s tickets for sale at 10s each, received unwelcome attention from the crowd, which was angered at his attempt at profiteering. Four constables and a sergeant had to disperse the crowd, whence he was allowed to escape to another gate. Some of the Bolton trippers did not see the match. They stood outside the Stadium and were almost beside themselves with joy when told that Jack had scored. Such is the magnetism of the Cup.

King George V shaking hands with the Bolton team before the 1926 final against Manchester City.

A rather bewildered-looking Joe Smith has a police escort with the Cup. His career with the Wanderers was coming to an end, though, and in 1927 he joined Stockport County for £1,000. He was Bolton's most consistent goal scorer until Nat Lofthouse, netting 38 goals in 1920-21. He won his first England cap in 1913, and continued his international career after the First World War. His connection with Bolton was to surface again, though - he was manager at Blackpool when they beat the Wanderers in the 1953 Cup Final. Another well-known player in the 1923 and 1926 Finals was Ted Vizard. He joined the club in 1910, and made his last appearance for the club in 1931 when he was 41. He won 22 caps for Wales.

Wanderers' captain Joe Smith fighting his way through the crowds who stayed to cheer him, in 1926.

TRIUMPHANT TOUR OF WELCOME

Bolton has never experienced such wild scenes of enthusiasm as swept over the town for the Wanderers' return. In regard both to the dimensions of the crowds and the vim with which they exercised their vocal powers, the demonstration easily excelled the great rejoicings of 1923. From Moses Gate to Bolton the crowds thickly lined the roadway, and many natives of long standing say they never witnessed the like. All along the route it was cheer upon cheer from lusty supporters, and the descent upon Bolton provided the most wonderful spectacle one could expect to see.

Along Manchester Road, Bradshawgate, Great Moor-st. and Newport-st. was the course taken to the Town Hall, and here the scene was a huge swaying mass of humanity - the women, as throughout the procession, holding their own with the men in their demonstrations of enthusiasm - everyone eagerly pressing forward to get a glimpse of Joe Smith, the Cup, and the players.

One man in 1926 who decided to follow the Wanderers to London, as he had done in 1923, by walking there was Bob Carr who beat his record of three years previously. On the following Monday, the paper reported . . .

FROM WEMBLEY TO BED

Laid Up after 215 Miles' Journey

Robert William Carr, of Newport-st., who left Bolton a week ago today to walk to London, arrived at Wembley Stadium at 12-30 on Saturday along with his cyclist pacer, Chas. Marshall, and witnessed the final from a half guinea seat "nice and comfortable" as he put it this morning when an Evening News' representative had a chat with him. He found Bob laid up, suffering from the after effects of his 215 miles journey by road.

All went well, said Bob, until Thursday noon between Daventry and Fenny Stratford. He had suffered from slight blisters on his toes before that, but those he cured.
On Thursday, however, the top of his clog began to chafe his left ankle, causing it to blister and swell, but he pushed on gamely. Then on Thursday evening the rain came down in bucketsful, and they were soaked in a moment.

On Friday night, despite his painful leg, Bob landed at Watford and completed his 12 miles' journey without difficulty. All along the road he had his "book" signed by residents and officials, and also by Bolton men passing in cars. This document is in the possession of his pacer, who is now accompanying the Wanderers on their triumphal journey homeward. It shows, he says, that he beat the record he set up in 1923.

Arriving home by train in the early hours of yesterday morning, he had to go straight to bed where today he was found nursing a badly inflamed leg, but he was quite resolved to be fit by the time the Wanderers return.

At Wembley, he sat besides James Sloan, who landed in London from Bolton on Thursday midday pushing a wheelbarrow, and Hugh Sloan arrived before the kick-off. He started from Blackpool on Tuesday.

Carr's well-worn clogs are on view in the window of his newsagent's shop.

19 AUGUST 1927

BURNDEN PARK LICENCE

On the application of Mr E. Fielding, the usual licences for the sale of intoxicants at Burnden Park, on the occasions of the Wanderers' first team and Central League matches, were granted by the Borough Magistrates on Tuesday. Mr Fielding pointed out that tea, coffee and foodstuffs were also supplied, and that last season the gate averaged 20,000 despite the unfavourable weather. The licence had been much appreciated. In reply, the Chief Constable, Mr S. Jackson, director, gave an assurance that the privilege would not be used on Christmas Day or Good Friday.

25 MAY 1928

TO COST £12,000

Bolton Firms to Build Wanderers' new stand

Bolton firms, Messrs Harry Peers and Co., Wm. Gornall and Sones, Ltd., and Messrs. Wm. Townson and Sons, Ltd., have secured the contracts for the building of the Wanderers' new stand, which is to take the place of the much criticised old stand at the east end of Burnden Park.

The contracts provide for a single stand to accommodate 14,000 spectators, of whom 2,500 can be seated in the back portion, and the remainder in standing positions, protected from the elements by a long, raking roof, which will cover the whole of the present "paddock", stretching to the rails. The structure will be rather larger than the old stand, and substantially built with concrete terracing, at an estimated cost of £12,000. Burnden Park will then have covered accommodation for about 20,000 spectators; it is probable steps will be taken to terrace the embankment under the new shelter, thus making that side of the ground more attractive to spectators than it has been since the ground was opened.

A 1929 cartoon about the Cup final.

Only three years later, April 27, 1929, came another great invasion of London, for the Final against Portsmouth, which the Wanderers won 2-0.

27 APRIL 1929

Bolton Wanderers' team, captained by a Bolton man, James Seddon, will bring the Cup to Bolton on Tuesday night for the third time in six years, and a great civic reception is being prepared in their honour. "I never had any doubts about our success", declared Seddon. "We played well within ourselves, and the great thing was that we kept our heads."

Both the Wanderers' goals were obtained at the same end where David Jack scored in the finals of 1923 and 1926, and in a match which produced plenty of good and interesting football, the Wanderers, after a disappointing first half, left no doubt in the minds of 92,576 spectators, who paid approximately £22,400 for admission, as to which was the better side.

The ground seemed firm, and all in favour of a fast game, and it is understood that the ball had been soaked in water for a time to prevent it being too lively. When the players went up to the Royal box for the presentation, the Prince of Wales, in handing the Cup to Seddon, congratulated the Wanderers "on having won the Cup so soon".

The Wanderers have now joined the select circle of clubs who have won the Cup thrice or more, the others being Aston Villa and Blackburn Rovers, each with six successes to their credit, the defunct amateur club the Wanderers, who won it five times, and Sheffield United, whose name has been inscribed on the trophy four times. Prior to this game 17 players had won three Cup medals. To the list must be added the names of Pym, Haworth, Seddon, Nuttall and Butler.

The 12-minute goal is London's popular description of the Wanderers' third successful Wembley game in a period of six years. It is true that the first and vital leading goal by Butler came within that distance of the final whistle, but goals were only a matter of time because "Pompey", after an opening that must have made their followers' hearts beat high with hope, had faded to almost nothing in the face of Bolton's half-back power and great defence.

Delayed the opening goal was, and therefore it was all the sweeter. In fact the Wanderers' chairman, seated in the Royal box, forgot himself and stood up shouting and waving his hat. Like the sportsman he is, the Prince turned and smiled, beckoned Mr Nichols to take a seat next to him, and confided that he "liked to see a man let himself go occasionally".

Harold Blackmore's truly-aimed arrow a short while later was a crowning glory for this young marksman in his most profile season for the club.

On the way up the special gangway to the Royal box for the Cup, the players were the recipients of hearty slaps from the spectators, and Alec Finney disappeared from view. His colleagues later said that he preferred to crawl up on all fours.

Teams -
Bolton: Pym, Haworth, Finney, Kean, Seddon, Nuttall, Butler, McClelland, Blackmore, Gibson, W. Cook

Portsmouth: Gilfillan, Mackie, Bell, Nichol, McIlwaine, Thackeray, Forward, Smith, Weddle, Watson, F. Cook

'BUFF' ON SALE IN LONDON

A special edition of the Evening News' "Buff" was on sale in the streets of the Metropolis soon after ten o'clock on Saturday night containing full details of the Cup tie at Wembley. The paper met with a ready sale amongst the Bolton excursionists, some of whom were rather sceptical as to whether the paper could possibly give a full account of the match. They were readily convinced, however.

Jimmy Seddon holds the Cup up high in 1929. Bolton-born Seddon joined the club in the 1913-14 season although he did not turn professional until 1919. During the First World War he served in France where he contracted "trench foot", something which troubled him in later years. He won three F.A. Cup medals with Bolton, and six caps for England, and left the club in 1932.

Another man who had great pride in the three 1920s Cup Final victories was goalkeeper Dick Pym - he kept a clean sheet in each Final. He had joined the Wanderers in 1921, for what is thought to be £5,000, won the first of three England caps in 1925, and played his last game in 1930, returning to the fishing industry in Devon where he had been brought up.

Little is known about this picture, except that it was taken probably in the 1920s during the celebrations for one of the three Cup victories.

30 AUGUST 1929

TERRACING AT BURNDEN COMPLETED

Three miles of concrete steps put down

Rapid strides have been made this year in completing the concrete terracing to the stand at Burnden Park. The main part of the structure (such as steelwork, reinforced concrete walls, joinery, roofing, glazing, etc,) was completed for the 1928-29 season, the seating at the rear of the stand having accommodation for 2,700.

The front portion was filled up and the ground allowed to consolidate as a foundation for the reinforced concrete terracing, just completed, which gives standing accommodation for 10,000 people. Ample entrances and exits have been provided, and everything possible arranged for the convenience of the public. Without doubt, the completed structure is the last word in football stands and will enhance the prestige of the club for their enterprise and foresight.

The terracing was completed in seven weeks at a cost of under £4,000. The terracing would, if laid out, mean three miles of steps, reaching approximately from Great Moor-st. to Station-rd., Kearsley, or from Bolton station to Dunscar car terminus.

In the process 2,200 tons of earth have been removed, 2,000 tons of concrete used, 125 tons of granite chippings from Shap, Westmorland. The work reflects great credit on all concerned.

A view of Bradshawgate, 1930s.

1930s

DATE	WORLD EVENTS	BOLTON EVENTS
1930	Uruguay win the inaugural football world cup when they beat Argentina 4-2 in the final.	Bolton had 22 cinemas (not including those in surrounding towns such as Westhoughton, Farnworth and Horwich).
1932		Fish Market on Bridge Street closed and moved to the Ashburner Street market.
1936	King George V dies; succeeded by son, Edward VIII, who soon abdicates to marry an American-born divorcée, Wallis Simpson, and is succeeded by brother, George VI. Jesse Owens wins four Olympic gold medals in Berlin, Germany.	
1938		King George V1 and Queen Elizabeth visited Westhoughton and Bolton.
1939	World War II Germany invades Poland. UK declares war on Germany.	The extension to the Town Hall and the Crescent were opened to house the museum, police, and magistrates' courts. Building them had provided eight years of employment for 800 Bolton men during the Depression.

At the end of the 1932-33 season, after 22 years in the First Division, the Wanderers were relegated to the Second Division after they finished 21st (for one home game that season, against Portsmouth, which the Wanderers won 4-1, a crowd of only 3,101 was present).

8 MAY 1933
A FIGHTING FINISH

The last League match of the season will be long remembered for a fighting finish that was all in vain (writes the Tramp). As far as it lay in their power, the Bolton team rose to the occasion in an eleventh-hour effort to save their position in First Division football, and they were denied complete success because others made a special effort too.

I should say their form against Leeds, allowing for the fact that they had only 10 men to beat for more than half the game, was as good as anything they have shown us this year, and for the players' sakes I am sorry it came too late to save the club.

They set about Leeds with gusto once Milsom had scored. That goal ended a period of hectic attacking, but rather nervous finishing, and once they had got it the Wanderers were a much more effective force, as their four further goals testified.

And Olympian added: Though the season was ended by Bolton Wanderers with a rousing victory over Leeds United, the worst fears of their followers were borne out, for all the four bottom teams were successful, leaving the Wanderers and Blackpool two points behind. So we shall have to be content with an inferior class of entertainment at Burnden Park next season.

Disappointing as that will undoubtedly be, it may prove a blessing in disguise if the necessary steps are made to strengthen the Bolton team. The vital weaknesses revealed during the last three months must be remedied before the team can have any hope of regaining its lost status. There is reason to believe that with experience Atkinson will become a very serviceable centre-half.

But two good extreme wing forwards, a strong, sturdy left-half who can support his forwards, and a right-back, are obviously required to give the team a reasonable chance of holding its own in the hurly-burly type of football in which the Wanderers will be compelled to take part next season. Upon the success of the management in preparing for the ordeal will depend the measure of support they will be accorded.

At the end of September, 1934, the Wanderers' were humiliated at Bramhall Lane when they were beaten 2-6 by Sheffield United. Would they take such a result lightly? Not likely - the Red Rose burst into flower again the following week when Bolton took on Barnsley and wiped the floor with them 8-0, a record League victory (although a couple of years previously they had beaten Liverpool 8-1). At the same time, Bolton became the first team in the League to claim 30 goals.

8 OCTOBER 1934
WANDERERS ESTABLISH A RECORD LEAGUE VICTORY

Barnsley owe Sheffield United a grudge. Throughout the last week the feeling grew at Burnden Park that something extra special had to be done to wipe out the memory of what happened at Bramhall Lane - and it was so. It took 21 minutes for the first goal to come, and with its arrival Barnsley's chance went. Westwood's first hat-trick for the club was an accomplished fact 18 minutes later, and in the period of its inspiration, on to the interval, the Wanderers played copy-book football.

Previously there had been a tendency to attack in penny-numbers, but once the Bolton men began to look for one another, they put Barnsley's best in the shade, all three half-backs moving up to make a smooth-working group of eight attackers delightful to watch. Only fine goalkeeping by Ellis, and more than once a spice of luck, kept the Wanderers' lead down to three at half-time so completely were they the masters of the situation. This was their best work of the match. The last 20 minutes or so of the first half, judged by the quality of play, was worth all the rest.
For the best part of the second half, they seemed to be going easy, and Barnsley took a fair proportion of the play. Then an avalanche of goals fell into the Barnsley net.
Five in the last six minutes of the game. Appropriately G.T. Taylor started the big push. He made a goal all on his own out of no chance at all, sailing in from the touch-line and forging a path up the middle before shooting the Wanderers' fourth goal. Again he showed opportunism a minute later

when, close in to goal, he converted a Cook centre. Shotton's mis-cueing of a Westwood centre made the sixth goal, and Westwood and Milsom rattled in the seventh and eighth with the Boys' Stand in a frenzy of excitement.

Barnsley took the beating well. Always trying, they preferred the careful pass to the indiscriminate lunge at man or ball, a different Barnsley altogether from the old Cup fighting crowd, and certainly not deserving of such an overwhelming defeat.

Teams -

Bolton: Jones, Smith (R), Finney, Goslin, Atkinson, Taylor (G), Taylor (G.T.), Eastham, Milsom, Westwood, Cook.

Barnsley: Ellis, Adey, Shotton, Harper, Henderson, Whitworth, Ashton, Smith (J), Finnigan, Andrews, Pedwell.

This 1933 page tells the story. Out of the F.A. Cup went the Wanderers, a 4-2 victory to Manchester City, but the match would be remembered because of the record crowd of 69,912 ("From the stand, Burnden Park made a wonderful picture, spectators not only filling the track and encroaching on the grass, but perching perilously on the top of the stands and bars, and even on the roof of the groundsman's cottage".) However, only four days later, at a re-arranged League game with Portsmouth which the Wanderers won 4-1, the crowd was only 3,101 - the lowest record attendance!

However, two years later the good times were back, promotion into the First Division, and a banquet was held to celebrate . . .

13 MAY 1935

MOST POPULAR TEAM IN COUNTRY

Do footballers benefit from a club's financial success? An answer was given to this question at the Wanderers' Promotion celebration dinner, given by the President, Sir William Edge, MP, at the Pack Horse Hotel last night when some 70 guests saw him hand benefit cheques totalling £1,950 to Jack Milsom, Bob Jones, and Ray Westwood.

This was the '"high spot" of a happy gathering. Another was when the President, after congratulating the team on gaining the prize it set out for by clean, sportsmanlike play, declared that their triumph was one of the most popular things that had happened in the football world for some years.

Sir William said he travelled up and down the country, and people in all stations of life had come to him and expressed their delight that Bolton's fine sporting team had succeeded in getting back to the First Division. Some of the heads of the football world were delighted, too. They had said the Wanderers would not only raise the standard of football and conduct in the higher division, and that was a fine tribute.

Mr G.F. Foweraker, manager, said at Burnden Park they were one happy band. He particularly wished to thank the captain, Alec Finney, who had the confidence of every player. "Whatever Alec says goes with them," declared Mr Foweraker, who went on to say that the Wanderers were the first club in the land to institute a system of paying players' wages through the bank as a means of encouraging them to save. Other clubs had imitated them and had claimed to be the first to do it. Bolton Wanderers began it years ago and had never had cause to regret doing so.

All the leading players were present, some of them after long journeys specially undertaken for the purpose. During the evening an entertainment was given by Messrs Alec Hill and Percy Rigby (vocalists), Mr Arthur Bewick (pianist) and Mr Graham Adams (entertainer) and the banquet, starting at 7.30 with a toast to the King, was not concluded until

11pm. It happily marked the end of another term in the Second Division and inaugurated what is widely hoped will be a triumphant re-entry into the highest class of all - the "promised land" of the First Division of the Football League.

Harry Goslin. He joined the Wanderers in 1930 for a £25 donation to Boots Athletic, a Nottingham club. In 1936 he was appointed skipper, and was selected for England's war time team. His last appearance for Bolton was at York in March, 1942.

On March 21, 1936, the Wanderers had in goal Fred Swift when they visited Manchester City. Fred's better-known brother Frank was 'keeper for City. It is fair to say that Frank came off somewhat better. City thrashed the Wanderers 7-0.

23 MARCH 1936
A SAD DAY FOR BOLTON FOOTBALL

If you have ever seen an overmatched boxer punched around the ring by a fast, hard-hitting, confident foe, going down first under a crack on the jaw, then from a blow in the body . . . pawing back feebly and being brushed contemptuously aside, then hitting the floor again after a rain of bewildering smashes from every angle - if you have ever seen a spectacle like this in the ring, you have a good idea what the second half at Maine Road on Saturday was like, writes "The Tramp".

Football, fortunately or otherwise, does not permit of retirements, otherwise the Bolton team would have been quite justified in giving up a pitifully unequal struggle, City did just what they liked, and Bolton couldn't so anything right. Defence simply went to bits. Overrun half-backs, and panicky backs, exposed their goal to the full might of the City attack and Swift, practically devoid of protection, failed completely to save his side.

It was a sad day for the goalkeeper, and all the more bitter, because he and his brother were "keeping" for the first time together in big football. Whilst brother Frank had one of the lightest afternoons he has known, due to the stingless character of the Bolton forward play, Fred had what was probably the worst experience of his career. Both his judgment and handling of the ball were faulty, and there appeared to be a serious lack of understanding between him and the backs.

At all events I feel certain Swift would normally have prevented all four second half goals, including a penalty. But weak as their last line of defence was, I do not say Swift caused the breakdown. The men in front had already been lost in the avalanche of City's supremacy. Frank Swift sat on his haunches, a spectator. Whatever his brother had done there was only one result. City were not wonderful; at times they looked it, but only by comparison.

A couple of days later these letters, among many others commenting on the match, appeared in the Evening News:

Sir, - Never have I seen Bolton Wanderers give such an exhibition as that seen at Manchester. I am not one who would attribute the failure to the defence, although goodness knows it did get rattled, and then fell to pieces. Attack is recognised to be a good defence. Well, Bolton had none. We have a centre forward who is better than three parts of the centres I have seen. Nine times out of ten he gets the ball head high. I seem to detect some kind of ill-feeling in the forward line. In only one case did I see any reasonable understanding, a pass given to Milson on Saturday, and that was from G.T. Taylor at outside-right, in the last five minutes. The directors must share the blame for allowing this state of affairs to exist. Internationals or not, if they will not play as a team, drop them. The City had no sulkers, they were triers, and gave their supporters something to shout about. Yours, etc., HARMONY.

Sir, - The directors must realise as well as us humble "bobites" that the team isn't good enough. The last day for transfers has gone, the team is in the dumps. A kind of "lump it or like it" suggestion to the spectators. Be fair to the players. It is their bread and butter. It's not their fault a few of them are out of their class. Yours, etc., ARTFUL.

The following year, Manchester City did it again. In what turned out to be a rather bad tempered game in the fifth round of the 1937 F.A. Cup at Burnden Park, in front of a crowd of 60,979, the Wanderers lost 0-5. But the "sportsmanship", or lack of it, was the subject of comment .

20 FEBRUARY 1937
WANDERERS' PLAYERS' LOSS OF CONTROL

Bolton 0 Manchester City 5

What Would Have Happened Had They Left the Field?

IT will be a long. long time before those who saw Manchester City's Cup contest with the Wanderers forget a bewildering last half-hour. From a game in a thousand, played with astonishing pace and packed with thrills, it deteriorated into a unpleasant burlesque in which the principal performers were Bolton players.

However much their supporters may have sympathised with the team about its bad luck - and most spectators agree that City were rather flattered to be in the lead at half time after the escapes Swift's goal enjoyed - no sportsman can feel proud of the attitude some of the players adopted afterwards.

Open defiance, insubordination, rough play, and a "score-as-often-as-you-like" air by certain defenders reflected no credit on the guilty ones. Getting rattled at the way events are turning, and at alleged "injustices" is no excuse for losing one's head and descending to childishness such as was demonstrated when players urged the referee to award a penalty kick against their own side; sarcastically applauding a decision in their own favour, and deliberately kicking a ball high into the crowd.

Surely the finest reaction to adversity, every time, is a redoubled fighting effort; a stoicism or display of Spartan courage such as many fighters in the boxing ring put in when the tide of battle is flowing strongly against them. Thank goodness the Bolton captain Goslin, and a few others revealed this trait and got on with the game as well as feelings would permit when some of his colleagues were inclined to leave the field and take others with them.

Do they realise what would have happened to them, and to the club had they gone off? The game would in all probability have been abandoned and awarded to their opponents, the players concerned would almost certainly have been suspended for a fairly long period, and Bolton Wanderers, a club that has always borne a good name, would have been in disgrace for years to come.

Happily for the club, the crowd kept its head better than some of those on the field - there was no invading of the pitch or attempt to molest the referee so there may be no serious echo, apart from the punishment of Anderson who was sent off without warning for an act of retaliation, of what was a regrettable chapter in the Wanderers' history.

A scene from a 1937 practice match at Burnden Park, showing a shot from Jack Milsom which he lifted over the bar. Centre forward Milsom joined the club in 1929 for £1,750 and was the only player to be Bolton's leading goal scorer in six consecutive seasons, between 1932 and 1937. His 25 goals in the 1932-33 season could not prevent relegation, but he was a member of the team which won promotion two seasons later. In 1937 he was sold to Manchester City for £4,000.

27 DECEMBER 1937

DISAPPOINTED WANDERERS

Christmastide is abnormal enough for professional footballers without such an experience as the Bolton players had at Burnden Park on Saturday, Christmas Day. Rarely have they appeared to be in firm command as they were against Derby County when, two goals up, with less than half the full 90 minutes played, the referee decided he could no longer carry on efficiently.

The Bolton players strongly held the view that the fog was no worse at that time than when Mr Ames made his decision to start the match. Furthermore, they declared they were able to see both goals from the centre of the field and to follow the flight of the ball quite well enough to play their game.

Harry Goslin, the former Boots Athletic player, who has proved such an excellent captain for the past 18 months or more, shared his team's annoyance at the turn of events, but had no criticism to level against the Derby players for not wishing to continue the match. "Any team two goals down away from home would have done the same," he said, "and that includes us."

But Goslin was firmly of the opinion that the abandonment was not justifiable in so far as conditions had not worsened. As the Bolton captain says, Mr Ames, having permitted 37 minutes' play, might at least have continued the remaining eight to half time (3pm), and been guided by the conditions prevailing at the time for restart. If he had taken this course, the match would have been carried through, for the fog thinned out rapidly, and at 3-30 had disappeared altogether.

The Christmas Day football crowd was bitterly disappointed. They saw little of the play, yet disagreed with the official decision to call off the match, and demonstrated volubly. Outside the ground a section of the crowd clamoured for a return of their money. That, of course, could not be acceded to.

When Alf Anderson arrived at Burnden Park in January 1937, he was welcomed by the manager Walter Rowley (pictured left, centre), and one of the fans' favourites of the day, Ray Westwood. He had been signed from Hibernian for £2,500, but his stay in Bolton was not very long. He played his last game for the Wanderers in a 2-1 win at Middlesbrough in February 1939, and then joined Third Lanark for a fee of £1,480. This action picture (above) was taken during Anderson's debut, in a 2-2 draw with Huddersfield at Burnden Park, and shows Bolton's Milsom's backheader which brought a goal in the last minute of the first half to give the Wanderers a 2-1 lead. The pitch, reported the paper, "had had no chance to recover from Wednesday's churning up, and today's rain left it in a dreadfully sodden condition".

5 APRIL 1938

STARS WHO ARE MARKED DOWN

Hound Those Responsible From the Game

One of the happiest "Annuals" for some years was that of the Wanderers at the Empress Hall last night, but opportunity was taken by the President, Sir William Edge, M.P., to condemn rough play. It was time the "star" players of this country - and Bolton Wanderers had some, he said - were kept continually out of the hands of the trainers.

He did not believe it was merely coincidence that crack players were marked down, and the sooner those responsible were "hounded out of the game the better". Football was a game, not a wrestling match or battle.

Sir William described the Wanderers as one of the most sporting teams in the country, and Goslin and Taylor as the finest uncapped players in the land. The meeting decided to send an expression of appreciation to the players for their efforts this season.

Some interesting remarks were made under the heading of any other business. Mr Dearden Cooke conveyed two suggestions from supporters, one that in carrying out its painting scheme at the ground, the club should paint all advertisements in club colours, and another that a narrow covering should be built over the railway embankment. Sir William said there were difficulties, but he promised that the directors' consideration would be given to this, and also to a suggestion from the same shareholder that no kick-off at Burnden should be fixed later than three o'clock.

The Bolton Wanderers' team 1936-37.

On April 14, 1939, The Wanderers' captain and others appealed to the 45,000 strong crowd at Burden because of the growing danger of war, asking those capable to join the Forces. The Evening News told the story . . .

14 APRIL   1939

Saturday afternoon's crowd at Burnden Park heard an appeal for National Service before the kick-off from the Wanderers' President, Sir William Edge, and the captains of the Wanderers and Sunderland teams. Before they came to the microphone placed in front of the centre stand, the band and drums of the 5th Loyals marched and counter-marched across the ground, and the players, in their dark blue training suits, lined up alongside the band.

Harry Goslin, the Wanderers' captain, went to the microphone first, and talked about the national emergency that may come. "But this danger can be met, if everyone keeps a cool head, and knows what to do", he said. "This is something you can't leave to the other fellow; everybody has a share to do.

"Get your name down straightaway for some form of National Service, and get yourself trained in the job you are best suited for. They will tell you all about it, either at the Labour Exchange of the A.R.P. headquarters on Victoria-sq."

Then Hall, the Sunderland captain, wished the appeal success. Sir William Edge, a former M.P. for Bolton, said that the F.A. had asked him to speak at Saturday's demonstration. Beside him stood the Mayor (Ald. Entwistle).

"I want to ask you a question," said Sir William. "Are we in Bolton, standing here on this ground, prepared as well as the Germans or the Italians to stand up for the security of our children?"

"Aye", came the answer from the crowd.

"We want more women drivers for ambulances," he went on. "There are women in Bolton driving for pleasure who could help here. And I appeal particularly to you sportsmen

on this ground to become volunteer firemen. Call at the Fire Station in Marsden-rd. on Monday or Tuesday night.
I promise you that some of the Wanderers will be there to welcome you."

Then the appeal ended with the singing of the National Anthem, led by the band and drums.

Following that appeal, a couple of days later, led by Harry Goslin, the whole of the Wanderers' team signed up into the Bolton Artillery at the Drill Hall, and were later called up for service in the 53rd Bolton Artillery, being involved in fighting in the Middle East, Italian campaigns, and the Dunkirk evacuation. Harry Goslin was killed in action in 1943. The rest of the first team squad survived, and many returned to playing professional football after the war. These pictures show the Wanderers at the Drill Hall, inspecting a gun, after signing on (opposite page), and then, early in the war. The Wanderers soldier-footballers were (from left, back row): D. Winter, H. Goslin, S. Hanson, G. Catterall, J. Ithell, J. Hurst. Front row: A. Geldard, D. Howe, R. Westwood, J.H. Roberts, T. Sinclair.

After Harry Goslin's death, "The Tramp" wrote: "He was one of the finest types of professional football breeds. Not only in a personal sense, but for the club's sake and the games' sake. I regret his life has had to be sacrificed in the cause of war. Peace conditions would, I think, have brought him big opportunities on the coaching or managerial side of the game, in which direction he had ambitions."

On September 3, 1939, the Wanderers played their last game in the League which, because of the outbreak of war, was to be suspended until further notice. They beat Portsmouth at Burnden Park 2-1 in front of a crowd of 12,992 spectators. Instead of a countrywide League, however, different areas formed their own Leagues, and Bolton continued to play, in the North West Division of the War Regional League.

13 DECEMBER 1939
LAW AND WANDERERS' SEASON TICKET HOLDERS

Judge's Decision in Test case

A case of interest to Bolton Wanderers' season ticket holders, and regarded as a test case concerning the question of any repayment, was heard at Bolton County Court today. Judgment was given for defendants, the Wanderers' Club. The plaintiff was James Henry Dilworth, 13, Arkwright-st., Bolton, who claimed 15s from the Wanderers Football and Athletic Club, Ltd. He alleged that this 15s was paid to the defendants upon a consideration which has in part failed.

Mr G. Keogh appeared for the plaintiff, and said that in August last the plaintiff purchased from the defendants a book of ground tickets entitling him to admission to the ground only. The price of the book was 18s. The normal price of admission to the ground was 1s for first team matches and 6d for reserve matches.

The book contained 48 tickets, entitling the plaintiff to attend 43 matches specified in the fixture list at the end of the book. The remaining tickets entitled him to attend such fixtures made after the fixture list had been published. The fixture list comprised 21 home matches between Wanderers first team and 21 other teams, which comprised the First Division of the Football League. The plaintiff would have been entitled to the League first team and reserve matches.

That was the consideration on which the plaintiff parted with his 18s. He thought he would see 21 First Division matches with all that term implied. He would have seen all the best

footballers in the country in one game or another. He would have watched teams struggling for points which affected the League championship. There was a thrill in watching all those games in the presence of large enthusiastic and often critical crowds. The plaintiff had used three tickets when war broke out. Immediately war came the remainder of the fixtures were abandoned and a revised fixture list was issued by the defendants. The country was divided into regions, and Wanderers fell into the North-Western Region, where there were only three other First Division teams.

Judge Crosthwaite said the facts of the case were not in dispute. There was no doubt at all that when Dilworth bought the ticket it was contemplated that the matches for which it would be available were first team matches in the First Division, and reserve team matches in the Central League. After Dilworth had attended three matches, the fixtures were abandoned by order of the Football Association, following upon an order made by the Secretary of State for Home Affairs under the Defence Regulations. In the book it was stated that the tickets were issued subject to the rules and regulations of the Football Association.

The question was, what is the position with regard to the money which Dilworth had paid for something which he cannot now obtain? What happened when the contract becomes impossible? In this case it became impossible because it became illegal - and neither party was at fault.

He thought that from the moment football became impossible Dilworth was unable to recover monies he had paid, just as the club would have been unable to sue for money if it had been due to them.

Whether that struck him or anyone else as being just or right was neither here nor there. Some might say that the burden should be halved, but he did not think we compromised our law. He believed there to be a definite rule and law in the matter, and there would be judgment for the defendants with costs.

In the 1930s, Humphrey Spender came to Bolton as part of a Mass Observation exercise in which Bolton became "Worktown". Among the hundreds of photographs he took was this one of good-natured spectators at Burnden Park.

Looking over the town from Deane, with mill chimneys standing out, 1940s.

1940s

DATE	WORLD EVENTS	BOLTON EVENTS
1940	Winston Churchill becomes prime minister.	
1941		11 people died and 64 injured when a bomb fell on the Ardwick Street/Punch Street area of Bolton. More than 1,500 Bolton men and women died in the Second World War. In one amazing money raising effort, £1,000,000 was raised in a week to buy a warship, HMS Dido.
1944	Allied troops invade France from Britain on D-Day (6th June) and begin to fight their way towards Germany.	
1945	Germany surrenders on 8 May. US drops two atomic bombs on Hiroshima and Nagasaki. Japan surrenders.	
1946		The Burnden Park disaster, when 33 people died.
1947		The last tram ran in Bolton, making its journey on the Tonge Moor line.
1948	National Health Service is established. London stages the 11th Olympic Games.	
1949		Field Marshall Montgomery given the Freedom of Bolton.

These days there is no need to explain the name of Nat Lofthouse to any football fan in the country - possibly not in the world - never mind Bolton, but although Nat signed amateur forms for the Wanderers in September, 1939, at the age of 14, it was not until March, 1941, that he made his first appearance for Bolton in a home match against Bury. The Wanderers won 5-1 (the previous week they had lost 4-1 to the same team!)

24 MARCH 1941
AMATEUR'S SUCCESSFUL DEBUT

Feature of the Wanderers' victory over Bury was the promising form of three local amateurs, of whom N. Lofthouse, a 15 years old centre forward, had the satisfaction of scoring twice in the second half. Well-built and fast, he may one day compensate the club for the loss of Lawton, like whom he played successfully for the Bolton Schools' team. Biggest success, however, was H. Cload, the 17-years-old Halliwell St. Thomas's left-winger, who revealed all-round skill against experienced players. Cload scored the Wanderers' second goal from Lofthouse's pass, a well-made chance splendidly taken. W. Grimsditch, Farnworth St. Thomas's goalkeeper, also justified his inclusion, and the introductions no doubt had something to do with the team's greater dash and liveliness.

May, 1945, and German prisoners of war helped clear the Burnden paddock of 24,000 baskets, Ministry of Supply material, at Burnden Park, ready for the first leg of the League North Cup Final, which the Wanderers won 1-0. The paper reported: "The baskets were neatly stacked in the stand behind, and made room in the paddock for 9,000 spectators. The prisoners of war did not kill themselves with work - in fact they refused to work at all when it rained! - but their contribution was an extra help."

A long line of supporters waiting to get their tickets for the Bolton leg of the Football League War Cup (North) Final, and one happy Serviceman with his two tickets.

In May, 1945, the Wanderers won the Football League War Cup (North) by beating Manchester United over two legs, the first, at home by 1-0, and the return match drawing 2-2. The Tramp wrote, after the second leg . . .

28 MAY 1945
WANDERERS' DRAMATIC CUP VICTORY

"A deflection by Barrass's head in the last half-minute at Maine-rd. brought the League War Cup to Bolton, but only super goalkeeping by Crompton deferred the issue so long. Let us get this game in the right perspective. With all due respect to Manchester United's pluck, they were for the most part struggling against a better team, and on the run of the game a truer result would have been 6-3 in the Wanderers' favour.

What happened, in a nutshell, was that the Wanderers, by superior all-round football, built up well-sustained attacks that failed by a hairsbreadth, or were thwarted by Crompton's uncanny positioning, while United raided in breakaways and snapped up a couple of chances, one of which Fielding made easy by "staying at home" instead of leaving his goal. They missed two others, one an amazing lapse before a gaping goal.

But against this the Bolton forwards twice hit the woodwork, with Crompton helpless, bombarded him with shots from all angles. It would indeed have been a miscarriage of justice if the Cup had somehow eluded them."

Another report on the day said: "The supporters of the Wanderers gave the players a boisterous welcome when they brought the Cup home. This very handsome trophy, which is now the property of the club, was held proudly aloft by the captain of the team, Harry Hubbick, surrounded by his fellow players in the open motor coach which brought the party back from Manchester. All the way from Moses Gate the streets were crowded with people, many of whom had decked themselves in the Wanderers' colours, and the players were loudly cheered. As the parade approached the town centre, the crowds became more dense and enthusiasm more marked. Such was the throng in front of the Pack Horse Hotel that the players had some difficulty, in spite of police assistance, in forcing a way through. For some time there were calls for practically all the players who had to show themselves at the upper windows."

The following week the winners of the North Cup played the winners of the South Cup, Bolton beating Chelsea 2-1.
"Olympian" wrote: For the second week in succession, Harry Hubbick, the Wanderers' captain, had the great pleasure of receiving a cup after the defeat of Chelsea in the charity match for sailors at Stamford Bridge. Now the League North Cup has a little brother to keep it company. This was a 100 per cent charity match. The clubs paid their own expenses, Chelsea footed the bill for match expenses, and the Greyhound Racing Association granted the use of the ground free of charge. A similar trophy to the one won by Bolton was handed to the Chelsea captain, and on each side 13 players and the trainer received five Savings Certificates

The Wanderers' triumphant return to Bolton with the League North Cup after the second leg against Manchester United, which ended in a 2-2 draw, giving the Wanderers an aggregate 3-2 victory. The pictures show Harry Hubbick (captain) holding the Cup as the team toured the town centre by coach, and the huge crowds that welcomed them in Bradshawgate (opposite page).

57

March 9, 1946 was to go down as the blackest day in the history of Bolton Wanderers, the worst disaster at the time in the history of professional football, leaving 33 soccer fans dead and more than 500 injured. In the first leg of the F.A. Cup quarter final the previous week at Stoke, Ray Westwood had scored twice in the Wanderers 2-0 victory. Now Stanley Matthews and his team had come to Bolton for the second leg, to win a place in the semi-finals. In the 5pm edition of the Evening News, "The Tramp" wrote of "Amazing Cup-tie Scenes at Burnden Park", and it was only at the end of his story that there was a hint of what was happening . . .

9 MARCH 1946
DISASTER

"Scenes unprecedented since the record crowd of 1932-33 season marked the return sixth round Cup-tie with Stoke City. A glorious day helped to make the event irresistible to football lovers of the North, and long before the kick off the overflow of spectators had reach the touch lines on two sides of the playing pitch. The mass of bodies at the Bolton end started immediately behind the goal net, and rose in a human terrace to the railway. There were all, the marks of Cup-tie enthusiasm and great good humour.

Teams -
Bolton: Hanson, Threlfall, Hubbick, Hurst, Hamlett, Murphy, Geldard, Howe, Lofthouse, Westwood, Woodward.

Stoke: Herod, Brigham, McCue, Mountford, Franklin, Kirton, Matthews, Peppitt, Steele, Sale, Baker

The Wanderers made the running and a beautiful piece of play by Westwood and Woodward on the left was broken up by Franklin, Stoke went on the attack and Hanson had to dive to a spinning ball from Steele which threatened to creep in. Stoke kept up the attack, and twice Bolton players were penalised for offences on Matthews.

The ball was extremely hard to move on the muddy surface, but the game was keen and interesting, with both sides attacking in turn. Unfortunately the crowd was now threatening to interfere with the match, which twice had to be stopped for the lines to be cleared of spectators.

On the second occasion, after a quarter of an hour's play, the referee called the captains together, and put a halt to the game until such time as the pitch could be cleared to his satisfaction. It appeared that too many spectators had been allowed into the enclosure, in addition to which there were stories, at the moment unconfirmed, of a wall having collapsed under the grandstand. After the players had filed off, the pitch at once became a mass of people who wandered all over it, crowding the goalmouth, packed the running track, and climbed everwhere they shouldn't be."

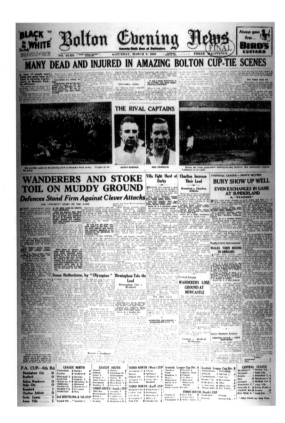

The Final edition of the Evening News of Saturday, March 9, 1946, which carried the first stories about the disaster (although the total number of dead were not known at the time).

A section of the crowd, with spectators even sitting and standing on the roofs.

When the Final edition of the paper was published that night, it was clear that a major disaster had happened, and that in his earlier story, "The Tramp" had pinpointed the wrong area of the ground:

MANY DEAD AND INJURED IN AMAZING BOLTON CUP-TIE SCENES

At least 17 people were killed and many more injured in amazing Cup-tie scenes at Burnden Park this afternoon. The crowd was so great spectators were trampled and others crushed in a barrier collapse. Two women are among the dead. Ambulances and private cars worked in relays to get the people from Burnden to the Royal Infirmary. All the injured people had been badly crushed.

Once the dead and injured had been rapidly taken away, the Chief Constable urged the resumption of play. The referee agreed because hardly any of the spectators - apart from those in the corner of the ground where the tragedy had taken place - were aware of what had happened, and to abandon the match might have led to disorder. Indeed, many of the spectators went home unaware of the catastropy until they read their copies of the Evening News. The match ended in a goalless draw, so Bolton progressed to the semi-finals, where they were beaten 2-0 by Charlton.

On March 11 the paper said: "The disaster stunned a town that had previously been keyed up to a state of nervous excitement by the prospect of Bolton Wanderers entering the semi-final by defeating Stoke City at Burnden Park. There were prospects of a large gate, but no-one anticipated that it would be marred by the tragedy which resulted in 33 deaths.

Evidence now goes to show that the accident was the result of excessive Cup-tie enthusiasm on the part of those who could not get on to the ground in the normal way. Statements issued by both the Chief Constable of Bolton (Mr W.J. Howard) and the directors of Bolton Wanderers show that thousands of people made their way on to the permanent way of the Bolton to Bury railway line that skirts the top of the railway embankment, They tore up the sleepers that form the fence, and forced their way on to the embankment at the back of the crowd already filling it.

Police controlling the crowds while rescue workers recovered the bodies of the victims.

The resultant increased pressure forced people against the steel barriers which eventually gave way, It appears that many of the victims were killed by being crushed against these barriers, whilst others were probably trampled to death by the crowd which inevitably surged over them from behind."

An inquiry was set up, and it was in July of that year that the Evening News was able to report on recommendations by King's Counsel Mr R. Moelwayn Hughes. He said that to prevent similar disasters the number of spectators allowed into grounds should be limited, and that clubs should be able to check the numbers entering grounds "by mechanical means".

This photo-diagram, taken by Evening News' Chief Photographer Jim Ashworth shortly before the disaster happened, shows how the tragedy occurred. Spectators at the point marked X were overwhelmed by the terrible pressure.

The Evening News front page of Monday March 11, 1946.

In January, 1947, Cup-tie fever was raging in the town, Manchester City were the visitors to Burnden Park in the fourth round of the FA Cup and this was the queue waiting to get tickets in advance - the first applicant was there at 5.50am. The paper said: "It is certain that if Burnden Park could accommodate 100,000, it would be full for the match." Note the prices: 1/3 (about 8p) for the ground, 3/- (15p) for the wing stand.

3 AUGUST 1946

PRIVATE BOXES AND TIP-UP CHAIRS AT BURNDEN

Setting about their work of reconstruction at Burnden Park dertermined to make it a football ground second to none, the Wanderers announce big alterations on the grandstand.

From a church at Rochdale and a cinema at Eccles, they obtained nearly 180 seats, mostly of the tip-up variety, and these are now set out on the first 13 rows of the stand. An innovation is the creation of a number of boxes or pens, some containing six seats and some four. These are, of course, hired en bloc for the season (£40 for six seats, and £27 for four) and represent a big increase on the old prices, but they are private enclosures, in the best positions, and are de luxe, even to carpets on the floors. The club sold these new seats almost at once.

Goalkeeper Stan Hanson signed as an amateur for Bolton in 1935, although after two months he turned professional. He made his League debut in 1936, but it was not until a couple of years later that he displaced Fred Swift. In 1940, he was one of the 13 Wanderers' players involved in the retreat at Dunkirk. In 1945 he was demobbed and continued his career with Bolton, in 1950 touring Canada with the F.A., and in 1953 kept goal in the F.A. Cup final against Blackpool. At the age of 40 he was given a free transfer to Rhyl and left Burnden in 1956. His ties to Bolton were not to be broken, however. He spent a couple of seasons taking charge of the Wanderers'"B" team, and then became postmaster at the Burnden Post Office opposite the ground where he stayed for many years.

"The departure of 'Ray' (William Raymond) Westwood to Chester closes another chapter in the club's history, and with some reluctance for many of us," wrote Haydn Berry in 1947. "Westwood, the only remaining playing link with the men who last brought Wembley glory to the club, although he had only just joined them at that time, was that rare type known as 'box office' Like the Matthews and Lawtons he had an appeal of his own, due to a graceful style of play and goal-scoring capacity. He played his first match for Bolton in 1931. He was a star in his own right, with three full international caps v Scotland, Wales and Ireland, and others v Continental sides, and I don't think it is too much to say that his wing association with Willie Cook was the last notable flank partnership possessed by the club in any way to be compared with past institutions such as the Smith-Vizard, Stokes-Marsh, Donaldson-Jones, White-McEwan, and Jack Butler combinations. "In his 17 years as a professional (six a 'dead' loss through war), Westwood played 338 senior matches and scored 152 goals. Figuratively his best season was in 1934-35 when his 30 goals in 38 Second Division games were a big factor in returning the Wanderers to the First Division, but we will always think of this man as the dainty dribbler who could travel faster with a ball than his pursuers without it, and who combined a body swerve with a rare eye for a chink in the best defences of his day."

18 MARCH
PLAYERS BOLTON WERE UNFORTUNATE TO LOSE

Bolton Wanderers have from time to time suffered heavy misfortune with players of great promise whose careers have been cut short by injuries, writes John K. Fletcher. As far back as 1910, they secured from Tranmere Rovers an inside forward, Harold Hilton, who would, I feel sure, have attained international recognition had he had the good fortune to escape mishap.

He showed such skill in a few games with the reserves that he was given his place in the senior team against Bristol City on April 9th, 1910, as partner to Joe Smith, then an outside-left. One of nine players the Wanderers tried in the inside-left position that season, Hilton quickly established himself as one of the best inside forwards in the country, his skill with the ball, an effective body swerve, and a deadly shot being features of his game.

When Ted Vizard arrived and could not be denied his place in the first team, Smith moved to inside-left, and Hilton crossed over to the right. But on December 9th, 1911, Hilton hurt a knee whilst playing against Notts. County on the Trent Bridge ground, and though he helped the Wanderers to beat Burnley 4-1 in a Lancashire Cup tie on the following Wednesday, the trouble was aggravated. Then followed a long spell of treatment, and he figured in few League games afterwards, his last appearance being on the Arsenal ground on November 8th, 1919, when goals by Vizard and Buchan earned a point.

It was obvious that his injury had shattered all hopes of his making a name, and in the end the Bolton directors gave him a free transfer. He was then re-engaged by his old club, Tranmere, but it was clear that his knee trouble was a sore and irreparable handicap, and he failed to repeat his old scoring feats.

In the winter of 1920, the Football Association sent a team on tour to South Africa, and two Bolton players, Joe Smith and David Jack, were included. The side won all their

matches, and in Test matches at Durban, Johannesburg and Cape Town, scored 15 goals against three. On returning to Bolton, Smith was full of praise for J.R. (Dick) Elvey, the Luton Town right full-back, who was one of the outstanding successes of the touring party, and the Bolton captain eventually persuaded the Wanderers' officials to seek his transfer. On August 28th, 1920, he made his League debut with the Wanderers against Manchester United at Old Trafford, and earned his first £2 bonus.

Seven days later, when the teams met in the return game at Burnden Park, he injured a knee, in his third game, and that to all intents and purposes put an end to his football. The Wanderers made every effort to repair the damage, but finally he was allowed to leave the club. On September 15th, 1922, the Arsenal decided to take a chance with him, and he went into training again, but it did not take long to convince both club and player that the future had no promise for him as a footballer.

When Bolton beat Arsenal 1-0 in 1948, Don Howe scored the only goal. The paper said: "After 11 years' wait, the Wanderers conquered Arsenal at Burnden entirely on merit. If their shooting had been as good as their approaches the score would have been a lot bigger."

19 NOVEMBER 1949
BOBBY LANGTON FOR BURNDEN PARK

Bobby Langton, Preston North End's international left-winger, today signed for the Wanderers after more than a week's talks between club and player. He will play against Manchester City tomorrow. The transfer, which has been effected with the utmost secrecy so that the player would not be prejudiced in the event of staying on at Deepdale, will have cost the Wanderers their biggest ever fee. It is thought to be as high as £22,500.

In November 1949, Field Marshall Viscount Montgomery came to Bolton to be created the 10th - and at that time the only living - Freeman of Bolton. Later that day he went on to Burnden Park where at first he saw a display of physical training by members of the Lads' Club (below), and then met the players (opposite page) before entering the directors' box to the strains of "Lillie Marlene". A few days later, the paper reported "A souvenir of Viscount Montgomery's visit has arrived at Burnden Park, and it should please the players as much as it is prized by the chairman, Mr Peter Duxbury. It is a letter from the new Freeman of the Borough, written in his own hand from his home and reads: "Mr Dear Duxbury, I am so glad you managed to hold Newcastle to a draw on Saturday. I had to leave at half-time, and up to then it looked to me as if you deserved to win. The great objective is never to be beaten by anyone on your home ground. Please tell your team how glad I was to meet them. I shall hope to see them in action again in due course. Yours sincerely, Montgomery of Alamein, Field Marshall."

Bridge Street, with the Palais dance hall prominent, 1950s.

1950s

DATE	WORLD EVENTS	BOLTON EVENTS
1953	Coronation of Queen Elizabeth II. Edmund Hillary of New Zealand and Tenzing Norgay of Nepal reach top of Mt. Everest. Hungary astonish England with a breathtaking 6-3 victory at Wembley.	
1954	England's Roger Bannister becomes the first man ever to run a mile under four minutes.	The new Queen was greeted by massive crowds on a visit to Bolton.
1957	Russians launch Sputnik I, first Earth-orbiting satellite and the Space Age begins.	A sewer caved in at Fylde Street, Moses Gate, wrecking 19 houses and making 400 people homeless.
1958		35 people died when plane travelling from the Isle of Man to Manchester plunged into Winter Hill in thick mist.

18 OCTOBER 1950

MR W.J. ROWLEY LEAVES THE WANDERERS

An association with Bolton Wanderers extending over 38 years was ended last night when the directors accepted "with deep regret" the resignation of the Secretary-Manager, Mr Walter J. Rowley, because of ill health.

When Bolton Wanderers secured his transfer from Oldham Athletic in 1912, neither player nor those who appointed him thought for a moment that he would one day become manager. A native of Little Hulton and a tailor's cutter by trade, he was a member of a football family. Throughout his career at Burnden, he was always a trier, rendering the club splendid service in all three half-back positions, and also at full-back. His playing career came to an end in 1924 and he left the tailoring trade when the Wanderers gave him appointment as coach. Later he became chief scout as well. In the Second World War he was engaged in the Admiralty Ordnance Department, and in 1944 the Wanderers brought him back to Burnden to succeed Mr C.E. Foweraker as manager.

In 1950, WILLIE Moir, the Wanderers' inside-right, was included in that position in the Scottish team to play England at Hampden Park. It was Moir's first (and as it turned out, only) cap. The paper said: "Moir, an Aberdeenshire man still at a sunny age, came to Bolton during the war. He signed amateur forms on April 27th, 1943, while serving with the R.A.F. at Weeton Camp, Blackpool, and turned professional very soon afterwards. Since first-class football resumed, he has made 128 appearances for the Wanderers and scored 49 goals". In fact, in the 1948-49 season, he topped the First Division scoring charts, with 25 goals in 42 appearances. In 1953 he captained Bolton in the F.A. Cup Final, but a couple of years later, after 12 years with the club, he joined Stockport County.

History was made at Burnden Park in October, 1951, when Raymond Parry, 15 years and 207 days old Derby ex-schoolboy international forward, was selected to play at inside-left for the Wanderers against Sunderland. He became the youngest player to appear in the First Division.

The paper said: "Those who have watched Parry in his six Central League games say his football is far more mature than his years. In his schoolboy international games he scored eight times and was so outstanding a footballer of the future that many of the big clubs, Derby County in particular, were bitterly disappointed when the Wanderers obtained his signature on amateur forms. He now works as an apprentice joiner at the ground. He will be 16 on January 19th next, so cannot be a professional for another 12 months."

He made one more first team appearance that season, then gradually settled into the side. He was a member of the 1958 Cup winning team, appeared twice for the England Under-23 side, winning the first of two full caps in 1959 when he scored in a 2-1 win over Northern Ireland. In October 1960, he transferred to Blackpool. He had scored 78 goals for the club and made 300 appearances. He is seen in this picture just after receiving the news of his 1951 debut, and being congratulated by Mrs Pickford, his Kearsley landlady, who was the wife of one of the club's scouts.

Improvements were being made to the playing pitch at Burnden Park in April, 1950. The pitch was being lengthened by seven feet and levelled.

BOLTON WANDERERS
JOIN THE
BOLTON WANDERERS
SUPPORTERS
CLUB
JOIN TODAY!

The Supporters Club is now a integral part of the Wanderers. But it was not always so...

21 JANUARY 1951
SHOULD WANDERERS RECOGNISE SUPPORTERS' CLUB?

Should the directors of Bolton Wanderers' Football Club "recognise" the newly-formed Supporters' Club?
Failure by the directors to support last night's presentation dinner, at which Nat Lofthouse was given a handsome grandmother clock in recognition of his first international cap, has brought into public prominence a difference of opinion on the point.

The Supporters' Club officials believe there is no reason why recognition should not be given, as it has to other similar clubs. The Wanderers say in effect, "We don't need a Supporters' Club, but we cannot stop you organising yourselves for your own purposes." And there the difference rests.

Last night's happy function, graced by the Mayor and attended by Ald Booth, M.P., Press guests and several players, with Tommy Lawton as the famous personality brought in to make the presentation, went off with complete success, in spite of the absence of an Burnden Park dignitary; but at the close, Mr L. Syddall, organising secretary of the Supporters' Club, gave a report of its aims and referred to the Wanderers' refusal to give recognition.

Several efforts had been made to gain this official recognition, he said, and offers had been made to form a deputation to meet the Board. This offer had been rejected.

Nevertheless, the Bolton Supporters' Club is here to stay, says the report. "At the moment, the Supporters' Club, with its 1,000 members, represents only a tiny section of the club's following, which this season stands at a steady thirty-odd thousand for home games. It is the ambition of the Supporters' organisation, however, to attain a membership of 10,000."

Whether recognition was being given or not, members were not giving in, and the picture (opposite page) shows officials of the Supporters' Club having a recruiting day in February, 1951. "Spectators found this signing-on post opposite the ground, and some 300 new members are reported to have been added to the roll," said the caption.

6 FEBRUARY 1951
WANDERERS' NEW MANAGER

A special meeting of the Wanderers' directors' yesterday afternoon appointed Mr W. Ridding, for four and a half years head trainer, to the vacant position of manager. Thus a stalemate of more than three months, since the resignation of Mr W.J. Rowley, during which rumour and gossip, in and out of print, have incorrectly anticipated the directors' choice, has been settled by a selection of a man from their own staff.

Mr Ridding has been a training specialist for some 16 years, and spent nearly nine years as a professional player. He is England's No. 1 trainer, the friend and confidant of many famous players, and a man well thought of in the hierarchy of the Football Association and Football League.

Bill Ridding, Bolton's new manager in 1951.

During the last century, before underground heating, the weather often played a major part in the football season. However, heavy snow wasn't enough to put off many matches. The picture on this page, taken in January, 1951, shows everyone buckling down to clear the pitch in preparation for the F.A. Cup match against York City, which the Wanderers won 2-1.

The opposite page shows another picture a gang of groundsmen forking the ice-pack at the Great Lever end in January 1953. "Burnden Park, scene of the Wanderers' third round F.A. Cup tie against Fulham, is a sheet of ice, in parts half an inch thick," reported the paper. "The Wanderers are battling hard to make a match possible so far as human hands or ingenuity can. An appeal has been made to Bolton Corporation to supply every brazier they can lay hands on." By the day of the match, a thaw had set in, but the match still had to be called off, because "it came creeping down from the hills, over the fields and into the streets - a murky fog which cut down visibility to a few yards." The game was eventually played the following Wednesday, and Bolton won 3-1.

Braziers were often used to thaw out the frozen pitch. (opposite page, insert) "Other methods have been tried out in various places, but an ideal way has yet to be found," said the caption in a 1950 booklet called "All About Bolton Wanderers", and reported in the paper. It was described as "an invaluable little booklet recently been published which, as its title says, is 'All About Bolton Wanderers.' With photographs and handy references for the 'facts and figures' boys, and notes about players past and present, it is a complete guide to Burnden. There is also a pleasant little essay on 'The Babel that is Burnden', which describes our football centre thus, 'Burnden Park - roistering, raucous Burnden, when 30,000 ordinarily quiet citizens cheer and curse, rant and rave, sway and shove, in keeping with the fortunes of the famous white-shirted Wanderers.

"The book can be had from local booksellers and newsagents at 1s 6d."

19 APRIL 1952
WANDERERS' BEST LEAGUE SEASON FOR 25 YEARS

That "double" over Fulham on Monday, bringing the points total to 46, has set a lot of folk hoping that after all this most successful of post-war seasons for the Bolton club will be crowned with half a century. Even the players are realising more than they did at the time what a wonderful opportunity of honours has been lost by a few poor performances.

"We must have dropped something like 10 points that could have been 'in the bag', and that is as good as saying we ought to be sitting comfortably on top instead of Manchester United," said Willie Moir this week. However, the 46 points gathered in is the biggest First Division harvest by a Bolton team in 25 seasons, not bad to be going on with. The last time it was beaten was in the 1926-7 season when the total was 48.

No Wanderers team has reached the half-century in First Division football since 1924-5 when 55 points were won in what is still considered the year of years, although it was not a cup winning season.

Backroom staff at the Wanderers in 1953 start sorting out the many thousands of applications for the Cup Final.

For many years the matches over the festive season included one on Christmas Day itself, and they were very popular with fans. In December, 1952, Bolton lost to Arsenal (so the rest of Christmas would have been miserable in many a local home!) and the paper reported:

27 DECEMBER 1952
CHRISTMAS DAY THRILLER AT BURNDEN

Bolton 4 Arsenal 6

IF it's goals that make soccer the magnet, then nearly 50,000 people at Burnden Park on Christmas Day saw soccer at its best. Inside a minute Willie Moir had lost a great scoring chance and then put his side ahead, both beautiful moves worthy of goals. Sparkling attacking play had Arsenal penned in their own half, but in characteristic Arsenal fashion they turned defence into attack when they drew level in the 12th minute. This was a damper for the crowd, but they had lots of consolation in store for both attacks continued to play fine, purposeful football replete with thrills. It was a little hard on the Wanderers, after Harry Webster had shot against an upright and Moir had seen a header beat the advancing Kelsey and curl outside an empty net, to find Holton driving home a short-range shot to give the Gunners the lead at half-time.

But two more goals in five minutes after the break, to Roper and Logie, emphasised the Gunners' mastery of the goalmaking art, and for a time demonstrated a clear superiority in all phases of the game. Many a side would have buckled at this stage but not the Wanderers. With the second half only ten minutes old, Lofthouse had banged in a second goal, and although Arsenal promptly added two more through Ray Daniel (a penalty kick) and Holton, the Bolton attack battled back with such spirit that the margin was again reduced to two by goals from Lofthouse and Moir.

With ten minutes left to play the match was more alive than ever and the crowd, revelling in the Wanderers' fighting qualities roared their approval when a penalty kick was awarded as Langton rolled over in a tackle. This was the great moment. A fifth goal now, with five minutes to play, meant there was still a chance to save the day. But Langton's shot from the spot was not far enough away from Kelsey and the goalkeeper smothered it round the post to safety. Kelsey had really settled the issue with that save, and indeed was a great factor throughout the match.

However, it is a testimony to the dash and opportunism of the Wanderers' forwards that they scored four goals and came near to getting many more.

Teams -
Bolton Wanderers: Hanson, Ball, Higgins, Wheeler, Barrass, Neill, Holden, Moir, Lofthouse, Webster, Langton

Arsenal: Kelsey, Wade, Smith, Shaw, Daniel, Mercer, Milton, Logie, Holton, Lishman, Roper.

Some of the thousands of Bolton fans who made their way to Maine Road, home of Manchester City, in March, 1953, for the F.A. Cup semi-final against Everton. The Wanderers won 4-3, with goals from Moir, Lofthouse 2, and Holden

1953 saw the first of Bolton's two appearances in the F.A. Cup final during the 1950s - but this one, against Blackpool, ended in tears after the Wanderers, winning 3-1 well into the second half, lost the match 4-3 in the dying seconds. It is recognised as one of the most dramatic and exciting Finals in history, and became known as the Matthews Final because of the magnificent part played by the Seasider in Bolton's destruction. Haydn Berry wrote in the Evening News:

4 MAY 1953

WANDERERS GO DOWN FIGHTING

Bolton 3 Blackpool 4

It was an extra thrill outside the stadium after what is being called the Final of Finals, to see the Bolton players leaving to cheers of many of their supporters. Sunshine roof flung back, the coach moved slowly away with the players on top, showing themselves and waving cheerfully just as if they had won the battle instead of losing it. That was the way to do it. No hiding away from the sympathetic gaze of the soccer legions for they had nothing to be ashamed of, this team of plucky fighters. All that was missing was the Cup - and they were unfortunate not to have that too.

As skipper Willie Moir said, in his remarks at the Cafe Royal banquet on Saturday night: "We lost because the game was five minutes too long. Every man in the side ran himself into the ground." This puts the whole situation into right perspective. Eric Bell's pulled muscle, reducing the team's strength to 10 men from the 20th minute (the team had to be reshuffled, with Bell having difficulty running being moved to the left-wing, Langton coming inside and Hassall at left-half) doubled the strain on all and the side just failed to hold out after achieving an apparently winning position of 3-1 with 20 minutes to play and 3-2 with only three minutes left.

Further knocks - Banks, Lofthouse, Barrass and Ball were all casualties - added to their distress in the final phase, and, of course, the brilliant play of Stanley Matthews exploited it and clinched Blackpool's dramatic victory. Stanley was a brilliant winger in the end, but this Matthews' performance should be considered in relation to the weakness of the opposition. He only ran away with the defence when the Bolton team was crippled and produced

nothing wonderful before that. But the ball-holding powers that he possesses, and his skill in 'drawing' a defence to him before crossing the vital pass, definitely turned defeat into victory where no ordinary player could have done so, and he was clearly the architect of victory."

And The Tramp followed it up with his comments: "In one of the most extraordinary transformations Wembley has seen, Blackpool took the Cup by scoring two goals in the last three minutes of the game. They owe their success to the brilliance of Matthews, but as much as to the injuries that beset their opponents. Hassall was the only real sound man on the Bolton left flank in defence and the brilliant dribbling of Matthews proved too much on the day."

Teams -
Bolton: Hanson, Ball, R. Banks, Wheeler, Barrass, Bell, Holden, Moir, Lofthouse, Hassall, Langton.

Blackpool: Farm, Shinwell, Garrett, Fenton, Johnston, Robinson, Matthews, Taylor, Mortenson, Mudie, Perrie.

Scorers: Bolton - Moir, Bell, Lofthouse. Blackpool - Hassall, Mortensen (2), Perry.

Another story in the paper reported that "While 12,000 to 15,000 Bolton supporters were at Wembley to be on the spot for this year's F.A. Cup Final, thousands more were gathered round television sets in homes all over the town to watch the Wanderers' first appearance at Wembley for 24 years. It was the new way to watch the Cup Final. At homes throughout the town, families and their friends saw acquaintances and well-known local people in the huge Wembley stadium. The commentator for the match was Farnworth-born Ken Wolstenholme.

THE FOOTBALL ASSOCIATION CHALLENGE CUP COMPETITION

FINAL TIE

BLACKPOOL v
BOLTON WANDERERS

SATURDAY, MAY 2nd, 1953   KICK-OFF 3 pm

EMPIRE STADIUM

WEMBLEY

Chairman and Managing Director : SIR ARTHUR J. ELVIN, M.B.E.

The last minute goal that gave Blackpool the Cup for the first time.

Another shot from Nat - but this one hit the post and failed to go in.

Seventy five seconds into the 1953 game, and a dismayed Blackpool goalkeeper Farm saw a shot from Nat Lofthouse at the back of his net.
It meant that the Bolton centre-forward had scored in every round of the Cup that season.

This party of Bolton supporters posed for an Evening News' photographer before entering the stadium in 1953.

Mrs J.H. Bowker and her husband wrote and painted on the window of their fish and chip shop in Egerton Street, Farnworth, a victory song for the Wanderers.

When the team returned home, they were given a great reception by supporters. (left) They appeared on the Town Hall steps (right) , and captain Willie Moir spoke to the crowds.

A page from the Evening News telling of the defeat.

9 MARCH 1954

BIGGEST EVER?

Has there ever, in Bolton Wanderers' long history, been a longer queue of ticket hunters than Sunday's? We can't remember one, although there were probably more people at the ground last April for the Cup Final ticket distribution.

Sunday's queue extended on the Manchester side to the greyhound track, after first doubling round Croft Lane, while the queue on the town centre side of the ground ran to the Queen's Cinema corner after travelling, dog-leg style, across the parking ground to Manchester Road. No wonder the sellers could not cope with their task at the office windows but had to open the match turnstiles!

Who would connect a line of people, starting at the end of Bradshawgate, with the football ground nearly half a mile away? We are coming to think it is not the players who in future should be known, and written about, as great Cup fighters; but their tough-fibred, long-suffering, incredible fans.

The scene outside Burnden Park in March, 1954, as people queued for the 3,000 ground tickets for the F.A. Cup tie returned by Sheffield Wednesday. Some even brought their prams with them. The match ended 1-1, and in the replay Wanderers went down 2-0.

30 APRIL 1954

WANDERERS DO NOT QUALIFY FOR LEAGUE BONUS MONEY

By the small margin of .008 of a goal, Bolton Wanderers lost the £220 bonus money that would have been awarded to them had they finished in the first four of the League. As the Wanderers lost to Huddersfield, who finished in third place, 2-1 on Saturday, they are fifth in the league table. In the first half of the game at Leeds-rd., the Wanderers were slightly inferior to the Huddersfield men and it was in the 20th minute that Huddersfield went ahead. Glazzard tried to dribble round Barrass, cleared him and then stumbled. The referee immediately gave a penalty to Huddersfield, which McGarry converted.

Lofthouse missed an easy chance to equalise six minutes later, and ten minutes from half time Cavanagh scored a second for Huddersfield. The situations were reversed in the second half and gave the Town's defence some anxious moments before Parry scored. He beat two men, and then placed a low shot just inside the post. The Wanderers failed to press home the advantage and could not score the vital goal which would mean bonus money.

Bolton Evening News

FIRST WITH ALL RESULTS

Green Final

No. 26,843   SATURDAY, JANUARY 2, 1954   TWOPENCE

WANDERERS RALLY AND BEAT BOTTOM CLUB

Stevens scores the winning goal

EXCITING INCIDENTS IN SECOND HALF

LIVERPOOL ....1 BOLTON WANDERERS 2

Our cameraman saw more than most spectators in the Gigg-lane gloom when he snapped Kelly's second goal for Bury against Hull City.

FOG STOPS GAME AT GIGG-LANE

Blackpool drop point

BURY SCORE FOUR AGAINST HULL CITY
Abandoned after 75 minutes

BURY 4   HULL CITY 1

North End just fail

This was the front page from January, 1954, of an edition of the Green Final, which was printed for only a few years.

MORE HOSPITAL BROADCASTS NEEDED

Once again a voice cries out from Wilkinson Sanatorium: "Give us the Wanderers' match broadcasts. "Since the hospital broadcasts started from Burnden Park two or three seasons ago an extension, especially to Wilkinson, has been asked for. Now the plea is such that something really must be done about it; but by whom?

The Wanderers, who defray the entire cost of the present broadcasts to the Royal Infirmary and Bolton District General Hospital (Townleys) are sympathetic towards the extension idea, but cannot undertake it at the recently increased Post Office charge of £200 a year for each new line. In fact, why should they, even if they were rich?

They are doing a grand job, with the help of volunteer broadcasters whose fidelity cannot be praised too much, providing match descriptions for two hospitals; but the obligation to provide the service should never be theirs at all. Perhaps it isn't anybody's, but surely there are funds in Bolton, and organisations behind them, to provide this boon for the sick and unfortunate at Wilkinson, Hulton-lane Hospital, and possibly to Blair Convalescent Hospital so that the club will not have the guilty feeling of letting someone down?

"The Wanderers' headquarters are fast becoming the Highbury of the North as the favourite centre of the B.B.C. and film sequence activities", said the caption to this picture in 1954. "Any day now a visit is expected from Arthur Askey in connection with his film 'The Love Match', but when Wilfred Pickles turned up unexpectedly today, Manager Bill Ridding and his staff adapted themselves with alacrity and the usual hospitality.

Wilfred slipped into a track suit and did a bit of sprinting as part of a "stunt", but his own facetious explanation of this was that he is going to Germany the week after next to entertain the troops and so he must be fit. His visit was in connection with one of the letters sent in to his television feature "Ask Pickles", by a 13-years-old Warsop boy, Michael Brightman, whose dearest ambitions in life were to meet Nat Lofthouse, his football hero, and to play for Bolton Wanderers. Michael and Wilfred had a good time at Burnden, the boy being granted his wish to meet Lofthouse and even being given the opportunity to wear the club 'strip'. And, of course, he collected autographs while the great opportunity presented itself - altogether a proud little boy. The picture shows Wilfred with the inevitable group of young autograph hunters."

In November, 1957, the Russian army team (CDSA) came to Bolton to play a friendly game. The night before the match a dinner was given for the visitors and "an introductory get-together over cocktails" set the tone for a happy function ending in a wholesale exchange of gifts between the parties. When it came to the game itself, though, it was a different story . . .

4 NOVEMBER 1957

QUICK TEMPERED PLAYERS SPOILED GAME: REFEREE MUST SHARE BLAME

Bolton 3 CDSA 1

A hard tacking tussle, with far too many unsavoury incidents went the Wanderers' way against the Russian Army team under the Burnden lights last night. It left the wrong kind of impression on neutral visitors and ended with players of both teams damaged. Nat Lofthouse was taken to the Royal Infirmary with delayed concussion. The Russian centre half finished the match after only nine minutes following a head clash with Lofthouse, but he was not in as bad shape. Bangs and bruises were suffered by almost everybody else in this unlovely display.

The Wanderers, faster, more direct and purposeful, were three goals to the good by half-time despite the substitution of Lofthouse by Gubbins with nearly a quarter of an hour to go to the interval; in fact the reserve man scored a fine goal with a close range volley shortly after coming on.

In the second half the Russians, with about six new men to freshen up their side did much better, and here Joe Dean came in to justify his place. In fact, Hopkinson could not have improved Big Joe's performance as he held and deflected short-range shots from centre-forward Busonov, Bubukin and Emisnev. Only one goal fell to the bald-headed inside right Bubukin, and it was a header after one of the few defensive slips the Wanderers were guilty of in the whole match.

A pity this event was spoiled by temper. The Wanderers, urged by many of us to make a real job of the game rather than just an exhibition, drifted into Cup-tie tackling when the far too complacent Dutch referee permitted the Russians to body-check and obstruct to their hearts content, and also gave too many decisions the wrong way. Tempers rose on both sides, and consequently the football suffered. If all games were treated this way, half a dozen officials would not be enough.

Goals came as follows: Parry (penalty) 26 minutes, Lofthouse 28 minutes, Gubbins 44 minutes. Bukukin 48 minutes.

Bolton team: Dean, Hartle, Banks, Hennin, Higgins, Edwards (B), Birch, Stevens, Lofthouse, Parry, Holden.

A page from The Buff, which for many years was the sports edition of the Evening News.

On October 14, 1957, floodlights were used for the first time at Burnden. "The weather did its best to spoil the switch-on," wrote Olympian. "The mist which hung over the ground was exactly what was not wanted, and whilst it was obvious that the lights would be first-class under normal conditions, visibility was not up to the desired standard last night. None of the 21,058 spectators had a clear view of the whole field." The friendly game against Hearts ended in a draw.

In 1957, trouble brewed at the Wanderers after Nat Lofthouse, still signed as a professional player, told the club that he wanted also to become licensee of the Castle Hotel, Crompton Way. The club refused permission, and a statement said "The Board find no justification for relaxing the club rule, which they feel sure serves in the best interests of the club and player". The row rumbled on for months, but in April of that year Nat re-signed forms for the next season, and at the same time got permission to run the Castle. Manager Bill Ridding issued a brief statement" "Both parties have come to a satisfactory agreement." Nat's comment, almost equally brief, was: "I am very pleased it is all over. I have been a one-man club all my career, and want it to continue that way."

The only conclusion to be drawn from this item of news, commented the paper, is that the 34-years-old club rule has been waived by the Board. So Nat got his pub . . . but his tenancy was to be shortlived. After only 19 months, and "of his own free will", he resigned because "my reasons are entirely to do with the health of my children, 10-years-old Jeffrey and five-years-old Vivien. We have come to the conclusion that the atmosphere in a pub is not good for the kids."

Wanderers' player Dennis Stevens said he was "amazed" when asked what he thought of his selection among England's 22 players for the World Cup preliminary series of three games, in 1957. The article about him said: "Few football recognitions have given more genuine pleasure to his team mates. Skipper Nat Lofthouse put it in a nutshell when he said 'If any lad deserves an honour, Dennis does for his play this season'. Nat added: 'I think I've only also been picked to daddy little Dennis. I think I'm there to keep an eye on him'."The picture shows Nat congratulating Dennis, together with team mates Ralph Gubbins, Harry Webster, Roy Hartle and Bryan Edwards.

Unfortunately, inside-forward Dennis did not get his cap. Later, he was a member of the 1958 Cup winning team, and in 1959-60, after taking over from an injured Nat Lofthouse at centre-forward, he was the club's leading goalscorer (14). He was sold to Everton in 1962 for £35,000.

Goalkeeper Eddie Hopkinson and his deputy, Nat Lofthouse, were the big stars in the Wanderers' 3-2 defeat at Wolverhampton in February, 1957. Before he was injured, Hopkinson prevented a goal-scoring riot by Wolves' bustling forwards, and Lofthouse kept up the good work later on, including, on this picture, saving a penalty from right-winger Harry Hooper.

In 1958 the Wanderers got to the Cup Final again, but on the way they had to beat League leaders and Cup favourites Wolves in the quarter-finals in a game which is said to be one of the most thrilling Cup ties ever played at Burnden.

1 MARCH 1958

BURNDEN GAME WAS ONE OF TENSE DRAMA

Bolton 2 Wolves 1

An early Cup Tie Special edition told of how Burnden "has emerged from a nightmare week of snow, ice and thaw to become a fit and proper place for the 'Little Wembley' battle. It will take the best Bolton can produce to beat the Midlands' idols and prevent them doing the double by winning the League and Cup."

That statement was certainly true. Hadyn Berry reported: "A happier place than the Wanderers' dressing room after the match could not have been found anywhere. Hand-shaking, patting on the back, shouts of congratulations, filled the air, and as the steam rose from the communal bath there rose also the singsong of the players who had triumphed over adversity.

For not only was Ray Parry - suffering from concussion and lying quietly in a darkened corner of the Burnden clinic while consciousness slowly returned - off the field for the last nerve-wracking 10 minutes, but, unknown to the crowd (and to the Wolves), Derek Hennin was suffering from a muscle pull from the fifth minute onwards, leaving the Bolton team with only nine sound men to hold the slender lead given them by the goals of Stevens and Parry against one to Wolves through Mason.

The secret of Hennin's handicap was kept because of the courage of the big right-half, and the industry of his mates, especially Dennis Stevens, who played the second half virtually in defence, concealed it; but this largely explains why the Wolves so dominated the game in the last lap. In keeping the ball out of their net the Wanderers had some fantastic luck; but there was some most determined goal-packing as well, and some goal-line resourcefulness that robbed the Wolves' marksmen of enough goals to win the game.

Roy Hartle, one of their fellow Midlanders, must have saved three himself, and we know Bryan Edwards kicked off the line early on, while Hopkinson, Banks and Higgins between them soaked up every inch of mud in the Great Lever goal mouth in making a human barrier against the Wolverhampton bombardment.

A stirring match, if ever there was one; many say the most exciting football match they can ever recall attending.

From Lofthouse downwards they were magnificent in their spirit. No bigger ordeal lies ahead. They don't come any bigger, stronger, or better in the Cup than the Wolves. They have come through their Cup crisis at the gateway to Wembley, and can go forward without fear to the end of this journey.

If these comments strike you as rhapsodising a football victory, let me tell you about Tommy Banks, as he came refreshed and glowing from the bath. Eyes sparking with honest delight, he said: I feel wonderful, wonderful. It's a feeling I can't describe. . all I know is that you can't buy it!" From a rugged Farnworthian, who calls a spade a spade, that was as near to poetry as sporting achievement will ever inspire.

Mo doubts about it, these Wolves were every bit as strong and tough a Cup side as they were expected to be. They were competent and businesslike in all they did, except goal scoring They also had the misfortune to meet a team as doggedly determined to win as themselves. Wolves were a bit quicker to the ball, most of the way, and that was the only point of superiority they could claim on the day. Bolton rose to the occasion and earned their semi-final reward.

Teams -
Bolton: Hopkinson, Hartle, Banks, Hennin, Higgins, Edwards, Birch, Stevens, Lofthouse, Parry, Holden.

Wolverhampton: Finlayson, Stuart, Harris, Clamp, Wright, Flowers, Deeley, Broadbent, Murray, Mason, Mullen.

Tommy Banks . . . "a feeling I can't describe."

When the Wanderers played Blackburn Rovers at Maine Road, Manchester, in the semi-final of the 1958 F.A. Cup, a young Ralph Gubbins, (pictured left, in an earlier league game) took the place of an injured Nat Lofthouse - and became the toast of the town when he scored both Bolton goals in the 2-1 victory. Haydn Berry wrote: "He wasn't everyone's choice, even as the stop-gap, but Gubbins, the slender winger turned centre forward, kept a cool head twice during fleeting moments of indecision by the Rovers' defenders and made neat little goals out of both situations. Did I say fleeting moments? I should have said magic moments, for these were indeed goals conjured up from nowhere by a lad who, without the brute strength and bashing style of some in his profession, is a true footballing type." Unfortunately for Ralph, Nat was fit again for the Final, so although he had got the team to the Final, Ralph did not appear in it.

Bolton's John Higgins shakes hands with Blackburn's captain before the semi-final.

The final a few weeks later was against Manchester United. It was shortly after the Munich disaster; the sympathies of the world were with United, but the Wanderers did not let that influence them. In the 1953 final against Blackpool Nat Lofthouse had scored within 75 seconds - on this occasion it took him three minutes, and he added another to give Bolton a well-deserved 2-0 victory. The F.A. Cup was back in Bolton. The cost of the Bolton team was just £110 - the total of the signing on fees!

MAY
BEST OF ALL CUP FORMULAS WON THE DAY

Bolton 2 Manchester United 0

THE black market in Cup Final tickets reached an enormous peak. Despite all attempts to check the traffic in tickets, open auctions were held along all roads leading to the stadium. The highest bid for a 3s 6d terrace ticket was £9. Stand tickets changed hands for never less than £20". It was obviously well worth paying that extra money.

Hadyn Berry reported: "It is not easy to decide where to begin these reflections on a famous victory that has written a new exciting chapter in the Wanderers' history. If you have not already read, or heard, enough about the match, it was won by the best of all Cup formulas - solid, unshakable defence, and scoring opportunism allied to the will to win.

Manchester United were not as good in any of these respects. In fact, they were not as good opposition as expected, even after allowing for their hastily-built force, and the Wanderers' win was their easiest of the series, apart from the York replay. This may be the main reason why the match was not one of Wembley's epics.

A workmanlike effort was required, not more, and the Wanderers produced it by pulling together as one man from the start. Skipper Nat converted his chances in his best style, Eddie Hopkinson pulled off two superb saves when they were needed, and enjoyed one fantastic spot of luck when Charlton hit a post. The big occasion also found two men in Bryan Edwards and Brian Birch pulling out an averagely good game. And Banks for me was the pick of the lot with an outstanding first half full of biting tackles, constructive placing and superb self-confidence that must

have been a great source of inspiration to his pals. Seconding him mightily was the man they thought might be too much of a heavyweight on that smooth Wembley turf, John Higgins; but Higgins just fooled them. A colossus in the middle of the field. But I hasten to repeat that this was a team game in every sense from number one to 11.

The scenes at the end had to be seen to be appreciated - Lofthouse leaping into Bill Ridding's grasp and Wanderers hugging one another. Then handshakes with opponents and, finally, the presentations and Nat sitting on John Higgins' broad shoulders holding the Cup aloft at all four corners of the ground for the crowd to get a close up.

At the Cafe Royal celebration banquet later, Nat Lofthouse rose to a great ovation, and said that by winning the Cup they had 'atoned for 1953' and gained the reward for careful planning. Football was a team game on park and off, said Nat, and they had that kind of team at Bolton, from top to bottom, from directors to ball boys.

'We went into the final as the Other Team', said the Bolton captain. 'This only gave us greater determination, and though we are sorry United could not crown their season with a win, football is a game where there can be only one winner, and I am proud to say that team was Bolton Wanderers."

Another columnist, The Pilgrim, said about the game that "Lofthouse receives a five-star rating for his performance, and I also rate two other Wanderers in the top-marks class - Banks, for as fine a display as one could wish to see, and Eddie Hopkinson, who was in his very best form. Hartle also had an excellent game, while the remaining members of the Bolton side played their parts manfully. Even Brian Birch, the youngster of the team, approached the final as 'just another game', and he was second to Lofthouse as the centre of danger for United."

Teams -
Bolton: Hopkinson, Hartle, Banks, Hennin, Higgins, Edwards, Birch, Stevens, Lofthouse, Parry, Holden.

Manchester United: Gregg, Foulkes, Greaves, Goodwin, Cope, Crowther, Dawson, Taylor, Charlton, Viollet, Webster. Scorers: Bolton, Lofthouse (2).

Reports of the Wanderers' coach, with the team standing half out of the open roof, being stoned by disgruntled Manchester United supporters as it passed through Salford on its victory tour home to Bolton are thought by some to have been one of the reasons for the long-standing rivalry between fans of the two clubs. But Haydn Berry talked the demonstration down . . .

MISSILE RAID REPORTS ARE UNFAIR

To talk, as some newspapers have done, about a "demonstration" or "attack" by "Manchester United supporters" on the Bolton team coach from Manchester is grossly unfair. I was in the second coach. I saw a shower of missiles thrown near Irlams-o'th-Height. The culprits were a few children. Elsewhere on the route people, many wearing United colours, applauded the Bolton team.

It is no exaggeration to say that the Wanderers were given two welcomes home last night, one in Manchester and one in Bolton. It is most unfortunate that the thoughtless action of a few mischievous children should put the only blot on a memorable evening. Happily, the players and officials who shared the barrage of turf, tomatoes, flour, and a few stones, took a light-hearted view of the incident, dusting the debris off their clothes and returning the "fire" with handwaves and smiles.

It was only on reaching the Bolton Town Hall steps and mixing with the players that we heard that one stone had broken a window and given the players' wives a shock. Mascot David Hartley was caught by a piece of glass that cut his finger. He soon forgot all about his injury as the coaches neared Bolton and excitement mounted. From Kearsley onwards it was a wildly enthusiastic multitude. Stops were made at both Kearsley and Farnworth for official welcomes by civic authorities. In Bolton, the team seemed overwhelmed. They went into the Town Hall for BBC interviews; the cheering did not cease, although after a few minutes it slowly faded. But it came back with greater zest when the boys re-appeared with the Cup.

A Heroes' welcome for the Wanderers

The crowd scenes as they appeared in the Bolton Evening News on Friday May 9th 1958.

A moment of glory for Derek Hennin as the team was presented to the Duke of Edinburgh before the match.

One of Wembley's most famous goals, and one which caused arguments long after the match, as Nat Lofthouse bundles Manchester United keeper Harry Gregg over the line to put the Wanderers two up.

The ball skims the post from a United shot with Hopkinson on the ground. On the right is Viollet.

Happiness on the faces of Nat Lofthouse and manager Bill Ridding as they hug each other immediately after the final whistle.

Nat Lofthouse, holding the F.A. Cup, leads his team mates at the Royal Box to receive their winners' medals.

Nat holds the cup aloft.

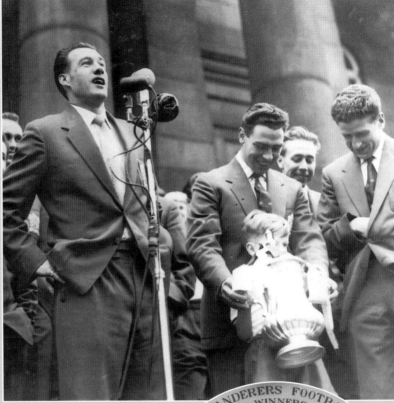

A massive crowd welcomed the team home after their triumph, and on the steps of the Town Hall Nat Lofthouse addressed them. The Cup is being shown to young mascot David Hartley.

A special plate to celebrate the victory.

Tommy Banks, the Bolton full-back, welcomed Wilf McGuiness, the only new cap, when England met the Wanderers in a trial match at Burnden Park in October, 1958. Looking on was England's captain Billy Wright. There had been a mid-day cloudburst, but the pitch was passed fit to use, and the full England team was paraded against a Wanderers X1. But it was not a full-scale match. Team manager Walter Winterbottom arranged for a 25-minute game, with a 10-minute break, followed by one or two practice moves. The 25-minute period ended with England two up. However, the teams continued to play match formation, although in the second half corner kicks were deliberately awarded and other opportunities taken to award free kicks. The final score was England 6, Wanderers 1.

Looking up Mawdsley Street from Great Moor Street, 1960s.

1960s

DATE	WORLD EVENTS	BOLTON EVENTS
1961	Moscow announces putting first man in orbit around Earth, Maj. Yuri A. Gagarin. East Germans erect Berlin Wall between East and West Berlin to halt flood of refugees.	19 people died in a fire at the Top Storey Club, Crown Street.
1962	The Beatles have their first Top 20 hit in the UK with 'Love Me Do'.	The construction of locomotives at Horwich Loco Works ended.
1963	President John F Kennedy assassinated; in Dallas, US. Lyndon Johnson becomes president. becomes president same day.	
1966	England win the world cup for the first time.	
1967	Israeli and Arab forces battle.Six-day war ends with Israel occupying Sinai Peninsula, Golan Heights, Gaza Strip, and east bank of Suez Canal.	
1968		Princess Margaret opened the Octagon Theatre.
1969	Apollo 11 astronauts—Neil A. Armstrong, Edwin E. Aldrin, Jr., and Michael Collins—take man's first walk on moon.	

Nat Lofthouse has been undoubtedly Bolton Wanderers' most illustrious and well-known player over the years. But in 1960, an injury brought his career to an end. At the time the Evening News wrote:

7 JANUARY   1960

LIONHEART LOFTHOUSE GOES INTO HISTORY

Nat Lofthouse, the living legend of Burnden Park, has passed from the active soccer scene. Nat will be missed by Bolton Wanderers and the club supporters who loved his tearaway, blood-and-guts attitude to the game which has earned him football fame as great as that of any of his contemporaries.

And indeed, the name of Nat Lofthouse will be put down in the history of the club alongside such never-to-be-forgotten giants of the past as Ted Vizard, Joe Smith and Jimmy Seddon. Many of the club's older supporters would perhaps challenge Lofthouse's right to be classed with such revered company, but the facts are incontrovertible. Nat Lofthouse, his fine international record apart, has been one of the game's greatest personalities.

The Lofthouse career is steeped in romance. It is the story of a Bolton lad who, by playing for his town's club, made his boyhood dreams come true. And during the 20 glorious years that have passed since the day he turned out for the first time in the famous white shirt of Bolton Wanderers, he has brought a dazzle of reflected glory to the club.

Nat has been essentially a one-club man, and in his career he has been capped 33 times for England, and, with Tom Finney, is the holder of the goal-scoring record for his country.

Season 1952-52 was probably the greatest for Nat Lofthouse. In that season he led England's attack in each of the three major internationals, and the climax came in the game against Wales when Nat produced what many critics regarded as his best-ever performance. Afterwards he was rated in certain quarters as England's greatest centre-forward.

A thrill for Lofthouse during 1952 was the memorable occasion when he scored six times for the Football League against the Irish League at Wolverhampton and was presented with the ball.

The feared Nat Lofthouse in typical fighting mood.

The honours continued to come Lofthouse's way, and in 1953 he was voted "Footballer of the year" by the sportswriters. It was about this time that the Italian club, Florentina offered Nat a three-year contract to go to Italy. He chose to stay in Bolton.

Probably Nat's finest hour in an international career crowded with highlights, was his game in 1952 against Austria when, seven minutes from time, the fabulous Lofthouse scored the winning goal against the so-called unbeatable Austrians. It was this performance which earned him the title "Lion of Vienna"

For the Wanderers, Lofthouse played 438 post-war League games. He scored 278 League and Cup goals, and this, coupled with the 52 goals he scored in representative matches brought his total to 330.

Counting the 107 goals Nat scored in wartime football, his gross goal count reaches 437, of which 385 have been scored for the Wanderers. During his career Nat had to take many hard knocks. One columnist wrote that he should have carried his own stretcher.

It is somewhat ironic that this wonderful player's career should be ended by an injury.

But what was that heading "Lionheart Lofthouse goes into history"? As it turned out, somewhat an overstatement. Nat continued at the club as assistant trainer. In 1967 he became chief coach, and later manager in succession to Bill Ridding. That did not last long, but he became caretaker manager on other occasions. In 1971 he left the club for a short period, but returned to become executive club manager, and later Life President. He has also been made a Freeman of Bolton and awarded an OBE.

After Nat's retirement the Evening News decided to compile "a book, handsomely bound, containing signatures of every football fan and well-wisher who cares to sign it" and it would be passed on to Nat. At the same time this picture was printed, of Nat taking "a close look at the apparatus that has been looking in his direction for so long." With him was Haydn Berry, who covered the Wanderers for the Evening News for many years, retiring in 1966 after he had reported on the World Cup Final at Wembley for the paper.

Bolton boss Bill Ridding greeted 16-years-old Francis Lee when he arrived at Burnden Park in 1960. In November of that year, he made his debut in the first team, against Manchester City, scored one goal himself and then provided the corner kick for Nat Lofthouse to put the ball in the net in the 3-1 victory (and also got booked for foul play!). The paper described him as "astonishing, baby of the battle but no pigmy among the giants . . . Lee was a revelation of stamina, spirit and football know-how, and completely justified those who were bold enough to 'risk' him in such a testing match and those who behind the scenes urged such a course." Lee signed professional forms in 1961, but his volatile nature led to him refusing to play after being dropped to the 'A' team. He made a number of transfer requests, and in 1967 Manchester City paid £65,000 for him.

In September, 1960, the Wanderers took part in the first League match to be televised. The previous day Wanderers' supporters were told in the paper: "Those who have neither the inclination nor the time to go to Blackpool tomorrow will be able to see part of the game on television, for this fixture is the first of those to be shown on the screen on Saturday evening." As for the match itself . . .

12 SEPTEMBER 1960

TV MATCH WAS NO ADVERT FOR FOOTBALL

When Bolton manager Bill Ridding described Saturday's winning performance as the worst the Wanderers have given in years he was both candid and justified by his candour. Neither the 22 players nor the 17,166 spectators would wish to go through that hour and a half's torment again in a hurry.

As an initial television showpiece, the Blackpool-Bolton game was poor advertisement for League football, lacking even the cup-tie tension of a typical Lancashire "Derby" struggle.

From start to finish it was scrappy in the extreme, and if there was a redeeming feature it can only be the consistently competent display of Jimmy Armfield, who was a very good back. Unfortunately his Blackpool colleagues failed completely to be inspired by his efforts and looked by far the poorest team the Wanderers have met so far this season.

In the form they showed against Spurs, Wolves and Birmingham the Wanderers must have won by a heavy margin, and it is sufficient commentary on their own standard of play on this occasion that the only goal of the evening only just beat the final whistle.

The question is why did the game sink so low? TV nerves have been suggested as part explanation, and there may be something in this theory; a much more important factor was the general inability to control a lively ball on a treacherous surface. No use saying "These men are professional exponents of the game, they should be able to master the ball". We know that normally they can do so. We must therefore look for reasons when all fail at once and give us a game that amateurs would not be proud of.

With thousands of other watchers I prayed for a bit of mud and a ball with some of the bounce taken out of it. We would have seen a different game altogether. That is why it is hoped the TV experiment will not be dropped because the curtain-raiser was a poor one. Many a good play has had a bad first night. The next League match televised - if there is a next - may be just what the viewers want.

10 SEPTEMBER 1960

WANDERERS SHOULDER A HEAVY 'BENEFITS BURDEN'

Blackpool 0 Bolton 1

It could have been the happiest day of Bryan Birch's life on Wednesday, but Spurs spoilt it by beating the Wanderers. In the dressing room in his jacket pocket reposed his first benefit cheque, £750 of it, and in his ears were the words of the club's vice-chairman, Ald Entwistle: "I hope you play long enough to get a second and third," writes Haydn Berry.

This was the 15th such payment by the Bolton club to members of the present staff, three of them being second benefits for the bigger sum, £1,000, to Bryan Edwards, Tommy Banks and Doug. Holden. Very soon a payment will be made to Neville Bannister, and Nat Lofthouse will be getting his third, this one another cool thousand.

Other Wanderers are coming up to a second, some to their first. I mention this to bring home to the watching thousands the money that is floating around in soccer, and the amount that goes in the case of a good club to the men who play the game. No club pays more benefits to the full amount or pays them more regularly than the Wanderers. But the number of qualifiers at present is a reminder that behind the policy and developing their own players, the Wanderers, and other clubs so-minded, shoulder a heavy benefit burden.

In other words, by starting their own lads off as professionals at 17, they must pay out benefits to all who qualify every five years, and that means pretty well every lad who makes the first team.

Wanderers players and officials before they left by coach on the first stage of a journey to France in August, 1960, where they were to meet Le Havre in the first leg of their Friendship Cup-tie. From left: Hartle, Higgins, Hopkinson, Parry, Deakin, Birch, Stanley, Hill, Banks, Mr C.N. Banks (chairman), Edwards, Bill Ridding (manager) and Bert Sprostron (trainer).

Burnden had been known for attracting massive crowds, but in the early 1960s things had taken a turn for the worse. In a report on the 1961-62 season, Haydn Berry said . . .

15 MAY 1962

BOLTON GATES AVERAGE IS ABOUT 17,000

Outstanding feature of any Burnden Park summary of the past season must be the great "fall out" of supporters. A check of the figures shows that the average worked out at just over 17,000 including season ticket holders.

From the signing of Wyn Davies to last Saturday there was an increase that took the figure up to 19,800, but this was due to a crowd of 34,366 for the visit of Manchester United, the season's biggest gate.

Only a grandstand finish saved the season from a playing point of view. One long black spell from November 11 to March 10 produced only four wins in 15 attempts, plus Cup defeat at Old Trafford. A much better sequence from April 4 onwards, when 11 points were gathered from seven fixtures, pulled the club's fortunes round and gave the creditable final record of one point per match for the season.

But once again the goal-getting department showed slender returns. It is no longer possible to win a top place without scoring freely. Something between 70 and 100 goals stamps the champions of today. The Wanderers scored 62, and with one of the soundest defences in the League, they still had a debit balance of four goals - 62 against 66.

As for the players, Eddie Hopkinson had a season as good as any that won him his 14 England caps; Bryan Edwards improved on a shaky start as pivot to become one of the most consistent in the League and he, along with Hopkinson, Farrimond and Rimmer, returned a full attendance record.

Roy Hartle, in more senses than one a big man in defence, and Fred Hill, were absent only once. As the one Bolton senior player called upon for international duty with the Under 23s, and as the leading marksman of the season with 14 goals, Hill added to his reputation among the leading forwards of Young England and the man most Burnden Park fans will always turn up to watch.

But let's hand a special word of praise to the "old man" of the team, Doug. Holden, who set off with three goals in the first three weeks (seven games), went down with appendix trouble, returned in six weeks and finished up second top scorer with 11 goals from 32 appearances, his best record in 13 years a professional.

Re-building in progress at the players' entrance to the pitch at Burnden Park in October, 1961.

A happy group of supporters at Burnden Park on August 19, 1961, when Wanderers were playing Ipswich. The crowd was only 16,708, and the result a goal-less draw.

In 1962, the Wanderers went on a tour of Greece, and found an unusual custom . . .

8 MAY `1962`
CAPTAIN'S USED HARD-BOILED EGGS TO 'TOSS UP'

Writing from Athens, a member of the Bolton Wanderers' touring party says that the result of the match with Olympiacos was very satisfactory. He says the Wanderers played really well under difficult conditions - a hot sun and a pitch devoid of grass - with the game controlled by officials whose interpretation of laws were very different from those in England, while the crowd was fanatical. The Wanderers were worthy winners by 2-1, Pilkington (penalty) and McGarry scoring.

Much is made in Greece, says our correspondent, of the great Church festival of Easter which is extended over a longer period in the Greek Orthodox and Byzantin churches than in the Western churches. The Greeks are intensely religious, and the church's influence touches life in many ways. This was typified in the Wanderers' matches, when the captains were given hard-boiled eggs with which to toss for choice of ends!

The eggs were coloured, one red and one blue, and it was a greatly astonished Brian Edwards who was handed an egg instead of the usual coin. The captains bang the two eggs together and the one whose shell is not cracked is deemed to have won the toss.

Several trips to places of interest have been organised. On a free day the whole party did a sight-seeing tour by coach of some of the principal archaeological sites and remains in Athens. The visit to the Acropolis was the titbit. On another day the whole party went by coach to Sonnion, a magnificent cape some 40 miles from Athens where the Temple of Poseidon stands. Unfortunately rain fell throughout the five hours' excursion, but it did not detract from the wonderful ride along the sea coast.

The weather during the winter of 1962-63 was so bad that for weeks no League Football could take place. At last, on February 16, 1963, the Wanderers were able to play Arsenal . . .

16 FEBRUARY `1963`
UNLUCKY DEFEAT ONE IN THE EYE FOR 'HOPPY'

Arsenal 3 Bolton 2

Defeat by misadventure in the closing seconds is the verdict on Bolton Wanderers' resumption of League football after nearly 10 weeks' lay-off through unfit grounds. A bitterly disappointing finale at Highbury brought Arsenal's match-winning goal after the Wanderers had cancelled out an early deficit and gone ahead after the interval. And it was a give-away in more senses than one.

To begin with Edwards went out to the touchline for a tackle and did, in fact, make it successfully, but was rather harshly penalised for pushing. Armstrong placed the free-kick badly, swinging it straight to Hopkinson, who would normally have "swallowed" it, as they say. But Strong challenged and so, Hopkinson said later, accidentally poked him in the eye - and in that involuntary blink the ball sailed straight in.

That was why Hopkinson was bent down, holding his hand to his face, as an almost unbelieving Arsenal team jumped for joy . . . and he was still a very unhappy player in the dressing room, taking the full blame for his mates' lost bonus.

How absurd when, undoubtedly, he was the star of the side, and the man who made it possible for the Wanderers to be heading for victory 10 minutes after the restart. This was when Butler hit his first League goal with a tremendous rocket from full 30 yards, after Hill had equalised McLeod's excellent goal for a rampant home attack in the 21st minute of the game.

This long-range shot, laden with the element of surprise, surely proves the point that goalkeepers are as fallible as any other human beings but, unfortunately, their mistakes - bad luck or errors or judgement - are more vital.

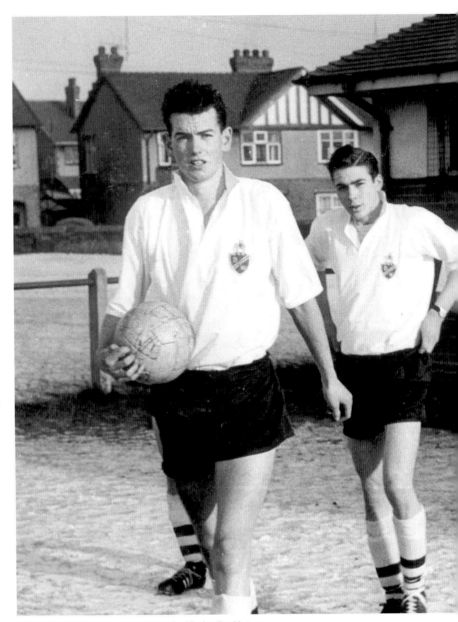

Napier, captain of Bolton Wanderers' under 18s, leading his team out for a match at Bromwich Street, Bolton, in January, 1963.

The season 1963-64 turned into a disaster. Despite a late flourish in which 10 points out of a possible 12 were won, defeat in the last two matches including going down 4-0 to Wolves at Burnden Park in the last game of the season, meant relegation from the First Division. A lot of soul-searching followed (although in future years, things were to become even worse!) . . .

27 APRIL   1964

DIRECTORS NOT TALKING ABOUT PLANS – YET

No sackcloth. No ashes. Burnden Park, now a Second Division citadel, was unchanged after the severest blow to Bolton soccer pride in 30 years. Relegation has left personnel there hurt and numbed.

Manager Bill Ridding put his reactions briefly: "I think the lads put up a wonderful fight to come back into the reckoning and only go down in the last lap. We are all sorry for the outcome and sorry for the disappointment to our loyal supporters. It is not by way of an excuse when I say I don't think any club has been as hard hit by injuries to key men as we have been, and this has definitely had a bearing on our ultimate fate."

Club captain Roy Hartle said he could hardly believe it. "If we had gone down at Easter before we started collecting points we would have been prepared for it. The position looked hopeless then, but after the fight-back to within one point of success with two matches to play it is hard to accept
the drop."

Roy said he could not stop himself thinking that only just over a week ago the Wanderers had a three points lead and appeared to be certainties to stay up."

Roy also felt sorry for the supporters. "After turning up like they did and giving us all they had got, they must be feeling badly let down. It wasn't by any wish of the lads that we didn't pull off a handsome win for their sakes as much as for our own."

As to what lies ahead no-one on the official side was prepared to talk at this stage. They know well enough that the new sphere of activity for Bolton Wanderers in 1964-65 is an exacting one little different in fact from the First Division, except, perhaps, that there are not as many outstanding sides.

The Evening News also reported:
MARATHON FIGHT A GREAT STRAIN ON BOLTON

Fighting for survival to the very last kick of the season - you could hardly have a closer finish to a 42-match marathon stretched over eight months of the year. But it is not something to be recommended. The strain has left its mark on quite a few people connected with Bolton Wanderers.

Though a shocking succession of injuries and mishaps made their struggle tougher, we all know that, even at full strength, the Wanderers fell short of top standard in several positions. Now the ambition should be to put this right to the limit of the club's potential in every way, finance no less than in managerial ingenuity and enterprise.

Readers have asked if there is any parallel to this season's late scoring flourish in post-war football. Well, it is only two years since the Wanderers, badly if not dangerously placed in the League table, finished a six-match series of games in the space of 17 days and netted 10 points. On February 17 their points totalled only 23 with 15 games left to play - and they wound up with 42.

In post-war football, perhaps the best comparison with this season was in 1947-8, when at Christmas they had picked up only 14 points from 23 fixtures. This season they had 13 at Christmas from 25 games.

27 DECEMBER 1964

SOCCER ROW INQUIRY

Police are investigation complaints that a youth was roughly handled by police during "amazing scenes" at Burnden Park on Boxing Day. After the incident - watched by nearly 25,000 spectators - members of Bolton Town Council and others in the stand protested. Scenes in the centre stand as players and officials left were described as "amazing".

Angry spectators were shouting and jeering, and a boardroom window was smashed. "If Bolton fans were not basically orderly types, I think the police would have been mobbed," said Counc. Frank Telford. The youth at the centre of the complaints was said to have been roughly handled by police after running towards referee Mr Don Payne, of Sheffield, at the end of the match between the Wanderers and Northampton. The referee had displeased local fans by decisions which culminated in the "booking" of Bolton full-back Syd Farrimond for throwing the ball away.

When Mr Payne blew the final whistle in the 0-0 draw, a number of youths ran onto the pitch and the referee was soon surrounded by police. After the incident in which police escorted a youth off the pitch (pictured) Counc. Telford and Counc William Magee, went to the Central Police Office to complain about what they saw, and because of the many complaints made to them by people in the stand.

18 FEBRUARY 1965

£100 PACKETS WAY OFF MARK

It is only a guess that any Bolton player will net £100 this week as his reward from the biggest game and the biggest "gate" for six years at Burnden Park. "A rough guess and way off the mark," says manager Bill Ridding. But he gladly admits that Bolton players will have their most profitable afternoon ever when they turn out against Liverpool in the F.A. Cup.

The reason is a bonus based on attendances, and this will operate for the first time in the grand manner. It could mean an extra £30 or £40 on top of normal basic wages, appearance money, and match bonus, and though the Bolton manager rightly declines to quote actual figures, it will bring Bolton players for once into the top clubs' money bracket.

With a capacity crowd of 58,822, and assured record receipts of £13,533, they have every right to be cashing in thus.

As for the actual match itself, "As Liverpool manager Bill Shankly admitted after the game, his sturdy Anfield boys, now in the F.A. Cup last eight, will have no tougher battle than the Wanderers provided before going down by the only goal of the match six minutes from time.

It was a hard, close, and often exciting tie and the League champions were only just able to pull through.

The crowd behaved itself perfectly. The only misfortune, the collapse of a section of fencing behind the Great Lever goal, when Callaghan scored, led to only one hospital case.

Police and ambulancemen quickly had the situation in hand, and the fence was put up again and kept in position by a shoring beam of timber while play went on."

Plenty of shovel work for these men outside Burnden Park in January, 1965.

January, 1966, saw Bolton bring off a "Giantkilling act" in the F.A. Cup when they beat First Division West Bromwich Albion 3-0. It was the fifth Cup meeting with the Midlands' side over the years, and the first time that Bolton finished as winners. The picture shows W.B.A. goalkeeper Potter making a desperate attempt to stop a shot from Lee going into the net for the 3-0 lead.

Hadyn Berry wrote: "A delighted team of victorious Wanderers, winners strictly on merit over more fancied opponents, and knowing well enough that they had done it in the way they intended to do, were still as surprised as the rest of us at the decisiveness of it.

As a very happy Roy Hartle put it: "We knew it was on if we got on top early and kept it up; but 3-0! Well, that was exceeding our highest expectations. It was a great team effort."

That it certainly was, and the result could have been even a bigger shock. Long before Albion, a completely shaken side, made two last, despairing efforts that almost brought two goals in the dying moments, the Bolton lead could have been five. As Hartle says, an all-out effort did it. On a hard soft-topped pitch, made for men prepared to take risks and suffer bruises, the Wanderers seized the initiative from the kick-off and never lost it, knocking all the confidence and rhythm out of West Bromwich with a display of fast, aggressive football.

There was no waiting for the ball, whether attacking or defending, no midfield gap for Albion to work in as some teams have been able to do against the Wanderers.

Francis Lee's first goal just before the break was the real clincher (Bromley had scored after 27 minutes), and his cheeky second, with only 22 minutes left for play, crushed West Brom utterly.

More than one Albion defender was convinced Lee in his dribble round three opponents brought the ball back into play from a foot the other side of the by-line, and in fact, seemed to be waiting for the whistle. Lee finished off his little gem of individualism by bringing the ball into the six-yard box and hitting it past Potter with the left foot.

As the referee pointed to the centre the scorer was mobbed by his team mates, and given an ovation by a crowd that was more demonstrative than at any time this season.

Their roars of "Bolton, Bolton' must have been heard way back in the town centre, and I can tell them it was sweet music in the ears of the players."

Sweating it out in the sauna in 1966 were five of Bolton's players, Dave Hatton, Gordon Taylor, Barry Fry, Brian Bromley and Eddie Hopkinson.

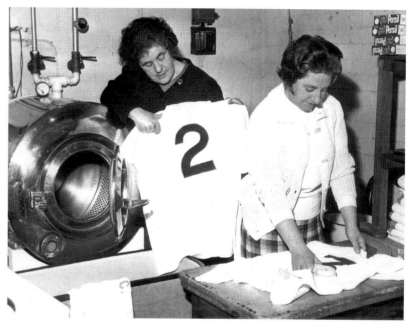

Those in the backrooms at the Wanderers rarely get public recognition, but in 1966 this picture of workers at work in the laundry at Burnden Park appeared under the heading "Keeping the Wanderers so lilywhite means a wash of 165 items', and was followed by the following article:

WHEN the roar goes up "Come on the Lilywhites' then it gives an extra special thrill to two women. For behind the immaculate appearance of Bolton Wanderers' five teams lie days of hard work for Mrs Ann Williams and Mrs Edna Wilcox. They are the women who make the 55 pairs of muddy shorts, 55 soiled jerseys, and 55 pairs of grubby socks, that appear in the laundry every Monday morning, look new again. And it is no mean feat, this mammoth task of washing, boiling and rubbing.

"But when I see the lads run on to the field and hear the crowd shout, I feel very proud and think 'that's my work,' said Mrs Williams. Besides this mammoth task, Mrs Williams also has to tackle a hundred towels and 'when the teams play extra matches during the week we have much more work to do.'

Mrs Wilcox, who does the ironing said: "I really like the work here. What with ironing, patching and darning, I'm kept really busy." When she leaves work she has to start washing and ironing shirts for her family. She said: "I usually laugh about it and when I start ironing at home I say to myself, 'well - it's a change'."

9 JULY | 1966

TRAINING MIX-UP FOR BRAZILIANS

In 1966, with the retirement of Hadyn Berry, Harold Hodgson (above) became the Evening News' Wanderers' reporter, following them for two years until Frank Booth (below) was appointed to the position (Frank then covered the "Burnden Beat" until 1979).

Brazil's World Cup team came to Bolton last night for their first pre-competition practice - and drove straight into a 'who plays where' controversy. The World Cup favourites thought that they were to train on the Burnden Park pitch; the Wanderers' management had already decided that the club's Bromwich Street practice ground would be used.

There was a meeting in the Bromwich Street pavilion between Wanderers' directors and officials and Brazilian team officials. It ended with Wanderers' chairman, Mr Ted Gerrard, offering the visitors full use of Burnden Park and its facilities.

The Brazilians went away and discussed the offer - then came back and said they preferred Bromwich Street. Their only additional stipulations were that they should have use of the medical room at Burnden Park, if needed, and that Coca-Cola should be served to the team instead of tea.

After sorting out the little local difficulty, Mr Gerrard commented: "The goalposts are not yet up at Burnden Park. And if the Brazilians had wanted to train there, we would have had to mark out the pitch and mow it. And we would have had to get the baths operating. Here at Bromwich Street we have excellent training facilities - there are none better in the country."

A number of members of the public saw the team at work, but proudest of the spectators was Gary Burke, a nine-years-old Bolton schoolboy, who ended up with a cut and swollen mouth after being hit by the ball. So enthralled was he in watching the world's master footballers going through their paces that he failed to duck a miskick by Brazilian ace Da Silva. His mouth bleeding, Gary was taken into the dressing room by Da Silva and Dr Nilton Gosling for treatment. But 15 minutes later his injuries were forgotten when he left the dressing room sporting a Brazilian lapel badge.

This line up of the Wanderers was taken at Burnden Park in February, 1966. Back row, from left: Bert Sprostron (trainer), Syd Farrimond, Wyn Davies, Fred Hill, Eddie Hopkinson, John Napier, Billy Russell, Dave Hatton, and (front row) Gordon Taylor, Francis Lee, Roy Hartle, Brian Bromley and Warwick Rimmer.

It was the first goal of the season as Rotherham's Les Chappell hammered the ball past Eddie Hopkinson to put the slick Yorkshire side ahead in August, 1966. The match ended in a 2-2 draw, but in the 71st minute referee Mr K. Stokes "awarded Rotherham a penalty and triggered off a whole series of ugly incidents which may raise the temperature, but which reflect badly on the game of soccer," wrote Harold Hodgson.

"It all started when Rotherham's inside right Bob Williams was impeded as he was bearing down on goal by the Wanderers' right-half and captain Warwick Rimmer. To me it looked an offence, but certainly no worse than anything that had gone before when Lee and Taylor claimed they had been legged up. If anything, an indirect free kick would have met the case.

"Syd Farrimond, Bolton's left back, evidently said as much in perhaps more forceful language and was sent off for what, in old-fashioned World Cup language, would be put down as "violence of the tongue'. A penalty it was, but Rotherham's right winger Barry Lyons, with a rare sense of justice, lifted the spot kick over the bar. Then for 10 minutes or so the game threatened to get badly out of hand as tempers rose and players on each side scythed each other.

"How many times the referee noted as players squared up to each other following fouls was not clear, but good sense prevailed and the players themselves apparently realised there was nothing to be achieved by such nonsense, and the game finished with a surprising degree of amity, although Mr Stokes was booed loudly as he was escorted off the field by the police."

At the beginning of 1967, some fans were so disgruntled by what was happening at Burnden that they threatened to boycott the club, and asked everyone else to do it as well.

10 MARCH 1967
FANS GIVE WARNINGS TO WANDERERS

The Bolton Wanderers fan revolt grew today with three more petitions, signed by more than 350 supporters, threatening to boycott games. The petitions - there have now been six in a fortnight - give the club a six-day ultimatum: "Sign new players before the transfer deadline - or we boycott your games."

The latest petitions, signed by 185 fans at Hick Hargreaves and Co., 100 at Montague Burtons, Halliwell, and 70 at Sunnyside Mills, follow three others from two Hawker Siddeley factories at Lostock and Farnworth, and Edbros at Bolton.

In a letter to manager Bill Ridding, the Sunnyside workers say: "This petition has been sent by 70 regular supporters who, for the past five or six years, have been getting quite plainly sick and tired at the way the Wanderers have been falling lower and lower in the First and Second Division tables.

"It is about time the management decided to buck up their ideas and do some spending on new and good players. We are not, by any means, blaming the team we have now. They do their best, but they are just not good enough for the First Division, which is where a team like Bolton Wanderers should be. We do not like to do this, but we are afraid that if you have not bought a player (s) we think good enough for First Division status, then we will boycott the Wanderers for good. You have six days left."

The Hick Hargreaves petition says: "At the moment the directors treat us as though they are doing us a great favour by allowing us to pay good money to watch Saturday fiascos. Therefore, if the directors make their usual excuses and do not make the side stronger and give it a more modern approach, the people who have signed this petition will stop attending."

A section of the crowd on the embankment in February 1967 when the Wanderers played Arsenal in the F.A. Cup. That match was a goal-less draw, but in the replay Arsenal won 3-0.

"Mitigation for moaning fans. Ordeal to test a 'Soccer Saint", read the headline for the match in March, 1967, when the Wanderers drew with Crystal Palace. "They don't breed 'em as tough as they used to," wrote Harold Hodgson. "In the old days the chilling effects of this cheerless goalless draw would have been shaken off in a jiffy with a therapeutic pint.

They just can't take it nowadays. Their constitution is simply not up to the sort of ordeal they had to endure on Saturday. A spineless, irresolute, sybaritic for these modern fans; they've gone soft; they wilt at the first sign of soccer hardship and go home like fractious children. They even slink off before the final whistle, furtive-like, glad when they've had enough.

"Mind you, the Crystal Palace game was a pretty stern test of anyone's loyalty to the game. The constant stream of misplaced passes was enough to disenchant a soccer saint, and this combined with the bitter weather has to be pleaded in mitigation for the moaners."

*The picture shows Crystal Palace "keeper John Jackson falling on a cross from Ron Phillips as John Byrom rushes to the challenge.

This was the view of the new supporters' club extensions at Burnden Park in August, 1967, which fans got when they arrived for the first home match of the season against Hull City (6-1 to the Wanderers). In November of that year, the £50,000 social club was opened by Wanderers' chairman Mr Joseph Battersby. Several hundred fans and several of the players attended the opening, and this picture shows Mr H. Wilcockson (seated left), chairman of the Supporters' Club, with some of the committee and guests.

These three Bolton Wanderers' players, Syd Farrimond, Charlie Cooper, and Freddie Hill had solved the knotty problem of what to do during the close season in 1967. They worked as labourers at a Bolton timber merchants. They were, in the language of officialdom, gainfully employed, and at the same time keeping their weight down and "making a bob or two."

WANDERERS' MANAGER RESIGNS

Ridding steps down

Bill Ridding resigned today as Bolton Wanderers' manager - a position he has held for 18 years. But he will be staying at Burnden Park as club secretary. He has held the dual job as secretary-manager since 1957, a position he has found too demanding.

Mr Harry Tyldesley, who succeeded Mr Joe Battersby as club chairman this week, said: "The position of secretary-manager is a particularly onerous one, and the work is too burdensome for one man to carry."

However, only a month later came the headline:

BILL RIDDING LEAVES THE WANDERERS
LOFTHOUSE PUT IN CHARGE OF TEAM MATTERS

"By mutual agreement, Mr W. Ridding has terminated his association with Bolton Wanderers F.C." That one sentence from the Wanderers' board ended an era at Burnden Park, and confirmed rumours circulating in the town for several days.

Today Bill Ridding, 22 years with the club as trainer, manager, secretary-manager, and finally secretary, waved goodbye to the Wanderers' party as they left for Bristol and finished collecting the personal effects he has accumulated during his reign at Burnden. The parting came after Mr Ridding had been called into a marathon six and a half hour board meeting yesterday afternoon. It also means a big break for Nat Lofthouse, who is now to be responsible for team selection and all team matters for the time being, until a new manager is appointed.

After an injury ended his football career at the age of 24, Mr Ridding took up physiotherapy and became Tranmere's trainer. He became England trainer and went to Brazil for the World Cup in 1950. He was appointed Wanderers' manager in 1951.

Here's a picture with a difference . . . a photograph of the photographers taking their shots of the Wanderers' team at the annual Press day in July, 1968.

The goal that never was. Despite claims by Bolton's two wingers, Terry Wharton and Gordon Taylor, that the ball had crossed the line before the Portsmouth goalkeeper collected, the referee ruled "no goal" in this April, 1968, match.

It was obviously a disappointment, but there was hope for the future. The paper reported: "If you can ignore the result - not an easy thing because this 2-1 defeat at the hands of Portsmouth extended the Wanderers' run without a win to 11 games - the clash with Pompey produced the best game seen at Burnden for too long.

"The Wanderers were distinctly unlucky not to at least share the points, and if the number of refereeing decisions which went against them is thrown into the balance, this is one Bolton should have won hands down.

"For once, this was a game which held the interest right up to the final whistle, and it is to be hoped that the result will not discourage the Wanderers from what could be the beginnings of a new attacking policy. It was a tonic to see the Wanderers' forwards surging towards the Portsmouth goal and cracking in shot after shot.

"The Wanderers had four appeals for penalties turned down, and again the decision went against them when they argued that a Gordon Taylor header had been over the line when George Ley cleared it. The Wanderers put up a spirited show, and there is consolation in that, although they perhaps could not match Portsmouth for method.

"Keep this up, Bolton, and the goals must surely come to end one of the worst runs that most fans can remember."

3 SEPTEMBER 1968

WANDERERS' PLAYERS COME OFF LIST

Ten Bolton Wanderers players have signed new contracts in a pay deal which brings the earnings of first team players more in line with one another, writes Frank Booth.

And if the team wins promotion, the players will share a bumper £10,000 bonus. At a marathon seven-hour Board meeting yesterday, the players were interviewed separately and all signed with the exception of inside-forward John Byrom. He is still thinking over the offer. This means that there is only Byrom on the transfer list at his own request.

Chairman Mr Harry Tyldesley said: "We have rewarded loyalty and consistency of service. This is a productivity deal linked with an incentive to play in the first team and get results. This is an act of faith. We have pledged a lot of money and we are gambling on success.

"The club is not as financially well off as it would like to be, and I was disappointed at Saturday's gate of only 14,636. It was the third lowest in the Division. We need 20,000 at Burnden." The new deal means that the Wanderers' players will be among the best paid in the Second Division.

The players who re-signed are Brian Bromley, Syd Farrimond, Roy Greaves, Dave Hatton, Freddie Hill, Eddie Hopkinson, John Hulme, Dave Lennard, Warwick Rimmer and Gordon Taylor.

"Nat's substitute game goes wrong", read the headline to the report of the Wanderers' 2-1 defeat by Cardiff City in December, 1968. "Bolton Wanderers' boss Nat Lofthouse took a brave second half gamble when he replaced £50,000 star Gareth Williams with 17-years-old Paul Fletcher in a bid to break down the opposition's tough defence," wrote Frank Booth.

"The gamble failed due to a cruel stroke of soccer misfortune. With 15 minutes of the second half gone, Mr Lofthouse brought off Williams and sent on Fletcher. But before the youngster had even kicked the ball, the Wanderers were reduced to ten men.

"Goalkeeper Eddie Hopkinson was the casualty, and he was carried off on a stretcher with a shin injury which he sustained as he attempted to prevent Cardiff's second goal. Hopkinson stayed off until eight minutes from the end, and when he returned to take over in goal from left-back Syd Farrimond, Bolton really started to play.

"Fletcher started to win the ball in the air against the tall, tough defence. He flashed a tremendous header narrowly past a post before outside right Terry Wharton hit a fine goal five minutes from the end. In the few minutes remaining after Hoppy's return we saw the Bolton forwards look more dangerous than they had all the game - and Cardiff were really relieved when the final whistle blew.

* The picture shows Cardiff's Ron Murray heading away a dangerous centre from Syd Farrimond, but conceding a corner.

Christmas time at Burnden Park in December, 1968 . . . Wanderers' officials and ground staff got together for a festive lunch.

18 DECEMBER 1968

WANDERERS GIVE TOP JOB TO LOFTHOUSE

Nat Lofthouse was today appointed team manager of
Bolton Wanderers - a job he has held on a temporary basis
since former boss Bill Ridding left the club in August. After
Mr Ridding's departure, Mr Lofthouse was put in charge
while the club advertised for a new manager. Then it was
announced that Mr Lofthouse would be team manager until
the end of the season, when his position would be reviewed.

Club chairman Mr Harry Tyldesley said: "We have relieved
him from his uncertainty. He will have a completely free and
unfettered hand to show our complete confidence in him.
We want the public of Bolton to cheer him and his team to
the echo. He is going to be the Lion of Bolton.

Cheers! Bolton Wanderers' players drink a toast to new boss Nat Lofthouse as he is congratulated by chairman Mr Harry Tyldesley after being appointed Manager of the club in December, 1968. Among the players in the picture were Gareth Williams, Eddie Hopkinson, Freddie Hill, John Ritson, Dave Hatton, and Terry Wharton.

27 JANUARY 1969

BOARD MUST GO, SAYS WANDERERS' SHAREHOLDER

A call for an extra-ordinary meeting of the shareholders of Bolton Wanderers was made today by a prominent shareholder, Ald Walter Walsh. He called the present Wanderers' team as the "worst he had seen in 40 years" and added that a meeting should pass a vote of no confidence in the board of directors.

"What can we do as shareholders to save this club?" he asked. "The policy at the top is wrong, and those at the top must go. I don't blame Nat Lofthouse. He isn't getting the support he deserves. All he can do is reshuffle the pack as far as picking a team is concerned. There were people coming to me after Saturday's disgraceful exhibition asking me what I could do to stop the rot. When ever I go into the stands I see defeat staring me in the face. We must act now. Are the board prepared to act now to save this club, or do they want the corporation to take over the land for housing development?"

Roy Greaves hits his third goal - and the Wanderers' fourth - two minutes from the end of the September, 1968, game against Sheffield United which Bolton won 4-2.

Bolton's new mascot was launched at Burnden Park with manager
Nat Lofthouse and players in February, 1969. The seven-feet-tall
Happy was pulled through the town centre on a horse-drawn cart.
From left are John Ritson, Eddie Hopkinson, manager Lofthouse,
Arthur Marsh, Paul Fletcher, John Byrom, Dave Hatton and
Terry Wharton.

16 OCTOBER 1969

'INFLUENTIAL' OFFER TO THE WANDERERS

Bolton Wanderers today received an offer of help from a local businessman of considerable influence. And if the approach had Wanderers' officials and players in something of a daze it had achieved its desired effect.

For it came from the Indian hypnotist Mirza, who wants to put the 'fluence on the struggling Wanderers' players. Bolton and Blackpool based Mirza has sent a telegram via his agent Bernard Wooley to Bolton manager Nat Lofthouse. It read: "Mirza, world famous hypnotist anxious to interview team selected for Saturday's match with will-to-win hypnosis method."

Mr Wooley, the northern showman with a ready eye for publicity, said at his Bolton office today: "Mirza is known and admired throughout the world and has followed the Wanderers' problems through the Evening News. If he can't instill the will-to-win confidence they seem to lack, nobody can."

Mirza said he would "take the players through the match before it is played while they are in trances, and then when they actually play the game they would feel the benefit by knowing exactly what they should do."

Manager Nat Lofthouse described the offer as as "an insult to the players, directors, staff of Bolton Wanderers and football in general .

"Our players are professionals, and this is an insult to them," said Nat, who does not propose even replying to the offer as a mark of his disgust.

Signing for the Wanderers in August 1969 were Joe Welsh (right), aged 15, and John McGill, 16, watched by chairman Harry Tyldesley and manager Nat Lofthouse. The Wanderers had faced some strong opposition from other top clubs to sign the couple from Glasgow. Joe could have signed for champions Leeds United, Cup-holders Manchester City, Chelsea and Sheffield Wednesday - and John had offers from Coventry City, Fulham and Kilmarnock. Why did they choose Bolton? Joe said that the Bolton youth policy swayed him. "I think I will have more of a chance here". It was also announced that the Wanderers had taken a Scottish junior club under their wing as a nursery side - Prestwick Star, one of the top sides in the Ayrshire and Glasgow districts, and John McGill is the first of their products to arrive on the Burnden scene.

Freddie Hill was a firm favourite with the fans during the 1960s. He signed for Bolton in 1957, and after only three seasons in League football was selected for the Under 23 side, and in October, 1962, won his first full cap, against Northern Ireland; he was selected again the following month against Wales at Wembley. At one stage, Liverpool offered to pay £60,000 for him, but he failed a medical because of high blood pressure, and he left Burnden in 1969 to join Halifax Town for £5,000.

The Wanderers on parade in 1968-69. Top row, from left are Bill Jones, Les Hudson, John Hulme, Syd Farrimond, Freddie Hill, Charlie Cooper, Eddie Hopkinson. Middle row: Dave Hatton, Bob Hatton, Warwick Rimmer, John Byrom, Gareth Williams. Front row: Gordon Taylor, Terry Wharton, John Ritson, Brian Bromley, Ron Phillips, Dave Lennard, and Roy Greaves.

Bolton Wanderers' Football Club was losing in the region of £800 to £900 per week. This was stated by director Mr W.G. Isherwood in reply to a question at the club's first public forum, held at Tonge Cricket Club in January, 1969. "This loss is based on our having gates of 12,000," said Mr Isherwood in reply to a question about the strengthening the team by buying players. "Recently we have only had gates of 8,000. We are in the unfortunate position, as are so many other Lancashire clubs, of having to develop the talents of young players and then selling them to exist." Director Mr Derrick Warburton, pictured here speaking, explained the club's youth policy and appealed for patience. "This is a long-term policy," he said, "and results cannot be achieved immediately. I feel that we have a lot of new blood, such as Mr Lofthouse, myself, and Colin Macdonald, and that we are bringing about these changes very quickly." Eddie Hopkinson was in full agreement. "There has been more effort in the past few months to sort out the team than there has been in the rest of the 17 years in which I have been a club member." Dave Hatton felt that the team members had all the necessary skill, but that they lacked confidence when playing in front of a home crowd. "Some of the lads have been frightened to go on the park, they get so much "stick' from the crowd," he said. "Some spectators just turn up to have a laugh. Our away record is as good as it has ever been."

The Wanderers' new all-white strip went on show for the first time in June, 1969, at the Balmoral Hotel, Bolton. Mr Alan Roberts, a partner with

Wanderers' star Gareth Williams in a sports outfitting business, showed the new colours to barmaids Mrs Brenda Welsby and Miss Mary Monahan.

17 DECEMBER 1969

NOW IT'S UP TO THE FANS, SAY BOLTON

The future of Bolton Wanderers Football Club lies very definitely with its supporters now. That was the message that came from the Burnden Park boardroom after yesterday's dramatic swoop to splash out £30,000 plus on Liverpool's former World Cup star Roger Hunt.

"We have done as you demanded. We have signed a big name. Now it's up to you," said the message in spirit, if not in precisely those words. The directors have indeed recognised their responsibility in coughing up the cash themselves for Hunt.

Chairman Harry Tyldesley said: "The success of this transfer is due to two things - the tenacity of Nat Lofthouse and the generosity of the directors. Nat has refused to take 'no' for an answer. He has got his teeth into the deal, and never let go. No praise can be higher for his handling of the whole matter."

Hunt arrived at Burnden promptly at 3pm, and within half an hour had become a Bolton player after 10 glorious goal scoring seasons on Merseyside. At 31 he believes he can take on a new lease of life with Bolton. "This is a great set up, and there is enormous potential here," he said.

Bolton attendances have slumped to between 6,000 and 7,000 in the last four home games, and are averaging around 9,000 at Burnden for the season - half the number Wanderers need to break even. The ball has been firmly planted in the court of the missing thousands.

The building of St Peter's Way, behind the Parish Church, 1971.

1970s

DATE	WORLD EVENTS	BOLTON EVENTS
1970	Brazil take football to new heights with a thrilling 4-1 victory over Italy in the World Cup Final in Mexico.	
1971		St. Peter's Way opened, linking Bolton town centre to the M-way system.
1972	Eleven Israeli athletes at Olympic Games in Munich are killed after eight members of an Arab terrorist group invade Olympic Village.	
1973	The UK joins the European Economic Community.	The pedestrian precinct was opened in Victoria Square.
1974		Announced that traditional Roman Catholic Walks (started in 1838) were not to take place any more.
1975		Wingates Band won British Open Brass Band competition.
1977	Red Rum wins his third Grand National. Britain's Virginia Wade wins Wimbledon.	Bolton Palais wrecked by fire.
1979	The Conservative politician Margaret Thatcher becomes prime minister.	

The end of the 1960s and beginning of the 1970s was a traumatic time as far as managers were concerned. Bill Ridding had resigned in 1968, and Nat Lofthouse replaced him. He was never comfortable in the job, and in 1970 Jimmy McIlroy, who had previously been chief coach, took over - yet within 18 days he had resigned! No official reason was given, but it is thought that he did not agree with constraints on him. Jimmy Meadows arrived in 1971, but lasted for only 11 weeks after receiving transfer requests from some of the top players, and seeing the team slump to the bottom of the Second Division. It was only when Jimmy Armfield arrived in May, 1971, that some sort of stability in the managership role materialised. The paper recalled: "Mr Armfield is the fourth manager to take charge at Bolton since the start of last season. Jimmy McIlroy came and went, and Nat Lofthouse held the reins at various times."By the end of Armfield's first season in charge, he had transformed things to the extent that only 41 goals were conceded, the club's best defensive record since 1925, although promotion was not won. It was under his guidance that the Third Division Championship was secured in 1972-73. In September, 1974, though, he accepted an offer as manager of Leeds United, but he left knowing that he had lifted Burnden out of one of its darkest periods. Ian Greaves had arrived in August of that year as Armfield's assistant, and now he was given the main role, a position he was to hold for six years, in 1977 winning the Manager of the Month Award twice, and in 1978 the Second Division Manager of the season. The Second Division championship was won under him in 1978. However, First Division success did not come, and he was sacked in January, 1980, with the Wanderers at the foot of the table.

Nat Lofthouse welcomes Jimmy McIlroy to Burnden.

Jimmy Meadows.

Jimmy Armfield.

Ian Greaves.

2 FEBRUARY   1970

FIRST PRIORITY . . . A SUCCESSFUL SIDE

Bolton Wanderers' chairman Mr Harry Tyldesley this week puts fans in the picture on work being done by his board, and spells out the policy which is aimed at putting the club back at the top.

He writes: "A decline from grace in the football world is seldom a sudden affair. In the case of Bolton Wanderers, the decline has been steadily progressive over the past 10 years. Where a policy of drift had almost produced a situation of disaster, the rise from the floor is likely to take time.

To steer the ship on a new course, the first necessity was to persuade the old board to purge itself. This was not an easy sea to navigate, but during the past 18 months four new directors have been appointed - Messrs W. Isherwood, D. Warburton, J. Banks, and E. Warburton. Having reconstituted itself, the board held a series of meetings when a new policy was thrashed out.

The actions decided upon were both short term and long term. In the first place we had to do something about making the players contented. Many of them, particularly the first team squad, had not signed on at the beginning of the 1968-9 season. The board made generous pay awards to the players. At this time we decided to make some new signings, with the result that Manning, Hurley, Boswell and Hunt have all been signed within the last 12 months.

Just to remind you, the board inherited a poor cash position. Indeed, the club was rather heavily in debt, so the directors decided to pump more funds into the club's coffers. Without this willingness on the directors' part we could not have bought Roger Hunt.

The board also did something for the immediate creature comfort and safety of our spectators. Last year the club spent over £5,000 on repair of the Great Lever Stand roof, and on repairing and strengthening the crush barriers. It is realised that other ground and stand improvements are imperative, and these jobs will be put in hand as and when cash is available.

It is also realised that the first priority is to secure a consistently successful side. To achieve this we shall spend when the cash resources are available, but it must be emphasised that we shall have to rely very largely on producing our own players. This explains why we have such a young reserve side.

But we are confident that, with patient persistence, this policy will pay off in the long run, and we anticipate that some of these young players who have gained such a lot of playing experience this season will shortly be available for the first team.

I would have the public of Bolton know full well that this board of directors, as at present constituted, is very much 'on the ball', and no effort will be spared to bring back to Bolton what we all want - a successful Bolton Wanderers."

Wanderer's head groundsman, Mr Fred Eckersley, with the help of two young players, Joe Welsh (left) and Willie Graham, prepared the pitch in March, 1970.

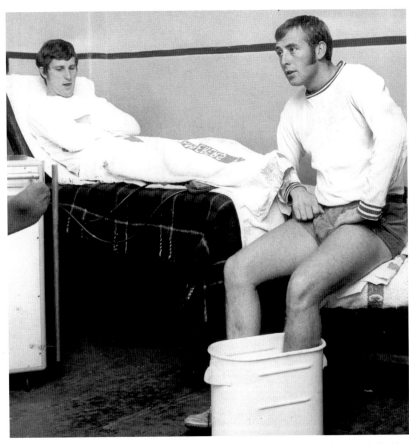

Back to business . . . Wanderers' players pictured on their first day back in training for the new season, in July, 1970. But the players did not spend the day standing around, with coaches Jim Conway and Eddie Hopkinson later putting them through hectic training routines at Bromwich Street.

Presumably they do things differently in 2004, but back in 1970 John Byrom used a bucket to bathe his injured ankle, while full-back John Ritson took his treatment lying down for a calf and ankle injury.

Determination shows on the face of Roger Hunt as he challenges Ron Atkinson during the Wanderers' game against Oxford United in September, 1970, at Burnden Park. Bolton lost 0-2.

Wanderers' youth manager George Taylor gave these young players a briefing in 1970 before a Youth Cup tie at Old Trafford against Manchester United. Among the players were skipper Don McAllister (next to Mr Taylor), then on his left centre-half Paul Jones, centre-forward Roger Denton, Stuart Bourne and Stuart Lee.

At the beginning of the 1970s, the Wanderers were in desperate straits and short of money. In 1970 they made an appeal for cash from the public, and were disappointed that the response only reached £22,212 in shares and £17,325 in loan notes - well short of the £170,000 target. Then there was a suggestion that the Council might take up £1,000 of the loan notes with money taken from the general rate fund. The club was hoping in vain . . .

8 OCTOBER 1970
NO WANDERERS LOAN, SAYS COUNCIL

Bolton Wanderers Football Club, in the red by £110,000, will not get a £1,000 loan from Bolton Council. Despite pleas for help for the Wanderers from both the Tory Group leader, Ald Edwin Taylor, and the Labour leader, Ald Harry Lucas, the Council voted against making the loan. Ald Taylor said: "If this council does not support the Wanderers, who is going to support them? Show the flag and give them some encouragement." He said that the success of Bolton was tied up with Bolton Wanderers. Ald Lucas added that £1,000 was a "very small amount" and that the Wanderers club was an important amenity to Bolton. "If they started to do better I am sure everyone would flock to Burnden Park. Don't kick a dog when it is down. Give the Wanderers a chance."

The Council heard that the Wanderers are £110,000 in the red, and losing £1,000 a week. They also heard that the club was "disappointed" by the public response to its recent appeal for cash through the sale of loan notes and shares.

Speaking against the loan, Counc. Frank Hall said: "Let us get our priorities right. This is not our concern or that of the ratepayers of Bolton. Football today is business, big business. Bolton Wanderers are in it to make money, and it is not for us to lend them money interest free."

The Chairman of the Wanderers, Mr Harry Tyldesley, hit back. "When the original statement was made that the Council might lend us £1,000 I refrained from comment because I thought it was a derisory offer," he said. "I thought that by showing reticence at that time, the Council might have second thoughts and increase their offer. I am bound to observe that I am not so disappointed as despairing of the Council's and the town's response. I would remind everyone that the directors have contributed more than half of the cash subscribed for shares. People talk about the Wanderers' 'rightful place' as being the First Division, but there is no divine right. It is now a question of survival, but the prime object of this Board is still the First Divison."

Wanderers' goalkeeper Charlie Wright gave his club's youth team a bit of light-hearted advice before the youngsters left Burnden for a tournament in Holland in 1972. After he retired in 1973, Wright, apart from a short period with York, stayed with the Wanderers, became first team coach and then, for a short time in 1985, manager.

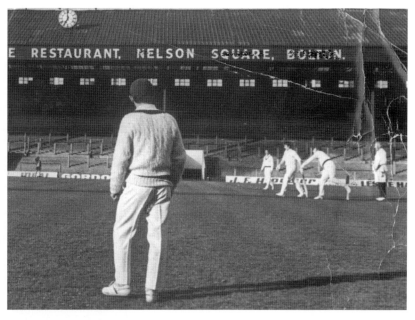

Eddie Hopkinson leaves the Burnden pitch after his farewell performance in his testimonial match in May, 1971. Players, including Portuguese World Cup stars Simoes and Eusebio, joined the 16,000 plus crowd in showing their appreciation of a great servant to the club. The goalkeeper had made 519 League appearances for Bolton since he signed in 1952 (and played in 58 Cup matches) had won an F.A. Cup medal in 1958, and 14 full caps for England. Injury had forced his retirement in 1969, but he then took on training posts at the Wanderers. The other picture shows Eddie at full stretch. In his later years he became a popular figure behind the scenes as a host in the hospitality suites, but died suddenly in April 2004.

What's this? Cricket? At Burnden Park? Well yes, because in May, 1971, as part of Eddie Hopkinson's testimonial, the Lancashire cricket team played a Eddie Hopkinson X1. The star of the night was Clive Lloyd, whose domination "scorched Lancashire to a seven wickets" win with a quickfire innings of 44, including six sixes. A couple of them landed on the Burnden Stand, while his longest hit soared out of the ground!

In January, 1971, the Wanderers fielded a team which included seven teenagers (Don McAllister, 17, Alan Waldron, 19, Paul Jones, 17, making his League debut, Jimmy Redfern, 19, Ian Seddon, 19, Paul Fletcher, 19, Garry Jones, 19) and the average age of the whole team was 20.

18 JANUARY 1971

BATTLING BABES REVIVE THAT OLD BURNDEN ROAR

The young Bolton Wanderers romped to a 2-1 win over promoting-chasing Sheffield United, and caused scenes of jubilation I have not witnessed at Burnden Park for years, writes Frank Booth.

A crowd of 9,854 played a great part in the side's win, spurring the "babes" on as the lifted themselves back into the game after going a shock goal behind after only 95 seconds. The Wanderers won through a superb display of grit, determination, and, above all, good skilful soccer. They were prepared to take on United in the skills of the game, and they came out on top.

The win was a tremendous boost for the Wanderers' youth policy, and this sort of display will certainly bring the crowds back to Burnden. It was a triumph for George Taylor and his scouts who found the youngsters, Jim Conway who had them in their early days in the Central League, Eddie Hopkinson who took over as they matured, and Nat Lofthouse who had the courage to put them in the side.

It was refreshing to see every Bolton player giving maximum effort. And one of the reasons for their win was because they refused to let United players settle on the ball. They were never given time to take control. Skipper John Hulme set a splendid example as he played "a blinder" in defence. He encouraged and talked to the youngster who willingly responded to every occasion.

Those who attended the game could count themselves fortunate. They saw what I believe was the start of a great revival in the fortunes of Bolton Wanderers.

Goals: Bolton - Seddon (19), Fletcher (79). Sheffield United - Tudor (2)

Paul Fletcher races clear of the Sheffield United defence to steer his shot past onrushing Alan Hodgkinson and into the net for the goal which won the match in 1971.

Teams -

Bolton: Boswell, Ritson, McAllister, Waldron, Hulme, Paul Jones, Redfern, Seddon, Fletcher, Garry Jones, Phillips. Sub: Hallows

Sheffield United: Hodgkinson, Badger, Hemsley, Powell, Colquhoun, Barnwell, Woodward, Tudor, Dearden, Currie, Salmons. Sub: Buckle.

Within a few months the Board, with new chairman John Banks, decided that they had to sell a number of players to keep the club afloat, but it was not until they sold Paul Fletcher in March, 1971, that the Buff headed a story by Evening News' sports reporter Frank Booth . . .

6 MARCH 1971

GREAT BETRAYAL

Bolton Wanderers sold 19-years-old striker Paul Fletcher to Burnley this week and kicked off one of the biggest uproars that I can remember in the town. Burnley paid £60,000 for Fletcher, one of the brightest stars of the Wanderers' much-publicised youth policy, and the deal sent a tremor of shock rippling through the club's supporters. For only four days before the Board decided to sell Fletcher, chairman John Banks had stated, for the umpteenth time, that the club's policy was to rely on youth.

This youth policy had been the crutch on which the club had staggered along for nearly three years. It had been the bandage which had held together the remnants of the club's support. Above all, it had been the ray of hope which had promised a brighter tomorrow for the faithful few.

The fans were led to believe - and I was led to believe - that the club had turned the financial corner. Don't forget that the cash from the pre-season share offer, some £45,000, was poured into the club's coffers, plus the cash for the sale of Gordon Taylor (£15,000) and Terry Wharton (£12,000). There was also a £19,900 guarantee from Board members. More than £90,000 ought to have put the balance somewhere near break-even, yet the club is still losing money, and I estimate this to be in the region of £800 a week.

But what happens now? Is it wise to spend on players who could be no better than the ones already on the books, and still go down? Or should the club soldier on, try to make the best out of what they have got, and, if the worst happens, use the cash to try to get out of Division Three? It is an almost insoluble quandary.

* Mr Banks said later: "It is only fair to tell the public of Bolton that there will be no signings. This club has to be run as a commercial concern, and the money we have will be needed to ensure League soccer in the town not only this season, but next season too. People must realise that we, as a Board, inherited what was virtually a bankrupt concern. It is impossible to put this right in a few months." Selling Paul Fletcher, he said, was a financial necessity.

PROMISES, PROMISES —THEN FLETCHER DEAL SHOCKS FANS

WYN DAVIES — Sold   FRANCIS LEE — Sold   DAVE HATTON — Sold   FREDDIE HILL — Sold   GORDON TAYLOR — Sold

FRANK BOOTH AT BURNDEN

GREAT BETRAYAL

BOLTON WANDERERS sold 19-years-old striker Paul Fletcher to Burnley this week and kicked off one of the biggest uproars that I can remember in the town.

Burnley paid £60,000 for Fletcher, one of the brightest stars of the Wanderers much-publicised youth policy, and the deal sent tremors of shock rippling through the club's supporters.

For only four days before the Burnden board agreed to sell Fletcher, chairman Mr John Banks had stated publicly, for the umpteenth time, that the club's policy was to rely on youth.

This youth policy had been the crutch on which the club had staggered along for nearly three years.

It had been the bandage which had held together the remnants of the club's support.

CONVINCED

And above all, it had been the ray of hope which had promised a brighter tomorrow for the faithful few.

General manager Nat Lofthouse and Mr Banks, together with other directors, had preached the youth policy until the fans were convinced that it was to be the club's salvation.

The game against Sheffield United, when the "kids" beat the promotion chasers 2-1, reinforced the thought that the policy might pay off.

And I cannot believe virtually overnight, Lofthouse and Mr Banks turned their backs on what they had said.

There was obviously more to it than that. But if the club's finances were in such dire straights that it was necessary to sell a young player, why was the public not informed of the likelihood before the event?

The fans were led to believe — and I was led to believe that the club had turned the corner financially.

HAD TO GO

As far as contracts of players are concerned, these expire in the main in June — and wages have to be paid from the last game of the season, May 1, with no cash coming in.

Players who are retained club have to be paid about the summer.

Don't forget that the cash from the pre-season share offer, some £45,000, was poured into the club's coffers, plus the cash for the sale of Gordon Taylor, £15,000.

More than £90,000 ought to have put the balance somewhere near the breaking-even mark, yet the club is still losing money and I estimate this to be in the region of £800 per week.

lines, I believe that the directors must have taken this into account and decided that someone would have to go.

I would also expect the board to be divided on the issue — especially in view of the youth policy statements which had been issued.

But having decided that Fletcher could be sold, why on earth did they sell to the first bidder? It was known that other clubs were interested in the player and this ought to have been turned to advantage.

As it stands, the fans feel that they have been betrayed. That not only have they lost one of their brightest hopes for the future, but they have seen him go at a relatively low fee.

Having said this, the fact remains that Fletcher has gone, and good luck to him! He is a player for whom I have the greatest regard and I wish him good fortune in his bid to save Burnley from relegation.

WHAT NOW

Obviously this is too great a task for any one player, but if he can help Burnley stay in the First Division, one would have thought that his value in Bolton's bid to stay in the

Second was more than £60,000.

But what happens to the cash now? Presumably, if the player was sold for purely financial reasons, a will have to go to settling good lump of the money the situation straight.

Don't forget that the directors had found the £12,000 to buy Roger Hunt out of their own pockets, and but for the money they poured in the share issue would not have got off the ground. Presumably, they felt, with good reason, that they were unable to put more cash into the club.

But what does one do with the remains of the fee? It is wise to spend now

on players who could be no better than the ones already on the books, and still go down?

Or should the club soldier on, try to make the best out of what they have got, and, if the worst happens, use the cash to try to get out of Division Three?

It's an almost insoluble quandary.

Before the Fletcher transfer exploded onto the scene on Tuesday, there were complaints about Monday night's friendly against Danish side Randers Freja.

First of all, a white ball was used in the same before got wrong, one was substituted. Then seven substitutes took the field without identification.

To make matters worse, Bolton played two players in No 3 shirts and two wore No 2s.

I know there were only 941 supporters present, but they had paid first team League prices, braved a blizzard, and deserved better than this.

QUOTE:

"BOLTON Wanderers is not a nursery for the more wealthy clubs. These youngsters are the launching pad for promotion".

—Nat Lofthouse, October 27, 1970

QUOTE:

". . . in the long run, we are going to have to develop our own players from promising youngsters, such as Paul Fletcher".

Derrick Warburton as a director

TERRY WHARTON — Sold

AND NOW . . . PAUL FLETCHER

Oh dear. As though being in the Second Division wasn't bad enough, the end of the 1970-71 saw the Wanderers drop even further, into the Third Division. Frank Booth reported on the last game, against Oxford, of that season when Bolton were again relegated.

MAY 1971

BOLTON BOW OUT ON A HIGH NOTE

Bolton 1 Oxford 1

Bolton Wanderers' Second Division campaign ended on Saturday when the Burnden boys grabbed a point. And if they can maintain this sort of form their hopes of bouncing out of the Third Division next season must look a little brighter. They created chance after chance, and did enough to win in spite of some terrific pressure from Oxford.

Roger Hunt snapped the Wanderers into the lead after only two minutes, when he scored at the second attempt from a Jimmy Redfern cross. Oxford had said before the game that they intended to finish the season with a good win, and they stormed back into attack. But they found Bolton 'keeper Alan Boswell in superb form. Bolton played some attractive football, and their best spell came shortly after the interval. Bolton ought to have been well in front, but Oxford equalised in the 61st minute when full-back Dick Lucas scored his first-ever League goal.

Redfern missed a glorious chance of putting the Wanderers ahead again after Hunt had teed the ball up for him in the Oxford penalty area. The winger leaned back and blazed the ball high over the bar when he had only Kearns to beat. Still the Wanderers pegged away, and twice Hunt was just wide of the mark with hard shots.

It was a thoroughly entertaining game, and for once the Wanderers could consider themselves unlucky not to win. Oxford came into the Second Division three years ago, and their first game was against Bolton with the result a 1-1 draw. What a co-incidence that the Wanderers' last Second Division game should also be against Oxford with an identical result.

Teams -

Bolton: Boswell, Ritson, McAllister, Waldron, Hulme, P. Jones, Redfern, Greaves, Byrom, Hunt, G. Jones.
Sub: Phillips

Oxford: Kearns, Lucas, Shuker, Roberts, C. Clarke, Evanson, D. Clarke, G. Atkinson, Skeen, Cassidy, R. Atkinson.
Sub: Sloan

Fans stream away from Burnden after a February, 1973, 1-0 F.A. Cup fifth round defeat by Luton, in front of a 39,556 crowd. Bolton may have been out of the Cup, but they were still favourites for promotion. The human tide that swept along Manchester Road afterwards brought traffic to a standstill.

Two years later, though, they bounced back into the Second Division . . .

30 APRIL 1973
BOLTON BEAT BARRIER - THEN IT'S A FIESTA

THE 2-0 victory over Brentford at Burnden Park was purely a curtain-raiser to the events which followed, when Bolton Wanderers received the Third Division Championship trophy. Vice-president of the Football League, Mr Sam Bolton, handed the Cup to Wanderers' skipper Warwick Rimmer and the players did a lap of honour to tumultuous applause. At the interval manager Jimmy Armfield had broadcast an appeal asking fans to stay in their places while the presentation was made, and it was not until the players were well on their way round the pitch that some youngsters spilled over barriers. They were quickly shooed away by the police with the minimum of fuss.

Mr Bolton later paid tribute to the behaviour of the supporters. "Their behaviour was excellent. We travel all over the place and we don't often see supporters as well behaved as these. They are a credit to the club and town." Then the celebrations began, and the players attended a champagne buffet organised by the Supporters' Club.

Four points separate the Wanderers from second club Notts. County who also make the climb into the Second Division. But spare a thought for Brentford, sent plunging into the Fourth Division, who stayed on the pitch after the game to add their congratulations to a side which is certainly going places.

Wanderers' skipper Warwick Rimmer holds up the 1972-73 Third Division Championship trophy after it had been officially presented to the team after the last game, against Brentford, which they won 2-0. The picture above shows Wanderers' senior players and coaches with the trophy. Back row, from left: Neil Whatmore, Ralph Wright, Roy Greaves, Paul Jones, Peter Nicholson, John Ritson, John Byrom. Middle row: Garry Jones, Charlie Wright, coaches Jim Conway and Eddie Hopkinson, trainer Bert Sprostron, Barry Siddall, Ian Seddon. Front row: Don McAllister, Jimmy Redfern, Alan Waldron, Warwick Rimmer, manager Jimmy Armfield, Stuart Lee, Ron Phillips, Paul Hallows.

14 JANUARY   1972

BURNDEN SCARVES SENT TO PRINCES

Bolton Wanderers' chairman, Mr John Banks, has sent two club scarves to Buckingham Palace for the young Princes, Andrew and Edward. It was decided to send the red, white and blue scarves after the Queen's Christmas broadcast, when references to Bolton Wanderers were made by both Prince Andrew and Prince Edward. During the programme the Princes were shown photographs of the Bolton Wanderers-Manchester City 1926 Cup Final, and Prince Andrew said: "Bolton Wanderers are now in the Second Division, or third."

An accompanying letter from Mr Banks said: "Your sons spoke felicitously of the Bolton Wanderers' team which won the F.A. Cup in 1926, and made somewhat sympathetic reference to the present team. To mark the occasion, the club has presumed to send to the two Princes club scarves as gifts in the hope that it will be a reminder of a happy Christmas occasion."

Something you do not see any more . . . Wanderers' players jogging round local streets as part of their training schedule. But in 1973 it was commonplace, as our picture shows - featuring the likes of Stuart Lee, Neil Whatmore, John Byrom, and Paul Jones.

25 OCTOBER   1972

BOLTON'S CHAIRMAN SOUNDS A 'CLOSURE' WARNING

Bolton Wanderers' chairman Mr John Banks told shareholders at last night's annual meeting that "gate" receipts are a staggering 40 per cent down on last season's at this stage. He agreed that it is a national trend, but said: "That does not help to solve out problem." And he handed out the warning that unless someone has the answer to this situation, football clubs will be closing down "faster than cinemas did in the last decade."

"It is unthinkable for a town the size of Bolton to be deprived of League football through apathy. I am informed that the public of Bolton are not interested in Bolton Wanderers' tickets, good value or not.

"We directors are very concerned about the image of our club. We are as hungry for success as you supporters. Are we being selfish to think that we are deserving of better support to get back in the Second Division? Perhaps so. We need more support."

Bobby Moore is remembered best of all because of his captaincy of England when they won the World Cup in 1966. Yet when 10 years later he came to Burnden Park as part of the Fulham team in a replay of the League Cup third round (the teams had drawn 1-1 at Craven Cottage), he was involved in a mass walk-off the pitch by his team after he had received a red card.

6 OCTOBER 1976
TIME STANDS STILL AND BOLTON CASH IN

Bolton 2 Fulham 2 (after extra time)

The match erupted sensationally at the end of normal time, wrote Frank Booth. The Wanderers were trailing 2-1 when the game reached 90 minutes, but referee Kevin McNally added time on for stoppages and time wasting. Bolton left-back Mike Walsh equalised in the 95th minute, and the Fulham players protested volubly. The game re-started, and eight minutes had been played when Mr McNally signalled the end.

This provoked further protests with manager Alec Stock and coach Bobby Campbell joining the Fulham players. During the melee around the referee, he produced the red card and directed Bobby Moore to the dressing room. At this point the rest of the Fulham team followed (as seen in this photograph),and retired to their dressing room leaving the bemused-looking Wanderers waiting for extra time which didn't look likely to be played.

But after an ultimatum from the referee, Fulham did re-appear, minus Bobby Moore and played the half hour extra time, with no further goals being scored. The Wanderers had agreed provisionally with Fulham before the game that if it ended in a draw, a toss of the coin would decide between Craven Cottage and Burnden Park for a further replay. But afterwards Fulham had a change of mind, and the match will be at a neutral venue.

Teams -
Bolton: McDonagh, Nicholson, Walsh, Greaves, P. Jones, Allardyce, Morgan, Whatmore, Taylor, Reid, Smith, Sub: Waldron.

Fulham: Mellor, Bullivant, Strong, Slough, Howe, Moore, Dowie, Evanson, Mitchell, Lacy, Barrett. Sub: Lloyd for Slough.

* In the second replay a couple of weeks later at St Andrew's, Birmingham, the Wanderers won 2-1, with goals from Paul Jones and Whatmore.

Bobby Moore walks off the field after his red card, followed by the rest of the Fulham team.

3 MAY

PAUL AIMS TO SCORE A HIT

Bolton Wanderers now have an official song, despite the breakdown of a competition organised last year to find one. The directors have agreed that "Here We Go Again", written and sung by Paul McLaughlan, of Heathfield Drive, Bolton, might just be the thing to spur on the "whites". Joining Paul on the record are local singers Paula Marshall and Dave Horridge. Dave also plays the drums. The song has already been played at Burnden Park and on local radio, and is proving popular with the fans.

By September, the paper told of how "The first 1,000 discs of the team song have already been sold, and the official launch last night at Astley Bridge Conservative Club - which backed the record by providing practice and recording facilities - was declared a 'fantastic night'. Another 5,000 copies are out on sale."

Celebrating the acceptance of their song by Bolton Wanderers, from left, singer Paul McLaughlan, promoter Bob Tomlinson, and Peter Fearn, who played in the backing for the demo disc.

A packed Railway Embankment at Bolton's second Sunday game, against Bristol City in January, 1974, which Bolton won 2-1. The attendance of 23,315 was the highest for a League game at Burnden that season, and bigger than five of the previous days' Saturday First Division matches.

The Burnden brigade posed for this photograph in August, 1974. Back row: Stephen Taylor, John Ritson, Peter Nicholson, Roy Greaves, Tony Dunne, Peter Olinyk.

Centre: Paul Jones, John Byrom, Sam Allardyce, Barry Siddall, Ian Holdbrook, Mike McBurney, Garry Jones, Don McAllister.

Front: Alan Waldron, Neil Whatmore, Warwick Rimmer, Jim Armfield, Ron Phillips, Malcolm Darling, Peter Thompson, Stuart Lee.

Bolton's 1973-74 top scorer John Byrom received the Player of the Year trophy from another sharpshooter, Manchester City's Francis Lee, who returned to his original club to present the Supporters' Club award. Runner-up was Peter Thompson, with Paul Jones third in a heavy vote. Also pictured were Wanderer' director Mr John Banks, president of the Supporters' Club, and Mr Harry Betney, club chairman.

Thousands of fans were still outside Burnden Park on December 27, 1975, when the game against Sunderland started, and club secretary Edward Rothwell appealed to fans to arrive earlier for big games. "It gives us no satisfaction to see so many people outside at the kick-off. We want them all in the ground. In the event, 42,680 watched the game, the biggest attendance for a League game since a visit of Manchester United 13 years earlier.

28 DECEMBER 1975
SAM SPECIAL PEPS UP SUPERWHITES

Bolton Wanderers scored their most important win of the season when they fought back from being a goal down to beat top-of-the-table Sunderland 2-1. For this was the game they really had to win after losing 2-1 at Oldham on Boxing Day.

And the large crowd made the atmosphere as tense and exciting as a Cup Final, with Sunderland bringing a big following to Bolton. Sunderland looked a very good outfit, although lacking to some extent a player to put his foot on the ball and slow things down. They seemed to play at 90 miles an hour, and this all-out workrate was reinforced by some ferocious tackling.

The Bolton midfield pair of Peter Reid and Roy Greaves did sterling work both in defence and pushing forward to help out the attack. And central defender Sam Allardyce had a fine game.

In the end it took an own goal to separate the sides, and it came only seconds before the interval. Tony Towers swung a free kick on the left over to the far post. Tony Dunne moved in towards his own goal, and helped by a push in the back by Bobby Kerr, headed firmly past Siddall into the net. It was just what the Wanderers didn't want, and it meant that they had a really tough job on their hands.

But they responded to the challenge magnificently, and the equaliser came in the 51st minute with big Allardyce coming in on a late run, for a Peter Thompson corner to send a bullet-like header into the top corner of the net.
The Wanderers struck the vital blow in the 70th minute with Byron unmarked to nod another Thompson cross past goalie Montgomery.

Teams -

Bolton: Sidall, Ritson, Dunne, Greaves, Paul Jones, Allardyce, Byrom, Whatmore, Garry Jones, Reid, Thompson.

Sunderland: Montgomery, Malone, Bolton, Towers, Clarke, Ashurst, Kerr, Finney, Holden, Robson, Henderson.

WHOOSH! The power of Sam Allardyce as he races in between Sunderland defenders Joe Bolton and Jack Ashurst to hammer in Bolton's first goal.

Byrom nods in the winning goal.

148

Brave Sam gets the vote from 'Doc', said the headline on this March, 1975 picture. "He makes Jim Holton look like Franz Beckenbauer," said Manchester United boss Tommy Docherty on Sam Allardyce after seeing the Wanderers' defender give a brave display in a match which United won 1-0. Big Sam played with five stitches in a gashed forehead, but shrugged off the injury. He started the game with a plaster, but soon had to have it replaced by a bandage which coach Jim Conway put on (pictured). However, Sam was still in the wars, and he was later booked for a foul on Stuart Pearson.

The Wanderers got a gate of about 20,000 one day in August, 1975, and there wasn't even a match. The big turn-out came during the first open day at Burnden Park. Boys, girls, mums, dads, grannies and granddads took a look behind the scenes at the ground, and "every door was open to the public". Eight local schools took parties to the ground, among them these pupils of St Matthew's School, Little Lever, taking the view from the directors' seats.

Despite a continuous downpour, a large crowd of enthusiastic youngsters, parents and fans turned up at Burnden Park in December, 1975, for a "Sportsnight with the Stars". Among the personalities on the panel were Ian Greaves and John Ritson of the Wanderers, Lancashire cricket captain David Lloyd, England Rugby League coach Alex Murphy, Lancashire amateur champion golfer Alan Squires, and marathon ace Ron Hill.

31 MAY 1977

BOLTON PRICES TO GO UP

IT will cost a minimum of 85p for an adult to watch Bolton Wanderers in the coming season. The club today announced its new price structure.

* Admission to the Railway Embankment goes up from 70p to 85p and juveniles and pensioners will pay 10p more at 50p.

* Cost of a Manchester Road season ticket is £35 as opposed to £30 last season, and a juvenile ticket is up from £13 to £15.

* Burnden Stand prices go up from £22.50 to £27 for adults, and from £11.50 to £13.50 for juveniles.

* Wing stand seats are up from £18 to £21 for adults, and pensioners will pay £2 more at £11.

* Match-day admission prices are £1.80 in the Manchester Road stand, up from £1.50 - juveniles 90p.

* Admission to the terraces is up from 85p to £1, and the "dad and lad" terrace ticket will be £1.30, with 50p for every additional juvenile ticket.* Great Lever End prices are 90p for adults and 50p for juveniles and pensioners.

* Terrace season tickets are up from £15 to £17, and ground tickets will cost £15, with juveniles and pensioners being charged £9.

BESIEGED BY SOCCER MOB

Bricks flung at coaches

COACHES taking Sheffield Wednesday supporters home after Saturday's League match at Burnden Park were besieged by mobs of missile-hurling fans, it was said today.

Two coaches were damaged by bricks and several Sheffield supporters were injured by flying glass, a Sheffield Wednesday fan club claims.

An inquiry into the incident is being held by fan club chairman Mr Fred Stones and there is a possibility of an official protest to both Bolton Wanderers C and Bolton police.

CAVALRY CHARGE "

Mr Harold Medlock, a -years-old driver of e of the supporters aches, said that the ar window of his ach was smashed by a orick.

He said: "I've never known anything like it in my life. We came out of the park and there were 300 or more of them waiting for us. It was like a cavalry arge or a scene from orea, they just kept ing at us," he aimed.

Mr Medlock claimed that he had been assured of police protection as they left the ground following the Wanderers 4-2 victory. But instead, he said, there was no protection and because of traffic hold-ups the coaches were "sitting ducks for the mob."

"They were throwing huge house bricks at us. It was a miracle that nobody was killed. Most of the bricks bounced off the coaches but in 20 years' driving I've never had to face a riot like this," he said.

Sheffield United Tours, who had six coaches at the ground, are making inquiries into the incident,

THE FOOTBALL HOOLIGANS

Sadly, the excesses of football hooliganism throughout the whole of the Leagues seemed to be in the 1970s and 1980s, and it was not a pleasant situation for the club or its vast majority of responsible supporters. It began to a small extent at the end of the 1960s, when stories appeared such as "About 20 Bolton Wanderers' supporters were ejected from Cardiff City's ground" and "Fines of up to £100 were imposed by magistrates on spectators who caused trouble at the Preston North End v Bolton Wanderers match . . " In later years, though, the problems increased with the paper reporting that "Bolton coach operators are refusing to take football fans to Old Trafford for the match between Wanderers and Manchester United because they fear soccer hooligans" and "The football season got off to a stormy start on Saturday when 15 fans, eight of them from Bolton, were arrested in the match at Oldham. Twenty other supporters, most of them skinheads, were ejected from the ground, and many others had to watch the game in stocking feet after police confiscated their 'bovver boots'.' A variety of weapons, including flick knives, umbrellas with sharpened points and sticks, were also taken off fans."

In 1972, rival fans fought it out in the middle of Bolton's busy Bradshawgate before the Wanderers' v Blackburn Rovers needle game, and after the return game it was reported that "stronger police guards on soccer specials could follow the wrecking of a diesel train by fans who went to Blackburn. The three-coach train was brought to a halt a mile from Trinity Street Station. Every window in one carriage was smashed, a sliding door ripped off, slogans daubed over compartments and seat cushions thrown out of the train during its 14-mile journey."

The ugly face of soccer rivalry was on show most weeks, fans were ejected from grounds and arrested, others fought in nearby streets and town centres. Then the police announced that "visiting football fans will have no more opportunities for pre-match rowdy behaviour in Bolton town centre. They will be shepherded immediately to Burnden Park after arriving at Trinity Street Station. Visiting fans will be kept away from the town centre." On one occasion

A young fan being searched by a policeman before he went into the ground before the September, 1974, game against Aston Villa.

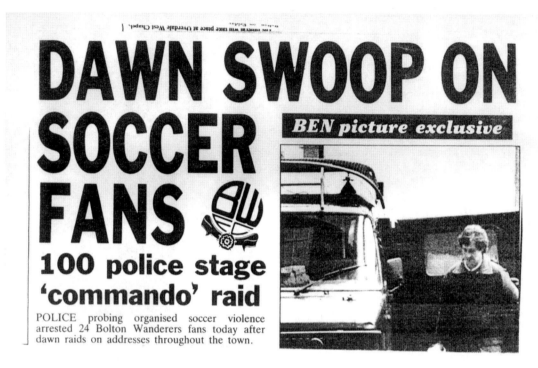

DAWN SWOOP ON SOCCER FANS

BEN picture exclusive

100 police stage 'commando' raid

POLICE probing organised soccer violence arrested 24 Bolton Wanderers fans today after dawn raids on addresses throughout the town.

though, about 60 rival fans fought a battle in the centre of the Burnden Park pitch before the match between Hull City and the Wanderers.

The worst possible situation arose in 1974 when in a pitched battle at Blackpool's football ground between Bolton and Blackpool fans, an 18-years-old Blackpool youth was killed. After the death (a Bolton youth was accused of the murder but was cleared after a trial) the Wanderers appealed for football and police authorities to lead the fight against soccer violence and hooliganism.

The troubles continued, though. In 1977, the Evening News reported: "It was a black day for Bolton Wanderers on Saturday. But it was a darker day for the town itself. Football violence reared its ugly head yet again, and the Wanderers' 1-0 defeat against Wolves was accompanied by scenes of soccer savagery both inside Burnden Park and in Bolton

town centre. Long before the teams kicked off, rival fans were already playing their own grim game. They were fighting in town centre streets, throwing stones and smashing shop windows. Shopkeepers have been repairing windows, and landlords counting the cost of hooliganism in their bars." In that year, the Wanderers also announced that in a bid to curb hooliganism they were to fence in fans behind the goals.

Hooliganism did not end with the advent of the 1980s, of course. The troubles continued, with headlines such as one in 1986 "Shame of Bolton soccer fans" about fighting at a "friendly" match against Blackpool, and the same year "Marauding fans beat policeman" which told of how a police dog handler was punched and kicked almost unconscious by hooligans in Bolton town centre.

Such stories became almost weekly, and in December, 1986, Nat Lofthouse laid down the law as part of the Wanderers' blitz on football louts. His message, which he gave from the pitch at half-time during a match against York City, was simple: "The manager and the team don't need you - and the rest of us don't want you." In 1987, the Wanderers issued a list of ten local soccer hooligans they had banned for life.

Yet in 1988 the headlines continued: "Fans in pub siege", about terrified regulars having to dive for cover as 400 Bolton soccer thugs raided a pub in a 60-minute reign of terror. Later that year, though, Bolton Wanderers teamed up with the police in a fresh bid to tackle a new wave of hooliganism and racism at Burnden Park. The following year the paper reported: "Police probing organised soccer violence arrested 24 Bolton Wanderers' fans after dawn raids on addresses throughout the town. The arrests follow months of undercover work by a special team of detectives. A frightening array of weapons including smoke bombs, martial arts equipment, ball bearings, chair legs covered in nails, rings with spikes and knuckledusters have been seized from some of the homes." In 1990, 34 Bolton football hooligans appeared in court in Britain's biggest ever soccer hooligan trial. They pleaded guilty to a total of 76 charges. Many of them were given fines and community service orders. Nine of them were jailed for a total of nearly 18 years.

That, and strong action taken by the police at Burnden Park, seemed to herald the end of a couple of decades of trouble; some remained though. Even in 1996 the headline "Yobs run amok" appeared, telling of how "Thirty hooligans were arrested in a massive police operation as rival soccer thugs were involved in a series of running battles in Bolton and Farnworth. The police team made the arrests before and after the Premiership clash at Burnden Park which saw the Wanderers crash to a humiliating 6-0 defeat."

Such stories have become fewer and fewer over the years, but those couple of decades or so were certainly a major black spot in the history of Bolton Wanderers.

In July 1977, the paper reported that "Work is underway erecting 8ft.-high fences to hold in football fans behind the goals at Burnden Park next season. The £17,000 project is an attempt to curb hooliganism after violent scenes during the Wolves and Chelsea visits to the Wanderers' ground last season." A spokesman said: "After the Wolves' fans ran riot the club felt there was no other choice but to fence in the two ends of the ground with unclimbable fences."

In 1986, Nat Lofthouse, who by then had been made club President, went on the pitch to lay down the law as part of the Wanderers' blitz on football louts. His message to the club's obscene chant brigade was simple: "The manager and the team don't need you - and the rest of us don't want you." Joined by Alf Davies, the club's Commerical Manager and several players, he made his personal plea from the centre of the pitch. Some spectators in the crowd tried to drown out their voices with "cat calls" and football slogans. But silence fell over the ground when Nat grabbed the microphone and ordered the fans to listen.

An historic moment as a mounted policeman on a white horse rides onto the Burnden Park ground in February, 1977, to help control fans who ran riot on the pitch at the game against Wolves. The incident was reminiscent of the time 54 years before when the famous "White Horse" at Wembley was used to control Cup Final crowds. This picture shows PC Barry Smith riding Bob Cratchett, a 20-years-old grey gelding which had been in police service since 1961.

155

Two legs from Wembley and then Europe, that's where the Wanderers stand today, wrote Frank Booth after Bolton had beaten Derby County 2-1 in the League Cup quarter-finals in 1976. The picture shows Peter Reid dribbling round Derby goalkeeper as the Wanderers mounted yet another attack on the Midlanders' goal, but it was Whatmore and Morgan who scored the goals. "The win was a tremendous test of character. They fought back from having a first half penalty awarded against them, and in the end they were streets ahead of their First Division opponents." * In the semi-finals, the Wanderers drew 1-1 at Everton, then lost 0-1 in the replay.

Wanderers' players and staff all set to leave Burnden for their German tour, in July, 1977.

The Bolton Wanderers' Instant Lottery kicked off in December, 1977. Manager Ian Greaves and several players launched the money-making scheme in Bolton's shopping precinct, and a total of 90 newsagents were selling the £1,000 draw tickets throughout the district. Soon afterwards there was a cry of "offside" from Bury F.C. because, they said, the Wanderers had been selling tickets in their town. The picture shows Ian Greaves (left) and team members Neil Whatmore, Jim McDonagh and Roy Greaves, buying lottery tickets from Tom Pritchard, secretary of the Leigh Newsagents' Federation, and Francis Walkden (right) secretary of Bolton Newsagents' Federation.

A foolish fan saw the second half of the match between Wanderers and Wolves in May 1977, from the top of one of the floodlight pylons. Was it worth the risk? Well, Bolton lost 0-1.

11 JANUARY   1978
CUP GLORY FOR BOLD BOLTON

Bolton 2 Tottenham 1 (after extra time)

Battling Bolton Wanderers earned a place in the fourth round of the F.A. Cup when they beat fellow promotion contenders Spurs at Burnden Park in a game that had just about everything. But it was not until the 14th minute of extra time that substitute Garry Jones headed the ball that finally sank the Londoners. Jones, who had replaced the injured Roy Greaves at the end of normal time, darted in to head past Barry Daines when John Ritson crossed from the right.

And while the goal finished Spurs, they deserve great credit for the part they played in two thrilling ties (the previous game had ended in a 2-2 draw). Both sides placed an emphasis on attack, and early on Frank Worthington went near with a cracking drive from a Neil Whatmore pass. Spurs looked very dangerous for a spell, then the Wanderers appeared to have taken the lead in the 34th minute when Morgan crossed for Greaves to head down. Peter Reid was there to slam the ball past Daines. But as the fans and players celebrated, the referee awarded a free kick to the visitors for an infringement in the box.

The Wanderers took the lead in the 51st minute with a gem of a goal. Morgan took a free kick some 15 yards outside the Spurs' box slipping the ball sideways to Ritson. The ball appeared to be too near a Spurs player, but Ritson got there first and sent a 25 yards drive flashing into the net. Incident followed incident in both goalmouths, but just as it looked as if the Wanderers were home and dry, the referee stepped in to award a penalty with just four minutes of normal time left for an Allardyce tackle on Perryman. Taylor banged the ball home from the spot, but their escape was short-lived with Jones's tremendous headed goal settling the issue just before the end of the first period of extra time.

Teams -
Bolton: McDonagh, Ritson, Nicholson, Greaves, Walsh, Allardyce, Morgan, Whatmore, Train, Reid, Worthington.
Sub: G. Jones for Greaves

Tottenham: Daines, Naylor, Holmes, Hoddle, McAllister, Perryman, Pratt, McNab, Duncan, Lee, Taylor.
Sub: Armstrong for McNab

* The Wanderers went on to beat Mansfield Town 1-0 in the fourth round, but then fell 0-2 to Middlesbrough.

In 1978, the Wanderers were back to the First Division again. They won promotion by beating Blackburn in the penultimate game of the season. The following week they played Fulham, and the goalless draw was enough to give Bolton the Second Division championship as well . . . little were they to know that over the next few years this was to be the ecstasy before the agony. Just another false dawn.

27 APRIL 1978

UP THEY GO

Blackburn 0 Bolton 1

They're back! Bolton Wanderers have finally returned to Division One. After 14 years "down under', the supremely happy Wanderers marched into the big league last night at Blackburn. It sparked off an orgy of celebration parties that went on well into the early hours.

A golden goal scored by Frank Worthington beat the Rovers, and he sent the thousands of Bolton fans who packed into Ewood Park wild with delight in the 33rd minute when he latched on to a Roy Greaves' pass. He appeared to have left it too late as the ball ran away towards the left of goal, but rifled a hard left-foot shot past the diving John Butcher.

The goal signalled the end of a long road for the Wanderers, who have endured a spell in the Third Division during their years out of the spotlight. And after two near misses it was third time lucky for the Wanderers, who took Blackburn by storm. After Worthington's goal the Wanderers never really looked back, although the atmosphere became very tense as time ran out. The final whistle went and the players and fans had at last cause to celebrate in earnest. It was a night of glory, and now the Wanderers can continue the good work with a win over Fulham at Burnden which will bring them the championship.

These pictures show the incredible scenes as fans swarmed onto the pitch at Burden Park after the last game of the 1977-78 season, and, at a civic reception given a few days later, Roy Greaves holding up the Cup as his team-mates waved to the crowds during a triumphal tour of the town on the top of a double-decker bus, and a jubilant Sam Allardyce holding the Cup aloft, on the steps of the Town Hall. The front page of the paper reflected everyone's delight.

Thursday, April 27 1978   8p

Well done ... from New Zealand

UP THEY GO!

Town cheers the happy Wanderers

THEY'RE BACK! Bolton Wanderers have finally returned to Division One. After 14 years "down under" the supremely happy Wanderers last night marched into the big league.

It sparked off an orgy of celebration parties that went on well into the early hours.

On sale now

Pat on the back from

Parties

Three days later . . .

TITLE IS ICING ON THE CAKE

Bolton 0 Fulham 0

Bolton Wanderers are the champions. They carried off the Second Division title in spite of being held to a goalless draw by Fulham. While the game is instantly forgettable, the scenes that followed it are not. The celebrations went on long into the night as the whole of Bolton paid tribute to their heroes - the players and management who have steered the town back onto the map. Incredibly, the fans kept off the field as the players went on a lap of honour as the news came through that Southampton and Spurs had drawn at The Dell to give Wanderers the title.

And when the players reached the tunnel to re-appear in the home directors' box, the gates were opened and the fans surged, by invitation, on to the playing area. The biggest crowd of the season, 34,110, had turned up hoping to see a feat of football culminating in the demolishing of Fulham, but that was not to be. Fulham had different ideas and showed that they are a very competitive young side brimful of talent. The final whistle brought relief for everyone at Burnden, and it was fortunate that one point was sufficient to land the title. No-one could blame the Wanderers for giving a poor display. The fact that they had won a place in the top three was sufficient, and in the end the title was just a bit of extra icing on the cake.

The campaign that faces the Wanderers in the First Division is to some extent a voyage into the unknown. I look forward to it, and I am sure the players and fans will do the same.

Ian Greaves leads the Bolton team out to tumultuous cheering at Burnden, said the caption to this picture in May, 1978. The occasion was a tribute to Wanderers' former international winger Peter Thompson. An incredible 20,516 spectators braved the incessant rain to watch an entertaining match between Bolton, the Second Division Champions, and Liverpool, the Champions of Europe.

The rivalry between the Wanderers and Manchester United has festered for a long time . . . few results in football give more pleasure than a Bolton victory in this local "derby". The destruction of United in December, 1978, was a good example . . .

23 DECEMBER 1978

WORTHINGTON THE STAR OF BRILLIANT WANDERERS

Bolton 3 Manchester United 0

It will be a long time before Manchester United forget the thrashing they received at Burnden Park last night - with Frank Worthington, Bolton's sharp-shooting scorer, as their leading tormentor. Worthington got the all-important goal after 11 minutes and followed it up nine minutes later with a second, to put him still further ahead in the First Division scoring charts.

Gowling put the issue beyond doubt in the 48th minute with number three. It was a great night for Wanderers in front of a 32,250 all-ticket crowd, when they seized their chance to put on a display which, for much of the match, had United struggling and reeling against aggressive, skilful, attacking play. From the 10th minute, when Jimmy Greenhough injured an ankle as a Ritchie effort was disallowed in a melee, United lacked any real focus in attack, hard as the promising young Ritchie tried.

After establishing a two-goal lead, Bolton took it easier for a while and gave some of the initiative to Manchester, and just before half-time McDonagh only just managed to touch McIlroy's corner over the bar, but in the 48th minute Bolton were home and dry.

Worthington took a quick throw-in on the left, Gowling chested it down and McQueen, who was six yards nearer to his own goal than Gowling, stood appealing for a non-existent handball as Gowling ran on and swept in a well-taken goal against his old club. As United tried for a consolation goal, Thomas twice shot into the side netting following good moves, although Coppell had a clear chance on each occasion at the far post.

But it was still Bolton who looked the top team, and with three minutes to go, Bailey could only palm out a Gowling centre. Worthington was lurking at the far post, and hit a

first time drive past Bailey, But Buchan was on the line to boot clear. United were certainly guilty of defensive errors - but Bolton must take credit for forcing the chances. Above all, it was Frank Worthington who destroyed United.

Teams -

Bolton: McDonagh, Nicholson, Dunne, Greaves, P. Jones, Walsh, Morgan, Reid, Gowling, Worthington, McNab. Sub: Whatmore

Manchester United: Bailey, B. Greenhoff, Connell, McIlroy, McQueen, Buchan, Coppell, J. Greenhoff, Ritchie, Macari, Thomas. Sub: Nicholl for J. Greenhoff

Gordon Sharrock took over as the Evening News' Wanderers' reporter in 1979, and has held that position to this day.

The new season was just round the corner when this team picture was taken in July, 1978. Back row: Peter Nicholson, Alan Gowling, Mike Walsh, Paul Jones. Middle: Ian Greaves, Terry Poole, Sam Allardyce, Jim McDonagh, Frank Worthington, George Mulhall, Jim Hedridge (physio). Front: Ray Train, Neil Whatmore, Roy Greaves, Peter Reid, John Ritson, Tony Dunne. Willie Morgan, Garry Jones and Brian Smith were still playing American soccer. Notice that only Manager Ian Greaves is looking at the camera. The reason? The players were in dispute with the Evening News in an early controversy regarding 'image rights'.

If there is one goal scored at Burnden which the majority of fans recall, it was that by Frank Worthington in April, 1979, against Ipswich Town. As it happened, the goal was televised and won the Goal of the Season competition. Everyone remembers the goal . . . but most forget the result of the match. That season, Worthington also topped the First Division scorers.

Teams -

Bolton: McDonagh, Nicholson, Walsh, McNab, Jones, Allardyce, Morgan, Whatmore, Gowling, Worthington, Smith. Sub: Nowak

Ipswich: Cooper, Burley, Mills, Thijssen, Osman, Butcher, Wark, Muhren, Brazil, Gates, Woods. Sub: Geddis

23 APRIL 1979

WORTHY MAGIC ISN'T ENOUGH

Bolton 2 Ipswich 3

If ever one moment of genius deserved to win a game of football it came after 38 minutes when Frank Worthington scored the most amazing of goals, writes Gordon Sharrock.

Unfortunately for the Wanderers, Worthington's touch of magic was not enough to prevent Ipswich Town earning a well-deserved 3-2 win, Wanderers' first home defeat since November 25 when Nottingham Forest won by a single goal.

It gave F.A. Cup holders Ipswich an impressive double over Wanderers, having won 3-0 at Portman Road in December. Ipswich deserved the points with an all-round display of attacking football, but it must be said that the usually sound Bolton defence was in a generous mood. Even Ipswich's two-goal hero Alan Brazil, who took his goals well, would have been quick to concede that things were made easy.

Even so, Worthington still stole the show with a memorable goal in front of England manager Ron Greenwood, a 20,000 crowd and, conveniently, the TV cameras. When the ball came to Worthington on the edge of the Ipswich area he had only one thing in mind - hitting the target. Back to goal, he juggled the ball with his head, twice with his left foot, then lifted it over his head before pivoting and firing a shot on the volley past Paul Cooper's left hand.

It was a goal which will always be remembered as one of the greatest.

Frank Worthington . . . scorer of a magnificent goal.

Another 'goal of the season' scored by Roy Greaves' snatched a vital point for Wanderers in a 1-1 game against Bristol City at Burnden in December, 1979. Roy, who had last scored a league goal 12 months previously, is seen here turning Bolton's despair into joy with his last-minute equaliser. No prizes for guessing Neil Whatmore's feelings at seeing the ball in the back of the net.

West Brom's young England defender Derek Statham moved in to challenge Bolton's Willie Morgan in this 1979 game which ended in a 0-0 draw.

Within hours of the last game being played at Burnden Park at the end of the 1978-79 season, the workmen moved in with their jack-hammers and bulldozers to make a start on an improvement programme costing close on £200,000, wrote Gordon Sharrock. "The work will, quite literally, take the Wanderers into the computer age and will bring the ground up to the rigid safety standards laid down in the latest Government legislation. And all for less than the price of your average first division footballer. When Wanderers won promotion to Division One the season before last, Burnden became a 'designated' ground. As such, the club is required by law to meet the standards laid down in the green code governing our major sports grounds. If the work was not carried out and the necessary certificate granted, the ground capacity would have to be reduced from 42,000 to 32,000 and that would mean the loss of vital revenue to the club. Lots of other improvements are taking place as well, but the most intriguing development is a table-top computer which will mastermind the new, intricate fire alarm system, and will monitor attendances. At a glance, officials will know exactly how many people are inside any section of the ground and whether that section is full and should be closed." The picture showed the new barriers on the Burnden terrace and fencing round the track.

Was it a penalty? Six minutes from the end of this game in December, 1979, Peter Nicholson was sent flying by Bristol City's Jimmy Mann. After the game one Bolton player joked: "If it had happened on the street the bloke would have been done for assault." Even so, the referee ignored Wanderers' appeals, and the match ended in a 1-1 draw.

The way we were: Looking down Knowsley Street, 1985, before the Market Place was built.

1980s

DATE	WORLD EVENTS	BOLTON EVENTS
1980	John Lennon of the Beatles shot dead in New York City.	
1981		Town Hall fire when the Albert Hall went up in flames. First Bolton marathon, with more than 8,000 runners cheered on by hundreds of thousands of spectators.
1982	Argentina invades the Falklands Islands in the South Atlantic. The UK dispatches a task force, which re-takes them.	
1986	Space shuttle Challenger explodes shortly after take off from Cape Canaveral. All seven crew members are killed. Manned space flights are suspended until September 1988. Maradona's hand of God goal against England in the World Cup.	
1988	Ben Johnson breaks the world record in winning the 100m - before being disqualified for failing a drugs test.	Queen opens Water Place and the new multi-million Market Place shopping development, together with the re-furbished Market Hall.
1989	After 28 years, Berlin Wall is open to West.	Nat Lofthouse is given the Freedom of the Borough.

If anyone had thought that previous decades had been roller-coasters, they hadn't allowed for the 1980s. Disaster upon disaster as the club slipped back into the Second Division, then the Third, and, horror of horrors, into the Fourth for the first time in the club's history. That wasn't all. That decade also saw more managers coming and going, rows and resignations in the Boardroom, despondency for Bolton. Fortunately, towards the end, things began to improve; but first the bad news . . . in 1980, only two years after hauling themselves out of the Second Division, the Wanderers' found themselves back in it . . .

6 MAY 1980

BOLTON BOW OUT WITH NO EXCUSES

Bolton 0 Wolves 0

Sadly Bolton Wanderers bowed out of Division One with a drab scoreless draw against Wolves at gusty, dusty, Burnden Park. There was an air of dejection and disappointment but no excuses from the players as they pondered their brief two-year spell at the top.

"There are no hard-luck stories", confessed goalkeeper Jim McDonagh, who has played in every one of the 84 Division One games since helping Wanderers to promotion. "We never really arrived - we never felt right," he added. And top scorer Neil Whatmore, whose goals kept hopes flickering at times, admitted: "We just weren't good enough. We got what we deserved because we didn't have good enough players." Whatmore had the chances to break the deadlock on Saturday and add to his season's tally, but the hard dusty pitch and relentless wind ruined Wanderers' hopes of bowing out on a winning note.

Whatmore went on: "Being realistic, I can't see us being good enough to get out of the Second Division at the first attempt. We need a couple of players with experience. The young lads have done well, but the Second Division is a very difficult League to play in. At times you have to go to places and battle with teams and forget good football. The First Division is fast and best for football - the Second Division is really tough. There's only one place to be and that's the First." Whatmore should know, because he was instrumental in helping Wanderers battle their way to promotion two years

ago. He realises that a team cannot merely rely on good football to break out of the Second Division stranglehold.

Teams -

Bolton: McDonagh, Graham, Nicholson, Cantello, Allardyce, Walsh, Nowak, Whatmore, Carter, Wilson, Bennett. Sub: Hoggan

Wolves: Kearns, Palmer, Parkin, Daniel, Hughes, Brazier, Hibbitt, Carr, Gray, Richards, Eves. Sub: Atkinson

Following that result, and the drop into Division Two, Gordon Sharrock wrote:

WANDERERS HAVE MISSED THE BOAT

Hopes of the big time, for the time being at least, lie in tatters. The dream has turned to a nightmare. The club now has the summer to contemplate its mistakes, its misfortunes, before getting down to the unenviable task of battling it out once more in Division Two.

Having struggled so long and hard in the first place to win promotion, the fans and the club know too well how hard that fight is going to be. I can't help thinking that the club, and the town for that matter, have missed out both on and off the field. No-one can escape blame.

Football is big business these days, and you don't get much bigger than the First Division. There are rich pickings in terms of prestige, both domestic and European and all the fringe benefits that go with soccer success.

Why did Wanderers deserve relegation? The board seemed to think it was the manager's fault, and with some reluctance, I would think, took the step of sacking Ian Greaves in January. It was reluctance which postponed the move back in November when, privately, they gave the manager and his coaching staff their vote of confidence. The delay, with hindsight, proved costly. By the time Stan Anderson took over it was too late, and all he could do was prepare for next season.

Had Wanderers shown a little more respect for the opposition they might not have gone 24 weeks without an away point. And what of the Division's leading goalscorer of

last season - Frank Worthington? He was sold in October after a mere eight appearances, three as substitute. The explanation from the manager was that Worthington had lost his touch. Whatever went on behind the scenes, I believe that Worthington was not given his chance on the field.

Then things got even worse. In the 1982-83 season, Bolton finished in 22nd place and relegation, and crashed into the Third Division for only the second time in the club's 109-year history.

16 MAY 1983
WHAT A WAY TO GO

Charlton 4 Bolton 1

Bolton Wanderers lost their Second Division lives at Charlton on a day of bitter irony and cruel coincidence. Hopes have foundered in the past and it was "The Valley of Death" once again with a 4-1 defeat, plunging Wanderers into Division Three and with the distinct threat that there is worse to come.

They ended a three-year struggle to avoid the drop losing on the same ground and by the identical score line as 12 years ago in the deciding game when they were last relegated to the Second Division. What a way to go!

Fate dealt Wanderers the cruellest of blows, handing them a survival lifeline before snatching it from their grasp in a dramatic late turnabout. It was all against form.

Ian Moore's 61st minute goal was his first for six months, while the collapse of the Bolton defence which began eight minutes later was completely out of character. The back four has been Bolton's strongest department all season. This time they collapsed like a pack of cards in a hurricane.

Mike Doyle, who goes into hospital for a knee operation next week, will have time to reflect on mistakes which presented Charlton skipper Derek Hales with two goals in a three-minute spell, ripping the heart out of Wanderers' last gasp bid for safety. In the 69th minute, with Wanderers clinging to their one goal lead, Doyle was at his positive best, charging to claim the ball and leaving two Charlton attackers in his wake. But his clearance was a poor one, and ex-Wanderer Don McAllister - a survivor of the Bolton side when they last dropped into Division Three - laid on the equaliser for Hales, who needed a pain-killing injection before the game. Dickenson, one of Doyle's victims, was limping back into position as Hales raced through, and was clearly in an offside position, as the Wanderers' camp claimed. But there

was no flag, and referee Clive Thomas may well have considered the Charlton full-back was not interfering with play.

Wanderers hadn't time to catch their breath before being punished a second time. Doyle was clearly irritated by a fierce and unsporting tackle from behind by Carl Harris when he slammed the ball down and mis-hit his hurried free kick. Hales cashed in again. This time Doyle, beaten for pace, could only take him down from behind, conceding the penalty. Hales placed to Jim McDonagh's right for the killer blow. Further goals from Steve Gritt and Carl Harris were merely statistics which added to Bolton's misery.

However, it was a fighting performance, and on the day Wanderers did not deserve to lose a game they approached with spirit and determination. But the hard facts are that the Wanderers are now paying for their inadequacies during this season and seasons past. They deserve to be relegated, and their position at the bottom of Division Two is a fitting end to one of the most traumatic periods in the club's history. Now the danger is that the Wanderers will find no safety net in the Third Division. Lessons must be learned if this slide is to be finally halted.

How prophetic that last paragraph was. Four years later, down went the Wanderers again after having to appear in the play-offs. In the first leg away at Aldershot, the home team had scraped out a 1-0 victory. Three days later it was all up to Bolton to take advantage at Burnden Park and ensure their survival in Division Three. It was not to be (even after extra time) . . .

10 MAY 1987

FOURTH RATE WANDERERS

Bolton 2 Aldershot 2

They had the hearts and voices of more than 7,000 fans to drive them on . . . the bravery of wounded hero Dave Felgate to inspire them, and two goals from Tony Caldwell to give them the breathing space of extra time. But none of it was enough. Wanderers finally submitted to relegation.

When the Football League kicks off its centenary season in August, Wanderers - one of the 12 clubs who were in it right at the beginning - will be playing in Division Four for the very first time. The brand new play-off system offered an escape route but no salvation for unhappy Wanderers, who could only manage a 2-2 draw on the day, conceding a 3-2 aggregate defeat at the hands of modest little Aldershot.

An afternoon of passion, drama and controversy ended with

demonstrations. Felgate, crippled with a foot injury he bravely carried for an hour and a quarter, had to be carried from the ground after the game and driven to hospital through crowds of angry fans who gathered on the Burnden Park forecourt. Supporters called for resignations and rumours spread that it had been announced on radio that Wanderers had sacked Phil Neal.

That was not true. At the same moment the manager was speaking to the players in the dressing room, recognising that while their efforts on the day had not been good enough, the real damage had been done earlier in the season.

They had indeed left themselves too much to do, but survival looked on the cards for a time as Wanderers stood all square in the tie. A heavy pitch didn't help, but the break came five minutes into the second half when the Wanderers broke out after a defensive scare, Colin Smith's desperate tackle sent Gavin flying, and Caldwell managed to compose himself for the penalty. What a relief! A goal at last for Caldwell after more than three months and a successful penalty after many misses. Now could Wanderers find another goal from somewhere without leaving the backdoor open?

The courageous, hobbling, Felgate somehow managed to keep the lead intact. And with some extremely tired legs to handicap them, Wanderers were clearly struggling. Brave

they may have been, but they looked ripe for the killing. The lethal blow came 15 minutes from the end of normal time when substitute Darren Anderson was first to react to Steve Wignall's free kick, and Felgate was beaten. It might as well have ended right there, even though Caldwell's second goal in the 81st minute gave the fans hope and took the game into a tense extra half hour, Aldershot had the massive psychological advantage of an away goal. When Glenn Burvill scored Aldershot's second equaliser 13 minutes into the added period, Wanderers didn't have it in them to come back again.

The supporters, who had been behind their team as long as there was hope, suddenly turned their attention to the directors' box and let fly with frustration and anger. They knew Wanderers were done for. The final period of extra time merely prolonged the agony.

Teams -

Bolton: Felgate, Neal, Scott, Joyce, Sutton, Came, Caldwell, Thompson, Elliott, Hartford, Gavin, sub Stevens (for Joyce, 76 mins).

Aldershot: Lange, Blankley, Friar, Fielder, Smith, Wignall, Mazzon, Burvill, Langley, McDonald, Johnson, sub Anderson (for Langley 8 mins).

The goal that sent the Wanderers tumbling into Division Four. Aldershot midfielder Glenn Burvill's shot flies into the Bolton net, and there's no turning back.

Don't get the impression, though, that it was all despair. In September 1983, for instance, the Wanderers beat Walsall 8-1 (Tony Caldwell scoring five, equalling the club's scoring record in one match). In the same month of the following year, against Plymouth, the team gave seven magnificent reasons why they shouldn't have been languishing at the bottom of Division Three, with Caldwell scoring a hat-trick.

24 SEPTEMBER 1984
SHOOTING STARS

Bolton 7 Plymouth 2

It was Bolton's first League win and their first goals on home ground, with Tony Caldwell, Jeff Chandler, George Oghani, and Warren Joyce cashing in to answer the critics who had been all too premature in writing them off. For hat-trick hero Caldwell, and two-goal Chandler, it was a personal score settled. They had been dropped in midweek as John McGovern took the drastic step of axing four senior players who had let him down at Rotherham.

The manager said he'd no regrets about leaving them out, and no qualms about bringing three of them - Bell returned in mid-field - straight back. And it paid off with the top score of the day in the Football League.

And while Caldwell and Chandler were proving their points, Oghani continued his amazing scoring run, playing a major part in the victory and in one of the finest goals to be scored at Burnden in recent years. Two minutes from time, with one goal to his credit plus a couple of close calls, Oghani latched on to a Caldwell pass that switched play from right to left. The striker set off on a mazy 50 yard dribble; having skipped through the entire Plymouth defence Oghani just couldn't manage to finish the job off himself. That was left to ever-alert Caldwell who slid in to complete a fine hat-trick. Seconds later Oghani was off again. But this time he settled for slipping the ball back for Chandler, whose 25 yard angled shot seemed to go right through the arms of emergency 'keeper Gordon Nisbet.

John McGovern was delighted Wanderers had answered their critics in such a devastating fashion. "Just because we have had a nightmare start to the season, you are made to feel like a criminal by some of the things people say about you," he commented.

Teams -

Bolton: Farnworth, Burrows, Phillips, Joyce, McElhinney, Valentine, Thompson, Chandler, Oghani, Caldwell, Bell.
Sub: Rudge

Plymouth: Crudginton, Nisbet, Uzzell, Harrison, Goodyear, Burrows, Hodges, Cooper, Tynan, Staniforth, Coughlin.
Sub: Rogers for Harrison

Tony Caldwell jumps for joy as he celebrates his hat-trick with Jeff Chandler during Wanderers' 7-2 win over Portsmouth. The display earned Wanderers the Fiat "Performance of the Week" award, which meant that a boys' club would benefit to the tune of £250 plus a full set of team strip.

In 1986, more heartbreak for the Wanderers. They had fought their way to Wembley for the final of the Freight Rover Trophy, only to go down to Bristol City. "It is better to have played and lost at Wembley than not to have played there at all. That is then only consolation for the Wanderers," commented the Evening News.

27 MAY 1986

FINAL HEARTBREAK BUT BOLTON PUT ON A BRAVE FACE

Bolton 0 Bristol City 3

Bolton Wanderers disguised their Wembley heartache and sportingly took their Cup Final defeat on the chin. It wasn't easy, but the fans cheered to the last as they watched their team lose to Bristol City. They had hoped for a triumphant return to the scene of past triumphs, but it was not to be. The Bristol City bogey struck again, and the London jinx stretched to 30 games without a win.

The convoy of more than 20,000 fans, who had travelled south brimming with optimism after the thrills of an exciting Cup run, came home crestfallen - many choking back the tears, others crying unashamedly. The only consolation was that they had seen their team at Wembley, and that is more than many other supporters can boast.

Wanderers shared in one triumph, helping put the Freight Rover Trophy - once much maligned - on the soccer map. Their very presence in the final boosted the attendance to 54,502 with gate receipts topping a massive £286,000. And they helped the competition live up to its reputation as the Family Final - friendly to the last.

As a spectacle and occasion, this was a hit. The day the Wanderers went to Wembley will live long in the memory. As a performance it was a let-down. Phil Neal's men didn't do themselves justice on the big day, and the bookies who had Bristol as red hot favourites, got it right.

The 3-0 scoreline reflected their superiority over the 90 minutes. Yet, as with all such occasions, it might have turned out differently. If a Tony Caldwell shot had been a fraction lower and the ball had deflected down off the crossbar and into the net instead of up and over the top, Wanderers would have been in the lead. Two inches made all the difference. And if Simon Farnworth's double-fisted

punch had not fallen perfectly for Glyn Riley, it would have been 0-0 at half time with all to play for. The two incidents were decisive. Instead of being a goal to the good or at least level at the change round, the Wanderers were trailing, disheartened and, as it transpired, unable to recover. The game ran away from them in the second half as Phil Neal sportingly conceded afterwards, Bristol were worthy winners.

The Wanderers' fans cheery reception as the City winners paraded the trophy was just as sporting as that of the Bristol supporters at the opposite end when the dejected Bolton players left the field.

The players knew they hadn't done themselves justice on their big day. They had the better of the early stages but never recovered from the psychological blow of conceding a goal just one minute before half time. Once in front on their first visit to Wembley, the Bristol City Robins went on bob-bob-bobbing along.

"We'll support you evermore", sang the Wanderers' fans as Asa Hartford led his disappointed team up the 35 steps to the Royal box to receive their losers' tokens. Derek Scott was second in line, followed by Simon Farnworth, who knew he could take the blame for that first goal; Steve Thompson, pulled off in the second half; Dave Sutton, doing his best to raise a cheer; youngest of all, Jimmy Phillips; Tony Caldwell, who was the last player to leave the field, making the most of his Wembley dream; the two Marks, Came and Gavin; disappointed but proud player-manager Phil Neal; star performer George Oghani, followed by subs Graham Bell who got on, and Sam Allardyce who didn't.

"My boys have given me one hundred per cent," Neal said later, "but I feel that Bristol were thoroughly the best winners, the better side on the day over 90 minutes."

Teams -
Bolton: Farnworth, Scott, Phillips, Sutton, Came, Thompson, Neal, Oghani, Caldwell, Hartford, Gavin.
Subs: Bell (for Thompson 73 mins) and Allardyce

Bristol City: Waugh, Newman, Williams, Curle, Moyes, Riley, Pritchard, Hutchinson, Harle, Walsh, Neville.
Subs: Llewellyn and Marshall

Bristol's Robert Newman chases for the ball with Bolton's Mark Gavin.

Some of the disappointed Wanderers players waving to fans at the end of the game.

A dejected Phil Neal leads Wanderers on a lap of honour.

The beginning of the end of the long nightmare, and a quick bounce-back . . . in 1988 the Wanderers finished third in the Fourth Division and were promoted. At last everyone could look into the future again with hope . . .

9 MAY 1988

HERE WE GO

Wrexham 0 Bolton 1

Bolton Wanderers are celebrating again - just a year after suffering the bitter blow of relegation. A win at Wrexham on Saturday, coupled with Scunthorpe's victory at Torquay, clinched an unexpected return ticket to Division Three for the Burnden Park club.

Most thought the final day of the season would leave the Wanderers facing the nerve-wrenching end of season play-offs. But 4,000 jubilant fans saw Robbie Savage's match-winner secure a dramatic victory. Player-manager Phil Neal, the most decorated player in England during his Liverpool days, ranked the success as highly as any in his career.

Amid wild scenes of tension, excitement and celebration, the happy Wanderers won one of the most dramatic promotion scrambles of all time. The entire Bolton contingent, players and fans, launched themselves into emotional scenes after the 1-0 win - correctly believing, but not knowing for sure, that Scunthorpe had won at Torquay to complete a winning combination that opened the door to the higher division.

But back in the dressing toom, where it was confirmed, there wasn't a single popping champagne cork to be heard. No-one expected to be celebrating because they all thought their promotion hopes rested on the play-offs. So no-one thought of bringing the bubbly.

So off they sped to Burnden Park to savour the heady atmosphere of winning the most frantic of last-ditch victories. It was one of those occasions that fans and players will never forget. Robbie Savage was the hero, smashing in the all-important matchwinner midway through the second half." The ball sat up nicely for me and I knew it was a goal the moment I hit it," he beamed. "And once we were in front I knew we would win it - no problem." Such

confidence! The rest of us had to endure 22 minutes of stomach-knotting tension, as the defence suddenly looked shaky. Nervous backpasses and silly fouls put Wrexham in sight of an equaliser, which would have broken Bolton hearts.

After the whistle the whole Wanderers' squad raced up to the directors' box - many had been stripped almost naked by the jubilant fans - to join in the celebrations. Defensive heroes, Welshman Dave Felgate celebrating on his native soil; Neal himself; a wounded Derek Scott; Mark Came, who admitted he didn't enjoy the game because of nerves; and Mark Winstanley, who again showed he is emerging as a player of the future.

The players, in various amounts of dress, acknowledge their fans (including a rather excited policeman) celebrating promotion in 1988.

In August, 1988, the Wanderers brought home another trophy, the Lancashire Manx Cup, one of the biggest trophies in football.

17 AUGUST `1988`

THOMAS THE SNATCH

Bolton 1 Preston North End 0

John Thomas landed one of the biggest trophies in football for Bolton Wanderers - with a little help from one of his old team mates.

But as Wanderers celebrated their victory over Preston in the Lancashire Manx Cup and skipper Mark Came carried off the 3ft. high cup, goal star Thomas refused to gloat. Thrilled as ever to be on the scoresheet, he took no special satisfaction in putting one over on the club who sold him to Bolton a year ago. "I don't think I've got anything to prove to Preston," he insisted. "I left there on good terms, and everyone there knows what I can do."

Wanderers found themselves in an awkward spot as they collected the massive trophy which was formerly the Lancashire Senior Cup and dates back to 1878. Everyone wanted to celebrate an exciting win against their famous old rivals, but they knew that apart from a £10,000 profit from their four games, the glory of winning a modest pre-season tournament will count for nothing once the real business of League football starts. "Let's not get carried away," was manager Phil Neal's way of bringing the revellers down to earth.

Nevertheless, Wanderers did all they needed to against the toughest opposition they have faced to date in their warm up for the Third Division. A crowd of 5,757, mainly from Preston, illustrated how serious the supporters believed it to be. And victory over this resolute Preston side is no mean achievement, anytime, anywhere.

Thomas and co-striker Ian Stevens ran themselves ragged to get anything they could out of Sam Allardyce and his stubborn, central defensive partners Jeff Wrightson and Bob Atkins - all for nothing until they finally got lucky with 20 minutes to go. After all the hard work it was a wayward backpass by Oshor Williams that handed Thomas his goal

on a plate. All Wanderers had to do then was survive a nervous finale.

Allardyce, once one of the idols of the Burnden crowd until his free transfer to Preston, went within an ace of producing one of his "specials" but unfortunately headed straight into Dave Felgate's hands after a long-distance one-two with David Miller. Wanderers worked hard for their first taste of success in the tournament. However, they still have problems finding the spark around the penalty area where they could be making more of the possession they enjoy.

Happy Wanderers celebrate their Lancashire Manx Cup win.

Three years after losing 3-0 to Bristol City in the Freight Rover Trophy final, Bolton were back at Wembley in the same competition, although it was now called the Sherpa Van Trophy. The opponents in the May, 1989 game, were Torquay, and when the southerners went ahead it looked as though 1986 might be repeated. No chance. Bolton came from behind to win 4-1 with what the paper described as a "champagne second half show". When the team returned home in glory, thousands of ecstatic Boltonians crowded the streets with "a glorious homecoming their Wembley heroes will never forget." The club was also having a good run in the League.

29 MAY 1989
WEMBLEY WONDERS

Bolton 4 Torquay 1

Hail the Wanderers - Wembley wonders in a five goal Sherpa Van Trophy final that put the sunshine back into soccer. Phil Neal's never-say-die battlers came from behind to clinch a glorious and worthy victory with a second half show that destroyed fourth division Torquay United and set a new club record of 20 games without defeat.

Torquay were Devon's first Wembley finalists, and gave the massed Bolton ranks a fright when Dean Edwards put them ahead in the 23rd minute. But Julian Darby, the only Bolton-born player in the line-up, started the revival and there was no looking back as Wanderers celebrated in the stadium where they were victorious in 1923-26-29 and 1958.

Jeff Chandler, confirmed in the team less than 24 hours earlier, is claiming the second goal as his, although the records may show that it was scored by Torquay's John Morrison. There were no doubts, though, about Dean Crombie's first-ever goal for Wanderers, and Trevor Morgan's, which wrapped up a great and well-deserved win.

Bolton had been the much more prominent side in the first half, showing hardly any signs of big match nerves. They were spraying the ball around confidently and making effective use of the flanks with skipper Phil Brown frequently worrying the Torquay defence with his overlapping runs down the right. Bolton played with a lot of passion, but although they were the better side they still had to be on

Julian Darby celebrates the equaliser with his team-mates just four minutes after Torquay had taken the lead.

A moment to savour - Bolton skipper Phil Brown shows the trophy to the Wembley crowds.

their guard to combat the threat posed by Torquay's lively front players. However, Steve Thompson made an impressive contribution in a Bolton midfield that gradually wore down Torquay.

Thompson was named Man of the Match - recognised for his quality play by adjudicator Lawrie McMenemy - and Dave Felgate made many vital saves.

Yet all the Wanderers, down to the late substitute Stuart Storer, were all heroes as skipper Phil Brown received the Trophy from Elton John, sending almost 25,000 Bolton followers wild with delight.

Teams -
Bolton: Felgate, Brown, Cowdrill, Savage, Crombie, Winstanley, Chandler, Thompson, Thomas, Morgan, Darby. Subs: Storer, Stevens

Torquay: Allen, Pugh, Kelly, McNichol, Elliott, Loram, Airey, Lloyd, Edwards, Weston, Morrison. Subs: Smith, Joyce

A couple of days later, the paper reported:
Thousands of ecstatic Boltonians crowned a jewel of a weekend with a glorious homecoming their Wembley heroes will never forget. Supporters young and old turned the streets into a blanket of navy, red and white as the triumphant players inched their way through the town in an open-top bus.

All along the short journey from Burnden Park the happy Wanderers were greeted with a crescendo of noise, which hit a climax as they turned into the Town Hall square where an estimated 5,000 people were waiting to herald Bolton's first Wembley victory for 31 years.

Rooftops, trees, street lamps and every other available vantage point seemed to be occupied by fans wanting the best view of the celebrations. Julian Darby said: "It's all been like a dream come true. To score for my home town team in a Wembley final and then to come home to a welcome like this."

A great welcome home . . . and some of the fans were determined to get the best vantage points.

There was as much drama off the field as there was on it during the 1980s, with boardroom changes, managers coming and going, and financial strife... even Pele came into the equation. It was, said the paper, "one of the most crucial times of the Wanderers' history".

IN THE HOT SEAT

In March, 1981, Derrick Warburton stepped down as managing director and chief executive (although he stayed on the board), and his duties were taken over by Brian Turnbull, who became vice-chairman. George Warburton, Derrick's brother, remained as chairman.

"Mr Turnbull is a young, energetic and very successful businessman. He is now taking on a new challenge and he must succeed, whatever the cost and however hard some decisions may be," commented the Evening News. "It would be a tragedy if all the rebuilding work of the 1970s were to be dissipated in the first two years of the eighties. The club owes it to the town and the fans to do everything possible to get back on an upward course, and this is Mr Turnbull's first task."

However, only 11 months later Mr Turnbull was on his way out. The man who was the club's largest single shareholder with 27 per cent quit because of a boardroom power-struggle in which the other directors vetoed his plan to raise cash for the club on a shares deal. With Wanderers more than £400,000 in the red, he had devised a shares scheme which would have raised up to £150,000. He had also carried out massive cost-cutting schemes including staff cuts and reductions in travel costs; those, together with other fund-raising efforts, had reduced a weekly loss in excess of £5,000 to near break-even point on gates averaging 7,000.

Mr Turnbull wasn't happy to leave it there. He would not accept defeat and called on the entire board to resign, leaving him to return and run the club. The other directors declined his offer, and issued the simple statement: "The board have no intention of resigning, and don't wish to be involved in personal squabbles."

Then in May of that year George Warburton also stepped down as chairman after eight years, staying on the board ("I thought it was time for a change") and the top post was taken by chief executive Terry Edge who declared that "I want

to see Bolton Wanderers back in the First Division and that will be the main priority."

He was still chairman in 1983 when a "mystery buyer" was hunting for Bolton shares and seemingly a controlling interest. "Put your money where your mouth is," Mr Edge told him. "If there's somebody out there with a lot of money to put into the club I'd be only too happy to speak to him. So far there has been no approach to me or to anyone else on the board." That was a story which disappeared fairly quickly . . .

By May, 1984, though, Mr Edge also stood down, because of personal and business commitments. "The board had

decided some time ago to re-introduce the old system of the chairmanship rotating among the directors on a two-year cycle," he explained. "It's been very hard."
So up stepped Neil Riley, former vice-chairman, to the top post, determined to "carry on the same policies of improving the team and the commercial side, and try to keep the club on a stable course." However, after his two years were up, Mr Riley also quit the Bolton board - because his fellow directors had failed to honour the agreement to rotate the chairmanship and share the responsibilities. He had been told that others weren't prepared to put the time in the job, and "I would sooner not be part of a board which cannot honour its agreements." George Warburton stepped back

All smiles in the boardroom in 1982 when chief executive Brian Turnbull (left) welcomed local businessman Terry Edge who had just been appointed a director at Burnden Park. Also pictured was chairman George Warburton.

into the position as a stop-gap, resigning after Bolton dropped into the Fourth Division, and in 1987 Barry Chaytow took over.

His first move was to quash any speculation about manager Phil Neal's future. "He has the full backing of the board," he declared. Phil Neal continued to have that support as the team floundered - but not from Mr Chaytow, and many fans.

Two years later, in February, 1989, the paper commented: "A successful town needs a good soccer team. Unfortunately Bolton is a First Division town with a Third Division football team. The glory days at Bolton are now little more than a distant memory, and the voices which once cheered another F.A. Cup victory or First Division triumph are raised against the board and manager . . . if the present incumbents of all positions at Burnden Park have the talent, the commitment and the resources to rescue Bolton Wanderers from the ever increasing mediocrity, then well and good. If they can't, they should make way for those who can."

Two days later Barry Chaytow quit the club after failing to get the backing of the board to sack Phil Neal. "There was no power struggle," it was reported. "Mr Chaytow simply asked his fellow directors to support his view that the team's current plight called for 'major changes' - namely the sacking of Phil Neal. But they refused. The power lay elsewhere in the boardroom, where five directors - namely

Sam Jones, George Warburton, Brett Warburton, Graham Ball and Gordon Seymour (Gordon Hargreaves was absent) - were against the chairman's view. He neither had the support of an ally nor the backing of a major shareholder to take on the rest of the board. The affair confirms the long-held view that the position of chairman of Bolton Wanderers, while placing the incumbent in the public firing line, carries no tangible authority."

Sam Jones then took over the position. Fortunately, generally speaking the whole situation was settling down again, and things were improving for the Wanderers, but the 1980s were a traumatic time in the Burnden boardroom.

Evening News, Tuesday, February 7, 1989

Evening News OPINION

Burnden crisis

A SUCCESSFUL town needs a good soccer team almost as much as it requires excellent shopping facilities, sensible local government policies and civic pride.

Unfortunately, Bolton is a First Division town with a Third Division football team.

The glory days at Burnden Park are now little more than a distant memory, and the voices which once cheered another FA Cup victory or First Division triumph are raised against the Board and the manager.

With only one win in 10 games, crowds have now dwindled to a hardcore of diehards while behind the scenes advertisements to buy shares are further evidence, should it be needed, of disenchantment.

Manager Phil Neal had a hugely distinguished playing career at club and international level, and is an ardent disciple of good football and professional attitudes. Regrettably, he has been unable to mirror his success on the field, off it.

Ultimately, though, it must be the Board who hire and fire managers, set policies, and make money available. It is their club and they run it — yet the Wanderers really belong to the whole of Bolton.

Bolton Wanderers would be nothing without the 3,500 faithful supporters who turn up for every home game, and many of whom follow the team away as well. It is they who are demanding action.

For them, it is bad enough having the likes of once second-rate footballing clubs like Millwall and Norwich looking down on everyone. But now they are having to suffer the additional indignity of seeing neighbours Bury showing us the way with good results and better attendances.

We do not speculate as to whose fault this situation is. We do not call for the head of manager Phil Neal. Managers always get the blame, and carry the can, but more often than not some of the responsibility lies elsewhere.

Money is available to buy new players to strengthen the team, we are told. But how much? And with such results why is it not being spent?

When Wanderers won promotion to the Third Division last season, the fans and the manager were promised that cash would be available to strengthen the side. Now we must see the colour of the Board's money in time to prevent the club making a rapid return to the Fourth.

What is needed at Burnden Park is determination and leadership on the field, and pride and vision off it. And for the sake of the town, as well as for the football club, it needs to come quickly.

If the present incumbents in all positions at Burnden Park have the talent, the commitment and the resources to rescue Bolton Wanderers from ever increasing mediocrity, then all well and good. If they can't, they should make way for those who can.

Sam Jones.

Neil Riley.

Barry Chaytow.

ON THE MANAGER'S SIDE

After the headlines screamed about Ian Greaves's sacking in 1980 after six years in the post (he added a little colour to what he termed "another soccer casualty" when he quipped: "As I was driving home I saw a funeral - so there's one bloke in Bolton worse off then me.") Stan Anderson, who had joined the club in 1978 as assistant to Greaves, was promoted. However, he was axed after only 14 months to make way for George Mulhall. George had previously been at Burnden under Ian Greaves between 1974 and 1978. When he returned in 1981, the club was in turmoil. The chief scout and chief coach had left, six players had been released on free transfers and a further six were available for transfer whilst cost cutting exercises continued. There was also conflict with the directors and in June, 1982, he left the club.

The board then decided to look for a player/manager, and John McGovern fitted the bill. An influx of young players between 1983-4 brought some good results, but there was a poor run the following season when the Wanderers finished near the bottom of the Third Division. McGovern had only played 16 League games in his more than two years as player-manager, and in January, 1985, out he went as well. Charlie Wright (former Bolton goalkeeper until he retired in 1973 with a back injury, then youth coach and chief coach; he left to be manager at York in 1977 without much success, and in 1981 had returned to Bolton as coach) was put in temporary charge with McGovern's departure. In December of that same year, though, Wright also left the club by mutual consent.

Stan Anderson with Jim Headridge (physio) and Tony Dunne (assistant manager).

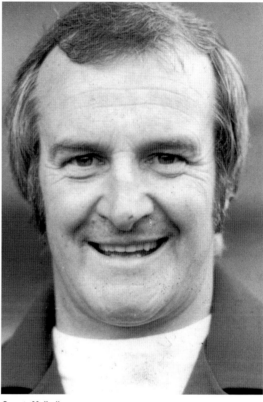

George Mulhall.

John McGovern, appointed in 1982 as player-manager, although by 1985 when he left he had appeared in only 16 League games. His place was taken by Charlie Wright, who was in the post for only a few months.

Then came Phil Neal, the Liverpool and England full-back ("He will be the sixth manager the Wanderers have had in as many years, and their 13th since the war," said the paper). In a book he wrote in 1986 he said that he had been staggered, on the day he arrived at Bolton, "by the shambles that lay before me." The wage structure, he said, in no way reflected the contribution that certain players were making to the team effort. "A young first team regular who has risen through the ranks to establish himself can be picking up as little as £80 a week while a senior pro, well past his best and probably picked up from his previous club on a free transfer, can be on a two-year contract at a basic wage of around £300 a week with a substantial bonus packet on top of that."

Neal was to prove an important lynch-pin in the improving fortunes of the Wanderers over the years.

Phil Neal, also a player-manager, appointed in December, 1985; under his guidance the team began to climb back up the ladder to the big time.

What happens when you sack a manager and are looking for another? Well, you might as well go for the big name, and that's exactly what happened when George Mulhall left Burnden Park in 1982.

1 JUNE　　　1982

BOLTON WANT PELE

Bolton Wanderers today sacked manager George Mulhall after less than a year in the Burnden hot-seat and then, in all seriousness, claimed that Pele was their next target. Wanderers' new chairman Terry Edge told an astonished news conference of the incredible plan to land the former Brazilian star - the biggest name in world football.

Club secretary Des McBain will fly to America, where he plans to set up a meeting with the soccer superstar to put forward the Wanderers' sensational approach. "I know it's a sensation," said Mr Edge, "but why not. That is how ambitious we are. Even if it's just for one year we believe Pele can bring the crowds back to Bolton and back to British football. I don't think Pele has ever been approached by an English club before. It's a serious proposition."

Sadly for Mr McBain, who was presumably looking forward to a trip to America (definitely sadly for Mr Edge, and possibly sadly for Bolton supporters as well), the following day the legendary Pele rejected the chance of becoming the new player-manager at Burnden. Pele, said Mr Edge, said he was flattered, but because he was under a long term contract with Warner Communications, he could not consider Bolton's invitation. "Now the Wanderers will be advertising the post," reported the paper.

WANDERERS WILL NOW ADVERTISE

Pele says 'No' to Bolton job

By ANDREW BUCKLEY

THE legendary Pele has rejected the chance to become the new player-manager of Bolton Wanderers.

The Brazilian star as expected turned down Bolton's offer to take over from George Mulhall who was sacked yesterday.

Now the Wanderers will widen their search for a new manager with former England players Mike Channon and Emlyn Hughes possibly on their wanted list.

Bolton will advertise the vacant post and will draw up a short list from the applicants.

quit Carlisle is another possibility. He is currently on holiday in Portugal.

The Wanderers may be

This was the cartoon view of the Pele situation which appeared in the Evening News in June, 1982.

If a club is in financial crisis, what do its directors do? Simple; think up a new idea, a lottery, make sure that it doesn't break the betting laws, and get enough people interested to make a profit. That's what happened in Bolton in 1982, and it saved the Wanderers from bankruptcy.

5 DECEMBER 1982

LOTTERY THAT SAVED THE CLUB

If there was one thing which helped save the Wanderers and ease the club's financial plight in the 1980s, it was the launch of the Lifeline scheme. Wanderers' could have gone to the wall for the princely sum of £500,000, and were sinking fast, but on December 5, 1982, the then chairman Terry Edge unveiled an ambitious plan to rescue the club from near-bankruptcy.

The Bolton chief press-ganged his fellow directors, management team, office staff, players and supporters - even the local media - into pledging £2 a week to form a private members' club that skilfully negotiated a way round the rigid laws governing lotteries and fund-raising. Burnden Lifeline was born.

The paper reported the next day: "Support is flooding in to save Bolton Wanderers from financial ruin. Within 24 hours of the Save Our Soccer call from the crisis-hit Burnden club, more than 1,000 people had pledged vital cash support to keep the Wanderers alive". "We are on our way," said a delighted Mr Edge.

Mr Edge refused to even contemplate the prospect of failure, appointing Nat Lofthouse to front the scheme and set about recruiting 6,000 members to save the club's financial skin. They would fall some way short of that initial target, but it soon became clear that the Wanderers were on to a winner. Thanks to Lifeline the club survived the financial crisis, eventually had the strength to bounce back - and even sold the concept to other clubs, at the same time developing an expertise that today makes them the third largest sports development in Britain behind Celtic, and seriously challenging Manchester United as the best in England in the weekly lottery stakes.

Before the match against Gillingham began in January, 1986, lifelong supporter Mrs Alice Frost, aged 88, picked the first three digits of the winning ticket number for the £30,000 house, then on the pitch at half-time the final number was picked. Alice is seen here with one of the balls, watched by Nat Lofthouse and commercial manager Alf Davies.

While clubs throughout the land are suffering falling returns in the lotteries market, Lifeline still thrives, 4,000 strong with many of its original members still paying £2 a week. It has now been overtaken by the Goldline draw, which has 14,700 members paying £1 a week, but Lifeline is still an important financial part of the club.

The prizes were certainly not to be kicked off the pitch - one couple won a £30,000 house (it might not sound much these days, but in 1986 you could buy a decent home with that); others won sunshine apartments abroad, and now, in addition to a weekly cash prize of £2,500, there is a new car to be won every three months.

Lifeline might have seemed to some a gimmick at the beginning of the 1980s, and the plan met a lot of sceptism at the time, but it turned out as exactly what it name says - a Lifeline for Bolton Wanderers.

In December, 1983, Bolton Wanderers paid tribute to the commercial agents who had worked so hard to make Lifeline's first year a success by holding a "Gala Night". Pictured with one group of the agents was commercial manager Alf Davies, and Nat Lofthouse, along with Wanderers' skipper Ray Deakin and new signing George Oghani.

14 SEPTEMBER 1982
FREE BEER OFFER FALLS FLAT

Free beer failed to tempt the Bolton public into taking part in a world record attempt. Two thousand free pints of beer were on offer at Burnden Park where Bolton Wanderers and their sponsors Ingersoll Rand hoped to break the record for the biggest "shout" for a round of drinks.

The existing record of 1,222 was the target, but there turned out to be only 136 takers, leaving the organisers with more than 200 gallons of best bitter on their hands, and the best part of £1,000 unspent.

One world record was already in the bag, though. It came in the shape of the international company's giant advertisement on the stand roof being recognised as the biggest of its kind. The sign measures 240ft. by 60ft., and took 800 man hours and 1,888 pints of paint to complete.

24 MAY 1983
BIG SEASON TICKET DEALS

The Railway Embankment of Burnden Park will be closed off to Bolton Wanderers fans next season. It will be "Visitors Only" on the Embankment as Wanderers bid to cut costs in Division Three. The minimum admission price goes up to £2, but there will be a better deal on season tickets which the club hopes will boost advanced sales.

The new minimum admission price in line with those at Bury and Wigan means a 10p increase for terrace fans, but for £2 (£1.10 for juveniles and pensioners) fans can now have the choice of standing on either the Manchester Road or Burnden Terraces or sitting in the Great Lever Stand.

The price of a seat in the Great Lever Stand has been slashed by 65p to encourage greater use of the facilities there. Concessions in what has become known as the Family Stand will continue, with an adult and two children admitted for the all-in price of £3, and groups comprising one adult and 11 children admitted for £6.50.

Prices elsewhere on the ground have been pegged at last season's level. Manchester Road and Burnden Stand admission will be £3.65 (£2.10 for juveniles and pensioners), with Wing Stand (Block "A") prices remaining at £2.65 (£1.55 for pensioners).

A season ticket for a seat in the two main stands will cost £55 if purchased up to July 17 - £58.50 up to and including August 21, and £65.75 after that date.

In the Wing Stand the respective figures are £40, £42.50 and £47.75, and in the Great Lever Stand and two terraces, a season ticket will cost £28 at the full discount price rising to £30.50 and £34.25.

All visiting fans wishing to stand and watch the game will be accommodated on the Embankment with one price of | £2 for all.

24 AUGUST 1984
WANDERERS' CASH RIDDLE

Bolton Wanderers, who are more than £500,000 in the red, have turned down a mystery man's cash offer of almost £100,000. The man has failed in a bid to get the Wanderers' directors to sell him a block of almost 30,000 unsold shares at a total price of £96,054. And he has accused the hard-up Burnden Park club of "looking a gift horse in the mouth".

But Wanderers' chairman Neil Riley explained today that his directors had no intention of negotiating such a major shareholding in the club with someone who prefers to remain anonymous. The man, who has insisted his identity remain a secret and has corresponded with the Wanderers through a local solicitor, says he is "astonished" by the club's refusal to take up his offer.

"We are constantly being led to believe that the Wanderers are in a serious financial position. It would have been in the best interests of the club to have accepted my offer." He insisted he was not attempting a take-over bid for the club. "My interest in Bolton Wanderers was only short term to help the club over its financial plight," he said.

In the early 1980s, during the cash crisis, a plan had been put forward to build a superstore on part of the Embankment end of Burnden Park, but part of the deal was also that a plastic pitch should be laid at Burnden which would also be used as a "community pitch." There was naturally a lot of opposition to the prospect of Bolton playing on a plastic pitch, from both fans and players, and the Football League came to Bolton's aid in December, 1987 (although the superstore building went ahead).

15 DECEMBER 1987

WANDERERS LET OFF HOOK ON PLASTIC PITCH

A plan to replace the hallowed turf of Burnden Park with plastic and turn it into a shared club/community pitch has been kicked into touch. The scheme was part of ambitious development plans at Bolton Wanderers' headquarters which included the building of a new Co-op superstore, and development of various community facilities at the club.

But the Football League changed its rules shortly after the deal was signed and outlawed plastic pitches for League clubs. If the club laid a plastic pitch now it could be expelled from the League, Bolton Planning Committee members have been told.

Now a new plan proposes that the Burnden Park ground should be left as it is, and a new £300,000 plastic community pitch should be built in Scholey Street. It gets the club off the hook and means the community pitch will still be provided as part of the plan. Some of the facilities envisaged in the deal, including a five-a-side pitch and improved gymnasium, are already well used, and the supermarket, on the site of the 1946 Burnden disaster, is due to open in the spring.

Bolton's newest sports centre has solved its all-weather pitch problems, reported the paper in November 1988. "Now the Burnden centre, which opened less than two years ago, boasts the same luxury surface that has replaced the grass at Preston North End's famous Deepdale ground. Soon after it was opened, the centre had problems with its plastic pitch. A new surface was laid, with the original manufacturers footing the £75,000 bill, and the picture shows Nat Lofthouse cutting the tape with players looking on ready to try out the new pitch. The indoor and outdoor facilities at the Burnden centre, transformed from the old dilapidated Wanderers gym have proved popular."

21 AUGUST 1989

WANDERERS WERE KNIGHTON'S FIRST CHOICE

Michael Knighton, the multi-millionaire who attempted to buy (unsuccessfully) Manchester United, tried to join Bolton Wanderers before he went to Old Trafford. Wanderers' chairman Sam Jones says the board treated Mr Knighton "with suspicion" when he offered to put money into the club at the height of the boardroom turmoil last season. They feared Mr Knighton, who claims to have £30 million to gain control of United, was linked with the deposed Wanderers' chairman Barry Chaytow. Mr Chaytow is now known to be the man who introduced Mr Knighton to Old Trafford supremo Martin Edwards on June 30. Mr Jones says that he and his directors were unaware that Mr Knighton could summon £30 million worth of backing, and quashed speculation that the 37-years-old Isle of Man tax exile tried to buy control of the Wanderers for £1 million.

"He wasn't really prepared to put much up," the Burnden chief explained. "He felt that his main asset was personal attitude and motivation - now he seems to have paid for the privilege." Had the Wanderers' directors passed up on a £30 million windfall? "Oh God no," Mr Jones exclaimed. "We wouldn't have let that pass us by. If he'd offered us £30 million I think we would be seeing more of him now. We never got to first base. We never got more involved than bits of talks. We felt he was interested in getting involved - then he disappeared."

These two pictures, taken a number of years apart, show Burnden
Park before and after the superstore was built.

In the early 1980s, the Evening News sponsored the Wanderers, the first time any newspaper had struck up such a deal with a Football League club, so the paper's name was carried across the country on the team's shirts. Wanderers were, in fact, pioneers on shirt sponsorship, and they put forward the original proposal to the F.A. in 1977; they were the first club to get permission to put a sponsor's name on their shirts. The paper reported: "Bolton Wanderers' proposal for advertising to be worn on players' shirts has been greeted with unanimous approval by other clubs. It might mean the financial salvation for some clubs in the lower divisions." However, deals with Bolton fell through and other clubs such as Liverpool and Everton then announced lucrative deals with national and international companies; Bolton never received the rightful acknowledgement for their pioneering move. The first sponsors for the Wanderers were Knight Security in 1980-81, followed by the Evening News the following year. However, for many years if a team played in a televised match, they were not allowed to wear a shirt wearing a sponsor's name - but it was only a matter of time before that rule was relaxed.

The goal that made history . . . What a finish. Bolton substitute John Thomas dives full-length to score a sensational goal with the final touch of the home game against Grimsby in October, 1981. But the goal, the Wanderers' 5,000th in League football was merely a consolation in the 2-1 defeat.

Wanderers' chief coach Walter Joyce gave some professional tips to a group of unemployed lads in 1982 at one of the special coaching sessions staged twice a week at British Aerospace sports grounds Lostock. The Wanderers were co-operating with the scheme on Tuesdays and Thursdays, aiding the unemployed under the Mayor's Charity Appeal.

A picture from November, 1980, showing "thinly-populated terraces at Bolton's game against Notts. County, serving a clear illustration of the problems soccer is facing with dwindling attendances. The gate was 7,344. The picture is certainly a sign of the times. At almost every ground in Britain nowadays, clubs are feeling the financial pinch. Not only Bolton Wanderers, but also the Manchester Uniteds and Liverpools are suffering in their own way."

Pictured limbering up during training in 1982 were Gerry McElhinney, Peter Reid, Steve Whitworth, and Tony Henry.

The Wanderers' full squad in 1988.

A 1994 view of open fields and the Red Moss tip at Horwich - the site where the Reebok Stadium was to be built.

1990s

DATE	WORLD EVENTS	BOLTON EVENTS
1990	World Wide Web debuts, popularises Internet.	Demonstrations in the town centre against the Poll Tax.
1991	UK takes part in US-led military campaign to liberate Kuwait from Iraqi occupation.	
1992	Prince and Princess of Wales agree to separate.	
1993		Princess Diana came to Bolton twice, once to open the Hospice, and later in the year to open the new £750,000 arts centre at Bolton School.
1996	Frankie Dettori rides all seven winners on the card at Ascot.	Bolton Royal Infirmary closed, and the new £45 million Royal Bolton Hospital opened its doors.
1997	Diana, Princess of Wales, is killed in a car crash in Paris.	It was decided that Sunday shopping should be a permanent fixture in Bolton. The Wanderers moved from Burnden Park to the new Reebok stadium.
1998		Middlebrook Retail and Leisure Park near Horwich was opened. The Valley complex followed a year later.

By the 1990s, things were definitely on the way up, although not without some major disappointments. In 1991 Wanderers got to the play-offs at Wembley against Tranmere, to see who would next season have Second Division status. It turned out to be a case of so near, yet so far, with Tranmere snatching the prize in extra time.

2 JUNE 1991

WEMBLEY PROVES A BRIDGE TOO FAR

Tranmere 1 Bolton 0

Wembley was just one hurdle too many for Wanderers to clear. They went there firmly believing they were rightful claimants to a promotion place. But they came away wearily cursing the play-off system for giving them the biggest disappointment of their football lives.

With 49 games played, their extended season had already stretched well beyond reasonable limits of endurance by the time referee Keith Hackett called an end to normal time. The further extension proved too much. Chris Malkin's goal, eight minutes into extra time, was the killer blow and the Bolton fans, who outnumbered Tranmere eight-to-one, sensed it. But they cheered on as Wanderers fought on - to the last.

It's a wonder that the likes of Thompson, Cowdrill, Brown and Darby found the energy to raise a boot, let alone drive shots agonisingly close to Eric Nixon's goal as a season of great expectations ended in even greater disappointment. In the end, the ultimate prize of promotion was decided by a solitary incident as players of two worthy teams dragged weary legs through the painful stages of Wembley cramp. Dave Felgate blocked Ged Brannan's shot, but was helpless when the rebound went straight to Malkin. That's how Cup Finals are decided - not promotion issues.

It's no wonder the losers are embittered by the experience. "I've already accepted the play-offs but I don't think they are right for English football," Phil Neal reflected sadly. "But even though all that hard work has come to nothing, we mustn't forget the good things we have done this season. We have had a really good season irrespective of us still being in the Third Division, and we have the nucleus of a really good side."

Neal knows the job of motivating his players after such a shattering blow will test all his managerial talents. Missing out on automatic promotion on goal difference was a major disappointment. They overcame that setback superbly, passing a tough semi-final test against Bury with great character. But they've been stunned with the result of this Final. Sadly, they couldn't produce the spark to do themselves justice when it really mattered.

Teams -

Bolton: Felgate, Brown, Cowdrill, Comstive, Seagraves, Stubbs, Storer, Thompson, Cunningham, Philliskirk, Darby. Subs: Reeves, Green.

Tranmere: Nixon, Higgins, Brannan, Irons, Hughes, Garnett, Morrissey, Martindale, Steel, Cooper, Thomas. Subs: Malkin, Harvey.

Alan Stubbs had plenty to look back on as the Wanderers' season ended in heartbreak and tears at Wembley. "It's going to be automatic promotion next year," he promised. Stubbs, supreme at Wembley as he has been in the run-in to the play-offs added: "We're too good for the Third Division. I'm gutted we didn't do it, but I'm sure we are going straight up next time."

Tony Cunningham challenges with Tranmere's Dave Higgins for a high ball.

Paul Comstive reflects on what might have been.

Whatever happened in those 1991 play-offs, there was going to be a medal. There was no trophy for the winners, and certainly nothing for the losers. But the Bolton players received an exclusive token in recognition of one of the finest achievements in the club's history.

REWARD FOR LONG PLAYING RECORD

The Burnden Park directors have had special medals struck to commemorate the 23-match unbeaten run that took the club from second bottom to second top of the table in one of the most remarkable transformations. When they went to Bury on October 13 they stood 23rd in the table with just seven points from their first nine fixtures. They didn't lose another league game until they came unstuck at Mansfield on March 12 - by which time they had confirmed themselves as a force in the Third Division promotion race.

Phil Neal had already had the distinction of seeing Wanderers set a club record 21-match unbeaten run in League and Sherpa Van Trophy games in 1989 - 20 matches up to Wembley and the first game of the following season. But League records are the ones that count, and half a season without having your colours lowered is an amazing achievement in anybody's book.

The 1990s saw five managers at the club - including a few months in 1995-96 when there was a "joint manager" experiment.

ON THE MANAGEMENT SIDE

The 1990s saw a number of changes of manager. Phil Neal bowed out in 1992, and according to the Evening News "his departure was undoubtedly prompted by the Wanderers' fans, who have clearly had enough after a six and a half year love-hate relationship, with protests at matches and letters to the paper reflecting their growing unrest towards the man who has taken them to Wembley, but never given them the greatest prize of all - promotion."

He was followed by Bruce Rioch, who in June, 1995, topped three seasons of wall-to-wall success by guiding the Wanderers to the Premiership - and 10 days later walked out of Burnden Park. It was thought at the time because he had been offered the post as manager at Arsenal, but he later claimed it was because of his father-in-law's failing health and the need of the family to move closer to him. If it hadn't been for that, he said in 1998, "I would still have been manager of Bolton Wanderers going into that 1995-96 season. I've said it before, and I'll say it again. Gordon Hargreaves and his board of directors were the best people I have ever worked for."

Colin Todd had been Rioch's No 2, but the club decided not to give him the top job automatically but brought in Roy McFarland in joint management arrangement. It was an experiment that faltered after six and a half months when McFarland was sacked, and Todd given the managership for himself. That lasted until 1999, when the dream management team of Sam Allardyce and Phil Brown came together for the Wanderers. It was a move that created further stability for the club, and was to see them eventually consolidate Bolton in the Premiership.

Bruce Rioch holds up a Wanderers' scarf outside Burnden Park in 1992.

Tea for two and two for the team - Roy McFarland and Colin Todd, the new management partnership at Wanderers kicked off their new joint career with a cup of tea in 1995.

PLAY IT AGAIN, SAM

Sam Allardyce, the towering figure at the heart of Wanderers' rise to the big time two decades ago, is the man Bolton chiefs have turned to in their bid to lead the club back to the top flight. Big Sam - the no-nonsense centre-half whose powerful performances made him a Burnden Park favourite in the late Seventies - became Wanderers' 17th post-war manager, to succeed Colin Todd who resigned three weeks ago.

Allardyce, who impressed in a two-year spell as manager of Blackpool between 1994 and 1996, resigned his job as manager of Second Division pacemakers Notts County last week. He was immediately installed as favourite to land the Bolton job, an appointment which was sealed over the weekend when his application arrived at the Reebok and he met new Bolton chairman Phil Gartside.

Phil Brown, who led Wanderers to four wins in his five games in charge as caretaker manager, has been promoted from chief coach to assistant manager, an appointment which brings together again the management team that took Blackpool to the Second Division play-offs of 1996. It is the second time that Allardyce has returned to Bolton, having had a second spell as a player in the mid-90s under Charlie Wright and Phil Neal.

He said: "I am thrilled to be back. This is where I began my playing career and I'm delighted to be able to put something back at this critical time for the club." And over the years, Sam has certainly put plenty back . . .

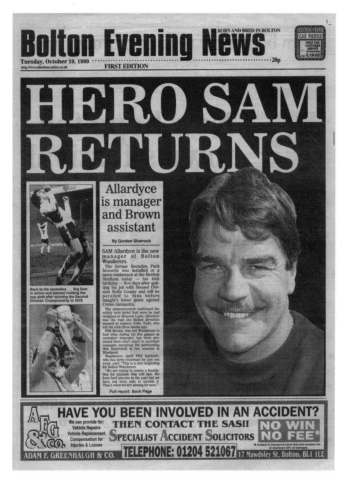

New boss Sam Allardyce and his assistant Phil Brown joined Wanderers' mascot Lofty the Lion on their appointment in 1999. Both Sam and Phil had played for the Wanderers previously, and Phil had been coach under Colin Todd since 1996.

IN THE CHAIR

Burnden Park was in mourning in December, 1990, when chairman Sam Jones suddenly died. He had, said the Evening News, become a respected, stabilizing figure at a time the Wanderers needed it most. Fellow director Graham Ball said: "With Sam's friendship came a wealth of football experience gathered over many years, quietly available in advice to colleagues or manager, whenever requested."

Into the chair stepped Gordon Hargreaves who led the club through nine of the most exciting years in its history, spearheading with fellow director Graham Ball the relocation from Burnden Park to the Reebok Stadium, and the Stock Market flotation in April, 1997. He stepped down in 1999, three weeks after the departure of manager Colin Todd, making way for Phil Gartside who then signed Sam Allardyce as manager, convinced him to sign a 10-year contract, and at the same time built a working relationship between the two of them which must be the envy of many other clubs.

In 2001, with the Wanderers in the First Division, an obviously frustrated Mr Gartside questioned whether the town of Bolton really wanted a successful football team. "The board are extremely grateful for the support we receive from the core support, which seems to have risen to an average of around 14,000. I wonder what we have to do to raise that number to the levels that other local clubs seem to attract." Fortunately, in 2004, that problem seems to be well in the past . . .

Gordon Hargreaves.

Phil Gartside.

24 SEPTEMBER 1991
BOLTON SUPER LEAGUE TARGET

Bolton Wanderers today pledged to make the Super League their No. 1 target. Burnden Park chiefs made their ambitions crystal clear within hours of the historic agreement in London.

One of the 12 original members of the Football League, Wanderers will play an influential part in determining how the remaining clubs will be organised when the premier clubs break away next season. But they refuse to lose sight of their burning ambition and the retention of the three-up, three-down system was music to their ears yesterday.

"The door is open to the premier league, and that is vital as far as we are concerned," said chief executive Des McBain after the meeting. "The carrot is still there with three-up and three-down. It is up to us now to be aiming for the higher rewards."

Wanderers' biggest fear during the protracted 'super league' wrangle was the threat of tight restrictions on promotion to the top flight. Now manager Phil Neal says: "All we wanted was a fair crack at getting there."

10 OCTOBER 1992
CHEAP DEAL FOR FANS

Bolton Wanderers have announced a new voucher scheme offering reduced price admission for League matches. The scheme is being introduced in response to appeals from supporters, in letters to the club, and the Evening News, claiming the £1.50 price increase imposed in the summer has been too much to bear. Burnden chairman Gordon Hargreaves said: "We have listened to what the genuine fans have had to say, and we are attempting to do something positive to help them.

Supporters who use the vouchers will save 50p per match. As a result, best seats will cost £8.50 and terrace admission will be £6.50. The scheme works simply. Supporters can buy a sheet of ten £1 vouchers for £5, which will be redeemable off the admission price at any home game. Fans using the vouchers must buy tickets in advance from the ticket office, but no later than two hours before kick-off on match days. Season ticket holders will not miss out. If they renew next season they will save an extra £5 in addition to the usual discounts on offer.

One of the greatest-ever victories for the Wanderers came in January, 1993, when they went to Liverpool in the third round of the F.A. Cup, and humbled the opposition 2-0 in front of the Anfield faithful - and on country-wide television and radio. It was a replay after a 2-2 draw at Burnden 10 days earlier, but this time there was no doubt who would come out on top."The defeat of Liverpool was not so much a shock, but an earthquake immeasurable on the Richter scale," was the description given by BBC Radio Five commentator John Champion. Even supercool Des Lynham was getting a little excited on BBC TV's Sportsnight: "That David Lee was a revelation," he said.

14 JANUARY 1993
ANFIELD SALUTES BOLTON HEROES!

Liverpool 0 Bolton 2

The date will be forever red in the Bolton Wanderers' calendar. It will go down in history as the night 8,500 Bolton fans, a magnanimous beaten manager, and the famous Kop, saluted each and every one of Bruce Rioch's heroes.

Bolton Wanderers, the club that in days long gone revelled in F.A. Cup glory, became true giant-killers for the first time last night. Every player outstanding in his own right, they outplayed the proud holders. Wanderers were in charge from start to finish, even before John McGinlay headed them in front so spectacularly in the third minute. When Andy Walker headed the second 11 minutes from time it merely confirmed their overwhelming dominance of an amazing cup tie.

They controlled the game, played the better football and quite ruthlessly embarrassed the most successful club side in modern times. Take nothing away from the Wanderers. Last night they damaged the bedrock of Merseyside football.

Those who saw it witnessed a famous victory, the upset of the season. What people might now start to acknowledge is that Wanderers can be a force in the game. But that is for the days to come.

The night that mattered saw Lee, in breathtaking menacing mood, set up one of the most comprehensive demolition jobs ever effected on the Liverpool side. He left Mike Marsh

for dead before delivering the perfect early cross for McGinlay to head home to give Wanderers a dream start. Lee was causing mayhem, bamboozling the Liverpool defence with a remarkable display. Wanderers never looked like surrendering what they had worked so hard to achieve. There were even signs that the Wanderers, who knocked the ball around confidently throughout were actually taking the Mickey with some sweet, sweeping, even arrogant passing play!

Teams -

Bolton: Branagan, Brown, Burke, Lee, Seagraves, Winstanley, Green, Kelly, Walker, McGinlay, Patterson. Subs: Reeves, Stubbs

Liverpool: Hooper, Marsh, Joes, Stewart, Pichnik, Bjornebye, Walters, Redknapp, Rosenthal, Barnes, Thomas. Subs: Hutchinson for Thomas 53 mins., Fowler

John McGinlay, David Lee and Andy Walker celebrate after the historic victory against Liverpool.

Promotion to the second tier finally came in 1993 with a victory over Preston in front of 19,000 cheering Bolton fans at Burnden Park. Wanderers were back in the big-time, and the town party that night was so large that Bradshawgate had to be shut to traffic. Who was the player who got that so-important goal? None other than John McGinlay, of course.

9 MAY 1993

MAC'S MAGIC MOMENT

Bolton 1 Preston 0

John McGinlay's name will go down in Burnden Park folklore as "The man with no nerve". The ice-cool Scot shut himself off from the tension and pressure to shoot Wanderers into promotion orbit. An entire season's work depended on the penalty 16 minutes from the end of the 46th and final League game - but there was no stopping McGinlay. "David Lee had the ball, then it went to Tony Kelly, but I was looking for it myself," he recalled of the fateful moment. "I just knew where I was putting it and thankfully it was the right decision. It was the most important goal I've ever scored, without any doubt."

It was a goal, THE goal, that meant Wanderers are back in the mainstream of English football after a decade in the backwaters. It was a goal that brought a just reward for a team that rattled off five straight wins, under the hottest pressure imaginable, to finish just three points behind the one-time runaway leaders.

It was a goal that confirmed that when the Burnden directors sought a new manager 11 months ago, they struck gold in the shape of Bruce Rioch. On the day, it was a goal that lifted the weight of nail-biting tension that had even the most optimistic - fans and players alike - wondering whether their moment of glory was going to be snatched away in one final twist to a dramatic promotion race. And they were against a team, Preston, fighting for their Second Division lives, who had to win to retain any hope of staying up.

This was an afternoon when quality and class came second to spirit and desire. Fortunately, Rioch's team has the lot - 48 points out of a possible 57 is proof of that. They have had an incredible season. Sixty games played, including an F.A. Cup run, capped by the biggest prize of all. It is a success they have yearned for since they bounced back from their first-ever season in Division Four in 1988.

In the end it hinged on one man keeping his nerve. McGinlay, who threw his treasured promotion-winning boots into the crowd at the end, couldn't care less about the manner of the victory. "This was a day," he said, "when the result mattered more than the performance."

Teams -
Bolton: Branagan, Brown, Burke, Lee, Seagraves, Stubbs, Kelly, McAteer, Darby, McGinlay, Patterson.
Subs: Green (for Darby 61 mins), Winstanley.

Preston: Farnworth, Callaghan, Lucas, Whalley, Kidd, Greenall, Fowler, Alnsworth, Norbury, Burton, Lennard.
Subs: Watson (for Fowler h.t.), Holland.

Agony for the Preston goalkeeper Simon Farnworth, but ecstasy for Bolton's John McGinlay as his penalty hits the back of the net.

The celebrations continued
when the team arrived at the
Town Hall a few days later for a
Civic Reception.

In the first of two appearances at Wembley within a couple of months, the Wanderers faced Liverpool in the final of the Coca-Cola Cup in April, 1995, and Liverpool got their own back for that famous Bolton win in the F.A. Cup tie in 1993. This time, Liverpool were giving little away, but the match enhanced the reputation of a Bolton team that deserved the rousing send-off they received from both sets of supporters at the end.

3 APRIL 1995

MAC KNIFES RICH BRAVES

Bolton 1 Liverpool 2

The pride of Bolton bowed to the Prince of Anfield in one of the finest ever Coco-Cola Cup finals. Steve McManaman showed the class that puts England's international future in exciting hands, but he broke Wanderers' hearts with wonder goals in the 37th and 67th minutes.

Yet, in a final that lived up to its top-quality billing, Wanderers made the Premiership side fight all the way for their sixth success in the competition. Alan Thompson's 69th minute goal will stand as one of the most spectacular at the famous old stadium.

The atmosphere was electric and the temperature on the pitch was topping 70 degrees. However, as expected of a team with nine wins over top flight opposition in the last three seasons, Wanderers were not in the least overawed or outplayed. Wanderers rose to the big occasion. Liverpool drew first blood, though, in the 37th minute.

John Barnes, playing the holding mid-field role he has grown into this season, fed McManaman who set off on a run that took him past Stubbs. With Bolton defenders tracking back, the Anfield youngster cleverly cut inside Green and drilled a low shot past the helpless Branagan. It was a stunning blow for Wanderers. The response was a concerted effort to snatch an early equaliser, but the Liverpool defence was having none of it.

In the second half there were touches of class about Liverpool's passing game and ability to create space, but both sides were contributing to an excellent final, which could have been all square if either Paatelainan or Thompson had got a head to a Lee cross.

Bruce Rioch leads his team out for the 1995 Coca-Cola Final at Wembley.

Branagan showed reflexes Peter Shilton would have been proud of on 65 minutes when he gathered a deflected header off Seagraves from Bjornebye's wicked cross. But the Ireland international was powerless to prevent McManaman doubling Liverpool's lead two minutes later. There was something ominous as the England star jockeyed Green on the left wing and, when the full-back committed himself to the tackle, McManaman took his chance brilliantly, striding inside and curling a right-footer out of Branagan's diving reach. Before the re-start, Bergsson replaced Green, and in almost fairytale fashion was responsible for laying on the goal that put Wanderers back in it almost immediately. The Icelander, making his Bolton debut, lobbed in a cross which Ruddock headed straight back at him. The sub returned the compliment with a header Paatelainan nudged towards Thompson who produced outstanding skills to score a goal to grace the occasion.

With his back to goal Thompson, who was in tears afterwards, controlled the ball on his chest, pivoted and blasted a spectacular left-footer into the top right hand corner of James' goal. The Bolton fans almost lifted the Wembley roof off as they sensed their never-say-die heroes might force extra time.

As the minutes ticked away the Liverpool fans sensed victory and struck up with the awe-inspiring "You'll Never Walk Alone". But still Wanderers searched for the equaliser, McGinlay and Paatelainan trying to find space in the middle against the three-man Liverpool centre back line.

In the dying seconds, Richard Sneekes, Stubbs and Thompson tried an innovative free kick followed by a long range Stubbs' effort. That turned out to be Wanderers' final flourish at the end of a game befitting the Wembley occasion, and justifying their right to play on football's greatest stage.

Teams -

Bolton: Branagan, Green, Phillips, McAteer, Seagraves, Stubbs, Lee, Sneekes, Paatelainan, McGinley, Thomspon.
Subs - Patterson, Bergsson, Davison

Liverpool: James, Jones, Babb, Scales, Ruddock, Bjornbye, McManaman, Redknapp, Barnes, Rush, Fowler.
Subs - Walters, Thomas, Chamberlain

High Fives: Creator Gudni Berggsson congratulates Alan Thompson on his spectacular goal.

Consolation for Gudni Bergsson (left) and Jimmy Phillips from manager Bruce Rioch.

Games don't come any hairier than the 1995 play-off at Wembley against Reading to determine who would spend the next season in the Premiership. The Wanderers looked down and out after Reading raced to a 2-0 lead, but in one of the greatest fight-backs ever seen at Wembley, including 'keeper Keith Branagan saving a penalty, they came out on top after extra time.

30 MAY 1995
WANDERERS' GREAT ESCAPE

Bolton 4 Reading 3

Wanderers made a nightmare start to their Premiership play-off dream day, giving away two goals in the opening 12 minutes. Bruce Rioch's men made a terrible opening when Alan Stubbs was penalised eight yards from goal for nudging a back pass to Keith Branagan.

Reading wasted the free kick, which Dariusz Wdowczyk fired straight into the back of Stuart Lovell. It was a short-lived reprieve, though, and Wanderers found themselves behind after just four minutes. Andy Bernal fed Lee Nogan who turned Stubbs, went past Scott Green and beat Branagan. It was a stunning early blow, but the response was swift, and Mixu Paatelainan felt he was fouled as he tried to get on the end of Green's deep cross.

Reading had their tails up, though, and in the 12th minute Green's foul on Royals' joint manager/boss Mick Gooding on the edge of the box led to a free kick which caught the Wanderers' defence napping. Simon Osbourn clipped the ball in and Adrian Williams got in front of a line of white shirts to knock a near post shot past Branagan.

With the sun breaking through the clouds, and sparked by their earlier successes, Reading looked sharper and able to create more space than Wanderers, whose sporadic attacks were less convincing. The Wanderers' fans were understandably subdued for spells, but worked hard to raise their team after Thompson, on a break on the left, landed a deep cross on top of the Reading net.

They were inspired in the 35th minute to see Branagan save Lovell's penalty, which could have effectively wrapped up the game. Referee Peter Foulkes pointed to the spot after McAteer tripped danger man Gilkes. Stubbs was booked for protesting, and the whole business seemed to be turning sour on Wanderers until Branagan threw himself to his right to punch away Lovell's penalty.

Wanderers started the second half with Fabian de Freitas replacing Neil McDonald in a re-shaped midfield. The Dutchman was in the action straight away, producing a cross from the right which Paatelainen met with a swinging right-footer which cannoned off a defender. Now with four natural attackers on the field, Rioch was obviously going for broke.

Wanderers continued to pile on the pressure, and in the 74th minute got the goal they fully deserved. McGinlay did well to find a space on the right and his deep cross was headed in at the back post by Coyle.

Branagan, who had kept Wanderers in the game with his first half penalty save, kept hopes alive again ten minutes from the end when he saved Lovell's point blank shot. With just four minutes to go, Bolton's magnificent army of support was rewarded when Thompson fed the ball forward for de Freitas to turn Wdowczyk and beat Hislop was a low left footer for a dramatic equaliser.

Mixu Paatelainen puts Wanderers ahead with a powerful header.

Bolton Evening News

> Tuesday, 30 May, 1995   > 26p

PREMIER MORNING SPECIAL

THE Wonderful Wanderers are in the FA Premiership, and the party is in full swing.
    Delirious players led the dancing around Wembley and the Carling conga throbbed right back to Burnden. This morning Bolton carried on celebrations that will not stop until the victorious team have been welcomed home tonight.
    Tens of thousands of fans will turn out to see the happy Wanderers take an open-topped bus ride from Burnden Park to the Town Hall, beginning at 6.30 pm.
    Their 4-3 victory over Reading at Wembley yesterday hit the jackpot for the Super Whites. They are where they belong, right back in the big time.
    We'll be dancing all summer long.

The Play-off Final story in full...Pages 2, 3, 4, 6, 16, 17, 28, 30, 31, 32.

Victory against all odds. . . a happy team celebrate.

In the opening minutes of extra time, Branagan made important saves to keep Reading at bay, but then Wanderers set about imposing their growing superiority. A minute from the end of the first extra period Wanderers produce the flowing football that has been the hallmark of their season to take the lead for the first time.

A slick inter-passing counter attack led to McAteer teeing up Coyle for a cross he hit to the back post where McGinlay headed the ball back inside for Paatelainan to head home. Then, with just two minutes to go, de Freitas scored the goal which completed one of the greatest come-backs in football history. Paatelainan broke into space on the right and crossed low and deliberately for de Freitas to hit his first shot against the post before composing himself to hit the rebound past the stunned Hislop.

It proved to be the cushion Wanderers needed, because in the dying seconds Quinn smashed Reading's third past Branagan to set up 30 seconds of a tense finale that saw Wanderers eventually joyous and triumphant.

Teams -

Bolton: Branagan, Green, Phillips, McAteer, Bergsson, Stubbs, McDonald, Coyle, Paateiainon, McGinley, Thompson. Subs- de Freitas, Dreyer, Shilton.

Reading: Hislop, Bernal, Osborn, Wdowczyk, Williams, McPherson, Gilkes, Gooding, Nogan, Lovell, Taylor. Subs - Quinn, Hopkins, Sheppard.

Sadly, life in the Premiership lasted only one season before in 1996 the Wanderers were again relegated.

6 MAY 1996
WE'LL BE BACK

That was the message spelled out loud and clear by Bolton Wanderers' fans who were down, but definitely not out, for the final Premier League game of the season at Highbury yesterday. But to any casual observer the Wanderers might just have won the championship as the loyal fans put their cares behind them and went into party mood when the final whistle blew.

Earlier they really had something to sing about as the Wanderers sparkled and went into an early lead. But then, like an action replay of so many games this season, Arsenal came back and ended up 2-1 winners. Many fans were in fancy dress, and others unfurled banners with the optimistic message "We'll be back", and "We'll meet again."

It was an all-too-brief, bitter-sweet, experience, but Wanderers have tasted the high life. Now, are they hungry enough to fight their way back to the Premiership table? They've been found wanting and, it must be said, they can have no complaints about losing their place among the elite of English football.

Nevertheless, they have had their appetites whetted, and it's hard to imagine anyone - players, management or fans - leaving Highbury without a backward glance and a deep-seated desire to make a quick return.

But as he sent his players away to lick their relegation wounds over the summer, Colin Todd rapped out a stern warning of the size of the task they face. Deeply disappointed at failing to consolidate after last season's promotion run, the Burnden boss cautioned: "They are in for a shock if they think that, just because they've been in the Premiership, they can just go out and waltz their way back.

"You've got to be hungry enough, make things happen, and batter down doors to get back up there. Next season is going

to be about attitude, the desire and the determination to make things happen for ourselves."

Teams -

Bolton: Branagan, McAnespie, Bergsson, Coleman, Stubbs, Small, McGinlay, Sellars, Curcic, Paatelainen, Andy Todd. Subs: Thompson for Curcic 69 mins., Blake for Coleman 87 mins., Green.

Arsenal: Seaman, Keown, Linighan, Marshall, Dixon, Merson, Platt, Parlour, Winterburn, Bergkamp, Wright. Subs: Hartson for Wright 58 mins., Shaw for Marshall 78 mins., Bartram.

On April 29, 1997, the Wanderers and Mosaic Investments merged to create Burnden Leisure plc, and the company was floated on the Stock Market. Under the terms of the merger, Wanderers' shareholders were to receive 1.135 new Mosaic shares for each ordinary share they held, and 11.350 for each special ordinary share.

30 APRIL 1997
WANDERERS' SHARE SPREE

Wanderers' soaraway success was heralded on the Stock Market today. Shares in Burnden Leisure kicked off at 69.5p. That was 18 pence up on the price Mosaic was listed at on March 6 when dealings in their shares was suspended.

They later settled at around 67.5 p, valuing the club at more than £60 million. Ordinary fans were among the first to buy themselves a slice of the action. City analysts suggest the debut price bodes well for the future of the new group, which will focus strongly on the fortunes of the Wanderers, but will also diversify and develop into broad-based sports, leisure and management group.

The good start reflects the incredible success the Wanderers have enjoyed this season, clinching a return to the Premiership at the first attempt, running away with the championship, and clinching a lucrative sponsorship deal with Reebok for their new £35 million stadium. It anticipates successful financial times ahead.

In the 1996-97 season, the Wanderers were in a class of their own. A 2-1 victory over QPR on April 7 ensured that they got a return ticket to the Premiership after only a year, finishing on top of the league 18 points ahead of their nearest rivals; but it was at the last ever game at Burnden, a win over Charlton on April 25, before the move to the new Reebok Stadium, when everyone wallowed in a night of nostalgia; "an essentially private affair, an occasion that belonged to Wanderers folk and their adopted sons - the old players who graced the hallowed turf and the current crop who have given today's fans a season to remember," wrote Gordon Sharrock.

25 APRIL　1997

WANDERERS' DREAM SHOW ON A NIGHT TO REMEMBER

Bolton 4 Charlton 1

Colin Todd looked back on last season's relegation today as he toasted his team's record-breaking title success. John McGinlay and Co. became the highest scoring team in Wanderers' history when they closed the door on 102 years of football at Burnden Park with their 4-1 victory over Charlton.

They are heading back to the Premiership as runaway Champions of the Nationwide League. John McGinlay, who wrote another chapter in the fairy tale that has seen him join the ranks of the Burnden legends in just five sensational seasons, put the gloss on one of the most memorable nights in the club's proud history with two vital late goals. Wanderers now go to Tranmere for the final fixture of the season, knowing they have given themselves a fighting chance of achieving the unique double of 100 points and 100 League goals.

Last night, Charlton didn't appear to have read the carefully-constructed script, though, and it wasn't looking so good when Mark Kinsella fired them into a 1-0 interval lead.

"The lads sat in the dressing room at half-time and we were all determined that it shouldn't end that way," McGinlay revealed. "We had to win our last game at Burnden Park. That determination helped us step up a gear in the second half, and we couldn't have stage-managed it better if we'd tried. This just has to be the best night of my life."

Wanderers players celebrate their elevation to the Premiership.

Champagne flows as Alan Thompson lifts the First Division trophy.

At the interval, Thompson changed his boots and the course of the game. The Geordie Boy sported a red pair supplied by his sponsors specially for the occasion in the first half before switching to more familiar footwear, and a minute into the second half he was turning away in celebration after his black-booted, right-foot, shot took a deflection past Andy Petterson. Taggart, though, reckons he will stick to his red pair after the sweetest of touches gave him his fourth goal of the season.

However, McGinlay stole the show with his two late strikes that eclipsed the 1933-34 team's 96 goals and set the new mark two short of a century.

Emotions ran high from start to finish. Roy Hartle, one of the so-called "hard men" of the 1958 F.A. Cup winning side unashamedly wept as he joined the many old favourites on a pre-match parade on the pitch where he spent 18 successful seasons. And Alan Thompson, young star of Colin Todd's record-breaking Championship side, choked back tears as the final seconds of the game ticked away.

Sentiment reigned at the end, too, when Todd sent three players up to receive the Championship trophy - club captain McGinlay, Gudni Bergsson, and Gerry Taggart, who has also worn the skipper's armband with distinction.

A satellite TV audience witnessed the historic scenes and Charlton did their best to spoil the party. But this was essentially a private affair, an occasion that belonged to Wanderers folk and their adopted sons - the old players who have graced the turf, and the current crop who have given today's fans a season to remember. Nothing was going to stop them bowing out in a blaze of glory.

It is a far cry from a year ago when they finished bottom of the Premier League, but Colin Todd put the transformation into perspective when he said: "You can't always go forward in life. Sometimes you've got to go backwards to go forward." Todd believes he is taking the Wanderers back to the top flight in far better shape than when they were promoted via the play-offs in 1995.

Teams -

Bolton: Branagan, Bergsson, Fairclough, Taggart, Phillips, Johansen, Frandsen, Thompson, Sellars, Blake, McGinley. Subs: McAnespie (for Bergsson 84 mins), Paatelainen (for Blake 86 mins), Sheridan (for Johansen 79 mins).

Charlton: Petterson, Robinson, Rufus, Balmer, Barness, Kinsella, Mortimer, O'Connell, Allen, Bright, Lisble. Subs: Chapple, Leaburn (for Lisble 66 mins), Nicholls (for Mortimer 66 mins).

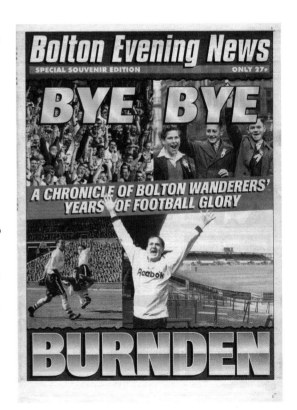

A week later, the Wanderers went to Tranmere in the hope of making more history, with 100 points and 100 goals. Unfortunately, it was not to be . . .

5 MAY 1997

THE TON-UP WANDERERS HAVE A PREMIER AIM

Tranmere 2 Bolton 2

Nothing could stop the corks popping to celebrate the most incredible season in the history of Bolton Wanderers. Fate's fickle finger - Lee Jones' boot to be precise - put a cruel twist in the tale and prevented Colin Todd's champions clinching the double they so richly deserved.

But the Wanderers' boss hoisted his paper cup high and confirmed its bubbly contents. "Of course it's champagne," he said. "We've been drinking it for weeks."

Todd was understandably miffed that a dramatic injury-time equaliser had robbed him of the distinction of managing the first team in English league history to reach 100 goals and 100 points in the same season. Yet nothing could dent the pride of the man who has masterminded one of the great sporting come-backs.

"Teams who get relegated don't find it easy to bounce back," he suggested as he put the last 12 months into perspective. They certainly don't finish bottom of the Premiership one season and recover so well that they win the title by 18 clear points the next - a record for the division, and an achievement Todd believes the fans and the town should take immense pride in.

"The fact that we didn't manage to get the 100 points we wanted was never going to spoil the party," said Todd, although with the seconds ticking away to the end of the game this magnificent free-scoring team appeared to have secured their place in history. John McGinlay (who else?) had set the ball rolling with the 27th minute goal that was to earn him the Golden Boot as the Division's top scorer. Rovers came back strongly and were good value for John Aldridge's equaliser from the penalty spot after Gudni

Bergsson's under-struck header left Keith Branagan little option but to bring down the Tranmere boss.

Wanderers now had to complete a century of goals if they were going to sign off with the win that would give them 100 points, and the magic moment came when Jamie Pollock appeared to pop up from nowhere to smash a Michael Johansen corner into the roof of the net and spark the wildest scenes of jubilation.

Todd even felt comfortable enough to send on Gavin Ward for the last couple of minutes to qualify for a Championship medal. But the unlucky keeper's first and only touch was to collect the ball from the back of the net after Kenny Irons' well-directed pass gave Jones all the space he needed to hammer home the equaliser. Branagan at his best couldn't have saved it and the goal was no reflection on Ward; it was just one of those sporting quirks.

So the Wanderers finished the season with 100 goals and 98 points - a magnificent achievement for a magnificent team and manager.

Teams -
Bolton: Branagan, Bergsson, Fairclough, Taggart, Phillips, Pollock, Frandsen, Thompson, Sellars, Blake, McGinley.
Subs: Ward for Branagan 88mins, Johansen for Blake 73 mins., Sheridan for Fairclough 35 mins.

Tranmere: Nixon, McGreal, Thorn, Rogers, Irons, O'Brien, Mahon, Jones, Aldridge, Branch.
Subs: Morrissey for Mahon 75 mins., McIntyre, Challinor.

The end of an era at Burnden Park after 102 years, as the cover of the last League programme shows.

It was the end of an era for the Wanderers, the closing of Burnden Park, although the last match which took place there before demolition was in July, 1997, a schoolboy game between Deane School and St Joseph's Horwich. The move to the Reebok was now a reality. It had taken more than seven years for Wanderers' state-of-the-art super stadium to get off the drawing board to fruition. It created vast interest in the town as the massive structure was put together, and special "viewing platforms" were erected so that members of the public could watch the progress.

1 SEPTEMBER 1997
SEVEN YEARS FOR DREAM TO BECOME A REALITY

Burnden Park's days first appeared numbered back in early 1990 when the club was linked with a possible move to a multi-million pound stadium on the Westhoughton/Hindley border, which was being planned for the Manchester Olympic bid. However, 18 months later the Wanderers' hierarchy were adamant the club would be at Burnden for the foreseeable future, and until at least until after the 1995 centenary.

Yet within a few months Bolton Council had revealed plans for a big money sports complex with Wanderers apparently key players in the scheme. In February, 1994, an artist's impression was released which showed a 21st century style stadium, planned for the Red Moss site at Horwich. Development also including possible leisure complexes, a multi-screen cinema, department stores and restaurants, with a total capital investment of around £40 million.

No formal decision to get involved had been confirmed by Wanderers, but they had hinted a move was inevitable with the announcement that it would cost in the region of £18 million to redevelop Burnden to an acceptable standard. One of the first obstacles was removed when Horwich Council voted in favour of the Red Moss plan.

In June, 1995, the Government cleared the way for the stadium, and Bolton Council gave their reserved approval before finally rubber-stamping the plans the following month. The first tangible signs of work saw Bolton's

During the last years of Burnden, work was progressing at Middlebrook with the building of the new stadium, seen in the background at the opening of the Visitors' Centre.

favourite son, Nat Lofthouse cut the first sod in November, 1995. Two months later the bulldozers were on site and work began on laying the playing surface.

Wanderers appointed Paul Fletcher (yes, the same man all the trouble was about when as a Wanderers' player he was sold in the early 1970s) as chief executive of the stadium complex. They also announced that they would sell off the name of the stadium to the highest bidder. October, 1996, saw the first steelwork erected, with the visitors' centre opened on site just before Christmas.

When Prime Minister John Major arrived in April, Wanderers announced that their major sponsor Reebok had increased their association with the club and the ground would be known as the Reebok Stadium.

Promotion back to the Premiership gave the Wanderers a tremendous double - back in the big-time and in a super new home.

Chief Executive Paul Fletcher as work progressed.

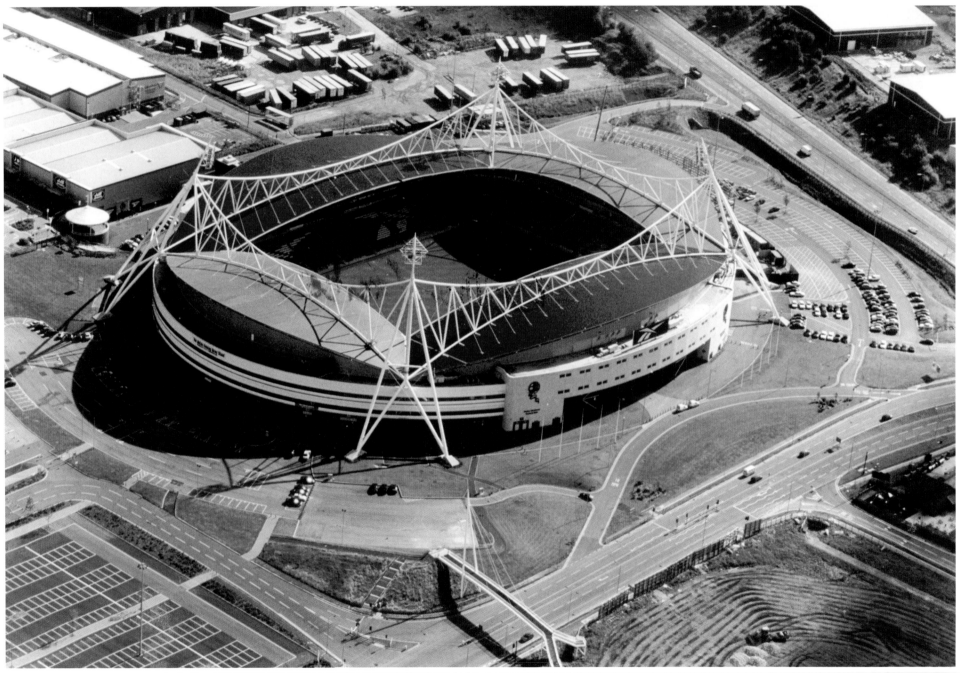

The impressive completed stadium from the air.

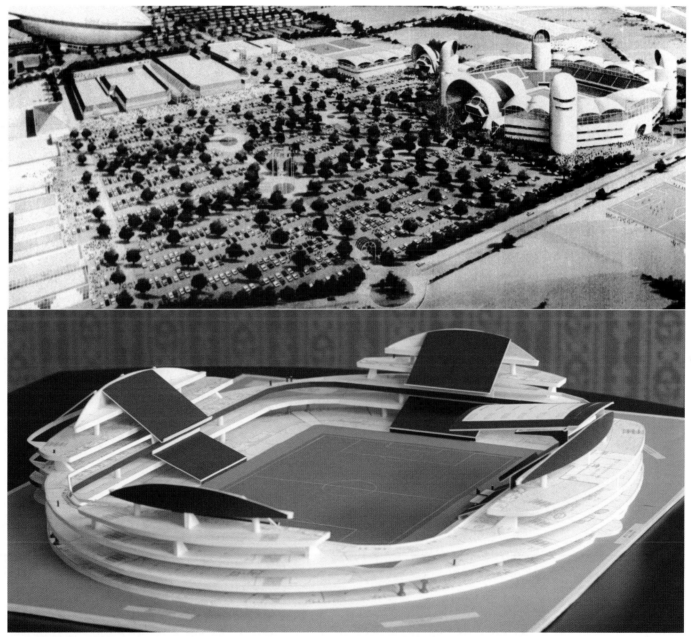

The present style of the Reebok Stadium was not the only one considered by the Board. Others included these two.

A wonderful £35 million new stadium the envy of many other Premiership clubs, and a place back in the Premiership . . . the Wanderers were riding high as they faced Everton in the first home match of the 1997-98 season.

2 SEPTEMBER 1997
SUPER STADIUM, SHAME ABOUT THE MATCH

Wanderers 0 Everton 0

Years in the planning, months in the building, an hour and a half of football was never going to do justice to the work that went into the magnificent Reebok Stadium. In the event, the game that heralded the dawn of a new era was a disappointing anti-climax.

It had its moments of controversy, and Wanderers can argue that they had the best chances to win it. But they were relieved to get the occasion out of the way with a point in the bag. Had they emerged unscathed they would have considered it a satisfactory night's work, but sadly the game had its darker side with record-signing Robbie Elliott stretchered off on the hour with a broken leg after an innocuous collision with Tony Thomas.

After starting the season with three away games, Wanderers had no significant advantage over their visitors. Strangers in their own home, they survived a torrid first quarter that saw them freeze like a mesmerised rabbit caught in a blaze of headlights.

"I'm just pleased we've got the first 90 minutes at the Reebok out of the way," manager Colin Todd said. "The lads will get a lot of confidence from taking a point under the circumstances. Nevertheless, we've got to stick the chances away when they come along. I couldn't believe the number of times they wasted possession."

Better teams than Everton would probably have punished the Wanderers more severely in that difficult early stage, but the tide turned approaching the half-hour when Nathan Blake was denied by his Welsh international teammate Neville Southall after Per Frandsen put him goal-side of Slaven Bilic.

The goal that wasn't . . .the ball was clearly over the line from Gerry Taggart's header, but the referee decided it wasn't a goal.

With Sellars missing a near-open goal just before half-time after Blake had caused chaos in the Everton defence, Wanderers edged it on chances alone. But the travesty of the night was when referee Steve Lodge and his linesman waved "play on" after a Taggart's header appeared to cross the line before Terry Phelan bundled the ball away.

"I thought from where I was standing that it had gone over," the big Ulsterman claimed, not knowing at that point that TV evidence supported his stance. Despite the disappointment of being robbed of the honour of scoring the historic first goal at the showpiece stadium, Taggart emerged with his reputation enhanced.

He won his personal battle with Duncan Ferguson, and inspired a defensive performance that, for all their possession, restricted Everton to just a couple of scoring chances. Todd might have been concerned that the accuracy and speed of his team's passing fell some way below par, but he saluted his defenders and Taggart in particular, suggesting he had emerged with flying colours from his head to head with Big Dunc.

But Taggart modestly refused to take the credit. "We had to play well as a team," he insisted. "It wasn't about me as centre-half, it was about the whole team playing well, and defensively we did. Gudni did his job against Barmby, and as far as the defence was concerned, everything went to plan."

Teams -
Bolton: Branagan, Phillips, Bergsson, Taggart, Elliott, Pollock, Frandsen, Thompson, Sellars, Beardsley, Blake.
Subs: McAnespie for Elliott 60 mins., Johansen for Frandsen 79 mins., McGinlay for Beardsley 81 mins., Andy Todd, Ward.

Everton: Southall, Thomas, Watson, Bilic, Pheian, Stuart, Speed, Williamson, Oster, Barmby, Ferguson.
Subs: Short for Watson at h.t., Hinchcliffe for Thomas 67 mins., Branch for Barmby 87 mins., Farrelly, Gerard.

The Wanderers had gained promotion in 1997, walking away with the First Division, but it was a different story the next season among the big boys, and they were relegated yet again. It was a cliff-hanger end to the season, and all hung on the results of the last match. Bolton played Chelsea and lost 2-0, and combined with Everton's 1-1 draw with Coventry, they were sent down on goal difference. Had the referee given Bolton their rightful goal against Everton in the first home game of the season (the first match at the Reebok) they would have survived. Ironically, as it was, Everton, who got a point out of that first match instead of three going to the Wanderers, were the team to stay up.

11 MAY 1998

WANDERERS GO DOWN FIGHTING

Chelsea 2 Bolton 0

They fought so desperately and bravely to pull off the Great Escape, but in the end it turned out to be a Bridge Too Far for the Wanderers. They took it to the last minute of the last game of the season before finally accepting their relegation fate.

An entire nation, apart from the blue half of Merseyside, wanted it to be so different, but the gallant fight for Premiership survival came to an end at 5.50 yesterday evening when referee Alan Wilkie blew his whistle at Stamford Bridge, and almost simultaneously Paul Alcock sounded his at Goodison Park.

It was high drama to the bitter end. They were not to know it at the time, but with 17 minutes to go, Wanderers were actually right on course. At that point Everton were leading Coventry but were destined to finish 1-1, which meant all Colin Todd's bravehearts needed was a point.

Even after Chelsea player-manager Gianluca Vialli gave his side the lead, it was only going to take one lucky strike to turn the nightmare into a dream - and didn't the Chelsea fans know it. In one of the most bizarre experiences ever witnessed at a Premiership game, they were on their feet

actually willing Wanderers to score - knowing an equalizer would send Everton down.

Almost predictably one last, desperate push left the back door open and young Jody Morris stole in. All that was left was to pray that news would come through from Merseyside that Coventry had snatched a last-gap winner. It was not to be. As the news sank in, grown men wept, torturing themselves at the thought of what might have been. Understandably, the disallowed goal against Everton on the opening night at the Reebok Stadium eight months ago figured prominently.

Relegation is never an easy pill to swallow, but on goal difference, and under these circumstances. . !

It was as though fate had decreed that the story of the season would be told in the final 90 minutes. Wanderers are where they are because they failed to take their chances

and were punished mercilessly when Chelsea took theirs. No recriminations, just the facts which Wanderers must accept in the way Barnsley and Crystal Palace already have.

It might seem tough getting into the Premiership, but it's even tougher to stay there.

Teams -

Bolton: Branagan, Fish, Bergsson, Taggart, Cox, Frandsen, Sheridan, Thompson, Phillips, Blake, Taylor.
Subs: Giallanza for Taylor 66 mins, Johanson for Bergsson 70 minutes, Salako for Sheridan 73 minutes, Todd, Jaaskelainen.

Chelsea: De Goey, Clarke, Laboeuf, Charvet, Granville, Petrescu, Wise, Newton, Morris, Hughes, Flo.
Subs: Poyet for Petrescu (HT), De Mateo got wise (HT), Vialli for Flo (HT)Lambourde, Hitchcock.

A hopeful crowd cheered their team on when Bolton played a cliff-hanger game against Chelsea in 1998, a game that saw Bolton relegated.

In 1999, though, the Wanderers got to the play-off finals against Watford at Wembley. Bolton was full of hope for a speedy return to the top flight, but the team lost and had to spend more time in the First Division.

1 JUNE 1999
COST OF FAILURE

Bolton 0 Watford 2

Bolton Wanderers were today counting the enormous cost of failing to find their way back into the promised land of the Premiership. Defeat by Watford in the Play-off Final at Wembley cost the club millions in guaranteed income, including TV and sponsorship payouts, plus a fortune in gate receipts. It will also increase speculation concerning the futures of the club's star names, with Per Franden and Mark Fish, neither relishing another season in Division One, having already been touted for summer transfers.

Even Colin Todd's tenure as manager was on the agenda as the tabloid writers stabbed in the dark, trying to second guess the mood of the powers that be at the Reebok stadium.

That was one of the main topics of conversation as supporters trudged away from Wembley, that and another exodus on the scale of that witnessed after the disappointments of 1996 and last year, when relegation from the Premiership led to the departures of Alan Stubbs, Sasa Curcic, Alan Thompson and Nathan Blake - all players who had their heads turned by the big money and the glory on offer in the top flight.

But Todd, bitterly disappointed at the result, refused to discuss the possible repercussions of his failure to take Wanderers back into the Premier League.

Teams -
Bolton: Banks, Cox, Todd, Fish, Elliott, Johansen, Jensen, Frandsen, Gardner, Taylor, Gudjohnson.
Subs: Sellars (for Johansen 67 mins), Hansen (for Gardner 88 mins), Bergsson.

Watford: Chamberlain, Bazeley, Palmer, Page, Robinson, Hyde, Johnson, Kennedy, Wright, Ngonge, Mooney.
Subs: Smart (for Ngonge 75 mins), Hazen (for Wright 87 mins), Day.

Gudjohnsen beats Watford goalkeeper Alec Chamberlain only to watch his first half effort go narrowly wide.

A dejected Claus Jensen hangs his head in disappointment at full-time.

Mark Came, Julian Darby and David Reeves celebrate Bolton's Lancs Cup win in 1990.

Thousands of fans queuing from Burnden Park along Manchester Road to town, all wanting tickets for the Bolton v Manchester United game at Burnden in January, 1991.

Alf Anderson, the Wanderers' winger of the Thirties, took centre stage at Burnden when in December, 1991, the recently-formed Wanderers' Association held their first Christmas get-together. The event brought together Bolton stars from every decade back to the 1936-39 days when Alf Anderson was left winger in the forward line that featured legendary players Jack Milsom and Ray Westwood. Alf was pictured flanked by familiar faces from more recent First Division days, Frank Worthington and Peter Nicholson, with a host of other famous ex-Wanderers.

If there was one man the fans really took to their hearts in the 1990s it was John McGinlay, seen here after scoring yet another of his fabulous goals (celebrating with Bryan Small and David Lee). He was signed from Millwall for £100,000 by Bruce Rioch in September, 1992, and became a goal-scoring machine hero in the five years before he left to join Bradford City, in 1997, for £625,000. In the 1996-97 season he finished top of the First Division scoring charts with 24 goals in a 30-goal league and Cup haul to help fire Wanderers into the Premiership. When he returned for a testimonial in 2,000, more than £20 million worth of Wanderers' "exports" also came back to salute him, including Owen Coyle, Tony Kelly, Andy Walker, Alan Stubbs, Keith Branagan, Jason McAteer, and Alan Thompson.

Wanderers are planning to screen their fourth round F.A. Cup tie at Wolves, reported the paper in January, 1993. Thousands of regular fans were certain to miss out on the real thing at Molineux following Wolves' refusal to increase Wanderers 2,400 ticket allocation. The all-ticket match was to be played before a reduced capacity of 19,000 because of building work at the First Division ground, but the Wanderers decided to hire a giant screen for Burnden so the fans would not miss out.

Prize guys! Reserve team manager Steve Carroll (centre right) receives the Pontins Trophy from League President Ernest Barron with squad members and Pontins officials looking on in June, 1995. The Reserves had clinched the championship for the first time in 40 years.

The Wanderers' Lofty the Lion has become one of the country's most recognised and cherished mascots in football over the last decade or so. He is, according to the Evening News, the pride of Bolton, and wherever he goes is the mane (!) attraction, even doing an Elvis impression to entertain the crowds.

In November, 1993, the Wanderers played the small club of Gretna in the F.A. Cup - and came within 11 minutes of one of the of one of the most embarrassing results in their history. Gretna were winning 2-1, and it was only a couple of late goals by Owen Coyle, in the 79th and 84th minutes, that got Bolton off the hook. His goals, wrote Gordon Sharrock, "banished the vultures who were ready to pick over the corpse of the four-time Wembley winners - beaten on their own ground by a team of no-hopers." So Bolton lived to fight another day. The pictures show Owen Coyle, all smiles after having hit the Wanderers' winner, and a letter which was sent to the Evening News from the Gretna club.

Thank you Bolton for a great day

● SIR: Through the courtesy of your newspaper may Gretna Football Club please be allowed space to thank most sincerely, Bolton Wanderers Football Club and supporters for the warmth of welcome, hospitality and standing ovation received at the end of last Saturday's Cup tie at your splendid Burnden Park.

GOOD LUCK

● It was a great pleasure for us to be taking part in a game with such a famous club as Bolton and we all really appreciated the way we were looked after by everyone concerned at the club, in particular, Nat Lofthouse and Des McBain.
● What lovely people you all are and how welcome you made us feel from the start to finish of the game. It was truely a day to remember for us from Gretna.
● At the end of the match our team was given a great standing ovation by your excellent supporters. It was a sporting gesture which brought a tear to many a Gretna eye. This will long be rememberd by us as a very special occasion in our history.
● In conclusion, may Bolton Wanderers now go on to win the FA Cup. All at Gretna will be rooting for you from now on — good luck friends, perhaps we will meet again. Who knows?
● Thank you from us all at Gretna. – ROBIN LOVE, on behalf of players, supporters and directors, Gretna Football Club.

The team wave to the fans at their homecoming after winning promotion in 1997.

The Wanderers 1997-98 line up. Back row, from left: Per Frandsen, Scott Taylor, Jimmy Phillips, Chris Fairclough, Greg Strong, Martin Doherty, Nathan Blake, Hasney Aljofree, Stuart Whitehead, Nick Spooner, John Sheridan, Andy Todd, Simon Coleman. Middle row: Ewan Simpson (physio), Colin Dyson (kit man), Bryan Small, Neil Cox, Gerry Taggart, Jamie Pollock, Gavin Ward, Matt Glennon, Keith Branagan, Robbie Elliott, Lee Potter, Scott Sellars, Michael Johansen, Dean Crombie (Youth coach), Steve Carroll (Reserve manager). Front row: Alan Thompson, Arnar Gunnlaugsson, Colin Todd (manager), Gudni Bergsson, Phil Brown (chief coach), John McGinlay, Steve McAnespie.

View of Bolton Town Centre at night taken from the top of Winchester Way, Top o' th' Brow, showing street lighting, in December 2003. The Town Hall and Parish Church can be seen in the centre.

2000s

DATE	WORLD EVENTS	BOLTON EVENTS
2000	Britain's Steve Redgrave wins his fifth gold medal at the Sydney Olympics.	
2001	Four passenger aircraft are hijacked and crashed into the World Trade Center in New York, the US Defence Department - the Pentagon - in Washington DC and into a field in Pennsylvania; 3,025 people are killed in the attacks. US leads massive campaign of air strikes against Afghanistan and later sends in special forces to help opposition forces defeat the Taleban regime and find Saudi-born dissident Osama Bin Laden, who is suspected of masterminding the 11 September attacks.	Bolton hailed as one of North-west's top tourist destination as figures for visitors crashed through 1,000,000 mark.
2002		Cycling and badminton competitions in Commonwealth Games held in Bolton area.
2003	Missile attacks on targets in Baghdad mark the start of a US-led campaign to topple the Iraqi leader Saddam Hussein. England beat Australia to win the Rugby World Cup in Australia.	Bolton celebrated 750 years since Charter granted. The Water Place closed because of its dilapidated condition.
2004	West Indies batsman Brian Lara smashes a record breaking 400 not out against England in the fourth test at Antigua. Arsenal become the first side to go through a league season unbeaten since Preston achieved the feat in 1888/89.	

In Sam Allardyce's first season as manager at the Reebok, his team got to the semi-finals of both the Worthington (League) Cup and of the F.A. Cup. But despite that seeming success, and the fact that they also appeared in the First Division play-offs, the year 2000 was not a good one for the Wanderers - a case of always the bridesmaid, never the bride. In January, the first leg of the Worthington Cup tie against Tranmere was at home - and the visitors won 1-0 on "a night of frustration for Bolton." The following week the Wanderers travelled to Tranmere, full of determination to make up for that previous match. But it all went wrong . . .

27 JANUARY 2000

WANDERERS' NIGHT OF SHAME

Tranmere 3 Wanderers 0 (Agg. 4-0)

Sam Allardyce found himself having to apologise to the fans as his team's Wembley dreams lay in tatters last night.

No doubt the manager will have had harsh words for his players in the privacy of the visitors' dressing room at Prenton Park. But on a night when the Wanderers were second best in every area - tactics, talent and motivation - it was fitting that the most damning indictment of their weak-kneed performance should come from the victorious Tranmere camp.

Liverpool's Republic of Ireland defender Phil Babb, who crossed the Mersey to answer John Aldridge's SOS, highlighted the key to his adopted team's walkover when he pointed out: "If you can't be inspired for a game like this, you're in the wrong job."

Babb's words should strike at the heart of every Bolton player who failed to produce even the basic essentials in the two legs of this Worthington Cup semi-final. Each time the glory was theirs for the taking and each time they let themselves down badly and let their supporters down even moreso. It was hard to imagine Wanderers playing worse than they had done in the first leg at the Reebok a fortnight ago, but they managed it.

Allardyce must know he has his work cut out getting a response from his players but it was to the 2,500 supporters who travelled to the Wirral in the hope of seeing their team

reverse the 1-0 first leg deficit that his attention turned. "My thoughts really go to the fans," he said, picking up on their frustration, disappointment, and in many cases, anger. "We didn't do them justice, and I apologise to them."

Supporters demand a lot from their team, and Bolton fans have had their expectation levels raised higher than most in recent years. Whether they are asking too much is a moot point, but you can't blame them for being optimistic and ambitious. It's certainly not asking too much of players to show passion and commitment, though. They are the basic requirements; if they aren't present, nothing else matters.

Yet that is precisely why it's Tranmere Rovers and not Bolton Wanderers who are now preparing for a trip to Wembley on February 27, their first appearance in a major cup final.

Teams -

Bolton: Banks, Holden, Bergsson, Whitlow, Phillips, Passi, Gardner, Elliott, Jensen, Holdsworth, Gudjohnsen.
Subs: Warhurst for Passi (53 mins), Johansen for Whitlow (67 mins), Taylor for Holdsworth (77 mins), Ritchie, Jaaskelainen.

Tranmere: Achterberg, Hazell, Challinor, Babb, Thompson, Taylor, Jones, Henry, Mahon, Parkinson, Kelly.
Subs: Black for Kelly (84 mins), Koumas for Mahon (85 mins), Allen for Thompson (88 mins), Santos, Nixon.

Michael Johansen cracked this first-half effort against the Tranmere post in the first leg of the semi-final.

A couple of months later, in April, 2000, Wanderers were at Wembley in the semi-final of the F.A. Cup, against Aston Villa. Neither team had netted the ball after 90 minutes, or after extra time (Dean Holdsworth missed a sitter nine minutes from the end), so it was all up to heart-stopping penalties. Holdsworth bravely stepped forward first for Bolton and scored, but he was the only Wanderer to succeed from the spot, and Aston Villa came out on top 4-1.

3 APRIL 2000

WANDERERS HOLD HEADS HIGH

Wanderers 0   Aston Villa 0 (Wanderers lost 4-1 on penalties after extra time)

Rarely in the long and glorious history of Wembley has a losing team left with so much pride. There were tears shed and some found it hard to keep their chins up but that was disappointment of defeat weighing too heavily on their shoulders.

Sam Allardyce and his players walked tall as they boarded their team coach knowing they had done their club, their town, and the Nationwide League proud in a semi-final in which they were only meant to be making up the numbers!

They were more than a match for their Premiership opponents, but one calamitous miss by Dean Holdsworth just nine minutes from the end of extra time let Villa off the hook, took the game to a penalty shoot out, and the world just came tumbling down around them. Holdsworth redeemed himself when he stepped up to beat David James to make it all square after Steve Stone had kicked off the penalty shoot out. But the Villa keeper, who was in goal when Liverpool beat Wanderers in the 1995 Coca-Cola Cup Final, saved the next two spot-kicks from Alan Johnston and Michael Johansen, and with Lee Hendrie and Gareth Barry tucking theirs away, it was all set up for Dion Dublin to assume the role of the fairy tale hero.

What is it about the F.A. Cup that produces such romance? Fourteen weeks ago Dublin was worried he would never play again - some said lucky to be alive - after breaking a bone in his neck. Now he's the toast of the Claret and Blues.
"It's Villa by a neck," one wag with a Brummie accent shouted, celebrating his team's good fortune with an irreverent but apt assessment.

It should never have got to that stage, though. Wanderers, revelling in the role of underdogs, produced a heroic performance that had their outnumbered but never outshouted supporters on their feet and in full voice right to the end.

The Wanderers were united in refusing to let any individual player carry the can for their F.A. Cup heartbreak. "I don't attribute any blame to anybody," Sam Allardyce said as he spoke with pride of the performance of his team which was more than a match for John Gregory's Premiership high-flyers for 120 minutes.

Bolton team: Jaaskelainen, Bergsson, Fish, Ritchie, Whitlow, Johansen, Jensen, Elliott, Johnston, Gudjohnson, Holdsworth. Subs: Warhurst for Jensen (62 min), O'Kane for Bergsson (91 mins), Banks, Passsi, Hansen.

Bolton's Dean Holdsworth looks dejected after his team lose on penalties.

In May, 2000, it was time for the First Division play-offs to see which team would be promoted to the Premiership, and in the semi-finals, Bolton played Ipswich over two legs. It was not a happy experience. The game at the Reebok ended as a 2-2 draw, after Wanderers had led by a couple of goals, with Gordon Sharrock writing that "if Wanderers are going to reach Wembley and keep their dream alive they are going to have to be at their best and beat a very good team at Portman Road", and Sam Allardyce insisting: "We're disappointed because we haven't won here on our own ground, but we're not out of the tie. It's not the end of the world. Our away form has been as good as our home form of late and we've been scoring a lot of goals." It was a massive game for both clubs, but Bolton felt that they were playing the referee as well . . .

18 MAY   `2000`
WHAT A BAD KNIGHT

IPSWICH TOWN 5 WANDERERS 3

(After extra time: 90 minutes 3-3. Ipswich wins 7-5 on aggregate)

Barry Knight had a lot of explaining to do as Bolton Wanderers surveyed the wreckage of their promotion dream and wondered what might have been. But the Kent referee, who turned last night's pulsating play-off decider at Portman Road into complete and utter chaos, refused to utter a single word to justify his one-sided view of events.

He declined to comment on his decision to award THREE penalties, or why he showed TWELVE yellow and TWO red cards to Bolton players, yet didn't see fit to issue so much as a single caution to the home side. He refused to react to claims from Sam Allardyce that he was "totally to blame" for a defeat that had cost Wanderers a place in the Premiership, and even remained tight-lipped when he was told the Bolton boss had accused him of holding a grudge against him personally and Wanderers as a club.

But Big Sam had his say right enough - to such an extent that he can now expect the Football Association to throw the book at him for launching such a vitriolic and detailed attack on the man he believes single-candidly denied his brave hearts a place at Wembley.

Allan Johnston volleys home Wanderers' third goal against Ipswich.

Allardyce, a semi-final loser for the third time in a magnificent but ultimately unsuccessful season - simply could not hold his tongue after seeing his promotion dream shattered in the space of 13 unlucky and chaotic minutes. Less than a minute of normal time remained when Northern Ireland international Jim Mailto rescued Ipswich with a dramatic equaliser to take a riveting play-off duel into extra time. And right before his eyes, the manager who had worked a tactical masterpiece saw his team reduced to nine men and trailing for the first time in the entire tie.

They had been robbed of a famous victory - a victory they genuinely and justifiably felt they deserved - by another worthy, never-say-die team. You don't deny George Burley and his boys their triumph after failing to clear the first hurdle of the play-offs for the last three years. Allardyce had the decency to wish the victors well and tip them to go all the way to the Premiership this time. But there were no niceties for Mr Knight as he let rip with an assault which, even by his own tough-talking standards, was ferocious.

"I totally blame the referee for this defeat," he said without qualification. "He could have done untold damage to this football club that will be felt over the next two years. You just don't know how long it will take us to get into this position again. He should be made accountable for what he's done. Words just can't describe how I feel. I don't think he should ever be allowed to referee a game again."

It was a sad and bitter end to an exciting season which promised nothing yet almost delivered everything. The 62nd and final game appeared to sum up the entire campaign. There was talent - stacks of it; but the special ingredient throughout the promotion push which has seen this team repeatedly defy its doubters and critics, is character, and it was there in abundance last night.

Holdsworth played as though his life, never mind his future, depended on it, and all around him was a "dogs of war" approach that saw Wanderers literally knock Ipswich out of their stride. Yet every time they got their noses in front they were reeled in again. Holdsworth pounced and then conceded the first of the penalties, which Magilton stuck away. Holdsworth struck again with a magnificent free kick, only for Mr Knight to

intervene again, awarding a second penalty for Ritchie's challenge on Stewart. Jussi Jaaskelainen came to the rescue, not for the only time in the game, but three minutes into the second half Magilton atoned for his miss to equalise for the second time.

Given the fever-pitched atmosphere, the needle in the game, and the magnitude of what was at stake, it was a credit to Wanderers that once Johnston had restored their lead with a spectacular strike, they not only took control of the game, frustrated the crowd and looked more than comfortable to be playing out time, they even fashioned a chance which would have given them game, set and match.

But with just five minutes of normal time remaining, Richard Wright - who had not impressed - got the better of a one-on-one with Claus Jenson in what turned out to be the defining moment of the match. You felt for the dashing Dane as Magilton's equaliser hit the back of the net.

Wanderers started extra-time a man down after Whitlow had been sent off for a second bookable offence, and within seven minutes they were trailing, Jamie Clapham converting the third of the penalties after Ritchie wrestled with David Johnston while the ball was in Jaaskelainen hands, and another man down as Elliott followed his captain on the long walk! Martin Reuser's goal in the second extra period was academic. The home fans had already started their celebrations. All that remained was for Mr Knight to show his 12th yellow card to Franck Passi.

Teams -

Bolton: Jaaskelainen, Bergsson, Fish, Ritchie, Whitlow, Johansen, Warhurst, Jensen, Elliott, Johnston, Holdsworth. Subs: Passi for Warhurst (71 mins), Phillips for Johansen (90 mins), Hansen for Holdsworth (101 mins), Farrelly, Banks.

Ipswich Town: Wright, Venus, Mowbray, Brown, Croft, Scowcroft, Magilton, Holland, Clapham, Johnson, Stewart. Subs: Reuser for Brown (65 mins), Naylor for Scowcroft (78 mins), Thetis, Wilnis, Branagan.

It may have seemed a long time coming, but the big moment arrived in May, 2001 - the Wanderers regained their rightful place in the Premiership with a stunning victory, although "tense, nail-biting stuff", over Preston at the Cardiff Millennium Stadium. It was seen not only as good for the club, but also as great for Bolton, with local business leaders predicting a multi-million boom-time for the town, with a revival for traders because of visitors and cash flooding to the area.

29 MAY 2001

SAVOUR THE MOMENT

Wanderers 3 Preston 0

A series of searching questions will be left unanswered over the next few days. Wanderers are back in the Premiership and, forgive them for not taking life too seriously for a while, they are going to party.

So don't expect announcements or even decisions on the future of key players' - Gudni Bergsson, Dean Holdsworth, Robbie Elliott, or Matt Clarke - who all figured in the dramatic play-off victory over Preston. Or the likes of Ian Marshall, Paul Warhurst and Nicky Summerbee who didn't have a part to play in the 55th match of the season but made telling contributions during the course of the previous nine months. They are all out of contract and need to sit down and talk turkey with Sam Allardyce.

But pinning the manager down on the matter of who stays, who goes, and who comes would be like asking a National Lottery winner if he wants the milkman to deliver two pints or three tomorrow morning. Wanderers have hit the jackpot and Big Sam and his players are going to savour every minute of it before they get down to planning how to stay in the Premiership for more than just one season this time.

After failing at the play-off stages in successive seasons, they finally made it - securing a place at football's top table for the third time in seven seasons. The two previous triumphs were celebrated and saluted - and rightly so - but when Michael Ricketts took the ball round Preston keeper David Lucas for the decisive second goal, just as the stadium clock was approaching 90 minutes, Wanderers banked a staggering £30 million.

Back in the Premiership, and the team celebrate with Sam Allardyce in May, 2001 after their victory over Preston.

It's the richest prize in sport, according to chairman Phil Gartside, whose confidence and faith in his manager has paid dividends neither could have imagined when they teamed up in October, 1999 - just 19 months ago!

Their target at the time - with the club deep in debt and low on confidence - was to achieve Premiership status and financial stability in five years. But Allardyce, who had previously been idolised by Wanderers' fans as Big Sam, the no-nonsense centre-half, has delivered in double quick time - and against the odds - to earn an even bigger place in the hearts of the faithful.

Forced to sell some of his most prized possessions - Gudjohnsen, Jensen and Fish - and having to beg and borrow players to rebuild his squad under the most severe of financial constraints, he has brought the good times rolling back and given the town, the club and its fans the exciting possibility of seeing the fabulous Reebok Stadium packed to capacity next season for the visits of Manchester United, Arsenal, Liverpool, Chelsea and the rest of the elite of English football.

Tensions were high and the pressure was on as an entire season's efforts and the keys to the riches of the Premiership rested on the outcome of just one match, but, after coming back from the dead in the semi-final against West Brom, Wanderers showed their quality, strength, resilience and tactical supremacy to see off the threat of a Preston side which had finished nine points below them in the regular season, but went into the winner-take-all showdown on level terms.

There were a few anxious and nail biting moments after Gareth Farrelly opened the scoring in the 16th minute, but Wanderers would end the game saluted as the better side; however, even they would admit they were flattered by the scoreline and that, until Farrelly sent Ricketts in for his 24th goal of the season and Ricardo Gardner applied the gloss finish with practically the last kick of the game, anything could have happened - and it nearly did.

If Matt Clarke (how valuable he proved after joining the Reebok ranks on loan from Bradford) hadn't hurled himself to his left to palm away David Healey's 69th minute shot, Wanderers could easily have been sitting and wondering about the £30 million that got away.

They'd created enough chances to have had the game in the bag long before that, but good saves from Lucas and a couple of hesitant finishes kept the fans in the 54,000 crowd - not exactly an impressive figure for a game that had so much riding on it - on the edge of their seats.

Not a lucky win, but Wanderers were assigned the lucky dressing room, their fans were at the lucky end of the stadium, and they had their lucky charm. Of his previous 23 goals, Ricketts had scored 13 coming off the subs. bench - and two in the regular season wins against Preston. Only a fool would back against him.

"It's as if it was written", he suggested before shooting off to join the party.

Teams -
Bolton: Clarke, Barness, Bergsson, Hendry, Charlton, Farrelly, Nolan, Frandsen, Gardner, Holdsworth, Hansen. Subs: Ricketts for Hansen (70 mins), Elliott for Frandsen (79 mins), Whitlow for Holdsworth (90 mins), Banks, Marshall.

Preston: Lucas, Alexander, Murdock, Kidd, Edwards, Cartwright, Rankine, Gregan, McKenna, Healy, Macken. Subs: Anderson for Cartwright (66 mins), Cresswell for McKenna (82 mins), Jackson, Moilanen, Barry-Murphy.

Once in the Premiership, despite money being tight, the Wanderers still found means of attracting some of the world's most famous players, including French former World Cup medal winner Youri Djorkaeff, Nigerian international Jay-Jay Okocha, and Ivan Campo from Real Madrid. The first big signing came in February, 2002 . . .

21 FEBRUARY 2002
MORE TO COME?

Wanderers unveiled the biggest name signing in their history, and then said there could be more to come. The Premiership-obsessed Whites appear determined to stop at nothing to preserve their status in the top flight.

Since the start of the year they have splashed out big time to bring former German regular international Fredi Bobic, current Danish midfielder Stig Tofting, and now the biggest name of them all, current World Cup and European Championship winners' medal holder Youri Djorkaeff.

Wanderers are believed to be paying him the biggest weekly wage in the club's history in the hope that he can keep them up over the last 12 games. But manager Sam Allardyce believes that is a drop in the ocean compared with what the club has to gain. "The deal is for the next four months which leaves the club with no financial commitment after that."

Suggesting that it might not be the last deal with three weeks to go before transfer deadline day, chairman Phil Gartside said: "If Sam comes to me with the right man and the money is right and the contract is right, then we will look at it. Sam will never stop looking for new player. That's the way he is, and he will try to convince me."

In February, 2002, Sam Allardyce pulled off a major coup with the signing of French World Cup winner Youri Djorkaeff. "In the terms of big signings, he's got to be the biggest by a mile," said club chairman Phil Gartside.

Getting into the Premiership is a difficult enough task as it is, but managing to stay there among the big boys who have lots of money to spend while you are trying to produce a winning team on a shoestring is even tougher. You've no need to tell that to Big Sam, or anyone else at the club. Both in 2002 and 2003 the Wanderers had a nail-biting end to the season to see if they would stay up - at the end of April, 2002, it happened without the Wanderers playing a match!

29 APRIL 2002
SAM-SATIONAL

Bolton was celebrating today after Wanderers achieved Premiership survival - without kicking a ball. The Wanderers had been hotly tipped for relegation all season, but the team's never-say-die performances earned the club another season in the top flight.

For manager Sam Allardyce, Bolton's survival has put him in the record books as being the first manager ever to take the club up and then keep them up in the Premiership. Manchester United's victory at Ipswich at the weekend guaranteed Bolton's survival, and for the first time ever Wanderers' fans cheered on as the team they considered their most bitter rivals won. There was a sense of poetic justice that Wanderers' survival was secured in Ipswich at the very ground where their promotion play-off dreams were so cruelly shattered by three penalties and a shower of yellow and red cards just two years ago.

However, reported the Evening News, Sam Allardyce revealed that he would not be dealing in big money transfers the next season. The Bolton boss, hailed for his success on a shoestring, does not expect to be joining the ranks of the big spenders until the club gets its finances back on an even keel.

And Gordon Sharrock, in his report of the next match, against Arsenal, which the southerners won 2-0, told of how the Wanderers had gone on a lap of honour.
"Players saluted supporters and the fans hailed their heroes who at the third attempt in seven roller-coaster seasons, had managed to avoid instant relegation. But no-one was under any illusions.

"The 90 preceding minutes proved that, while they will again operate in the same division as Arsene Wenger's Arsenal, no way can they consider themselves in the same league! How fortunate they were to have already been assured of survival because, with the Gunners in this form and on the crest of a 10-match winning wave, there was not the slightest chance of them toppling the Champions-elect and returning the favour Sam Allardyce felt they owed arch-rivals Manchester United.

"Although the Wanderers have taken points off all the main contenders in this remarkable season, they are still light years away from competing consistently - week in week out, season in season out, with the elite."

Another result of Bolton's great 2002 season was a hairy one. Football pundit Mark Lawrenson had constantly tipped Bolton to be relegated (among many other cynics, it must be said, but all they did was help motivate the Bolton team) and promised that if the Wanderers retained their place in the Premiership he would have his moustache shaved off. No way were the Wanderers' supporters going to let him get away without paying the price - and so off came his quarter of a century old facial hair - and he looked so much better he hasn't regrown it! Artist Kevin Collins produced this super cartoon.

Glory boy Kevin Nolan celebrates after turning the "Theatre of Dreams" into a nightmare for Manchester United at Old Trafford in 2002, scoring the only goal of the match. The previous year he and Michael Rickets had scored the goals that gave Wanderers an historic 2-1 win at Old Trafford - the first time in 22 years that Bolton had beaten United.

At the end of the 2003 season, the tension was even worse, with the result not known until the last minutes of the season. It was either Bolton or West Ham to go down. The Wanderers were playing Middlesbrough, West Ham playing Birmingham - fortunately Bolton held their nerve and won 2-1 while West Ham drew, which meant safety for Bolton for at least another 12 months, a third successive season of Premiership football. Sam Allardyce commented: "I am completely drained, emotionally unstable, absolutely delighted and relieved." So were the players and fans, who had suffered with him . . .

12 MAY   2003

WHITES' DAY OF DESTINY

Wanderers 2   Middlesbrough 1

It was Wanderers against the rest of the world and there was only going to be one winner. The Bolton fans and local media were a rare breed as they were the only people who wanted Wanderers to beat West Ham in the fight to avoid the drop.

But from the moment Per Frandsen turned into Roy of the Rovers and almost broke the net after 10 minutes it was going to be Wanderers' day. As always on these dramatic occasions there was a spell when fans with heart conditions would have been advised to look away. Wanderers' Premiership existence and possibly their long term destiny came down to one game, and Wanderers played it true to the script of the whole season - with drama, passion, and an irresistible will to win.

As always Wanderers had to do it the hard way and in the knowledge that if they survived they would be seen as the bad guys who had sent everybody's favourites West Ham down. Everybody, that is, except the highly-charged Wanderers' fans who almost raised the Reebok roof with their passion.

Frandsen's strike sent the White hordes delirious. And they had only 80 minutes left on the clock to run down. Eighty became 70 when Jay Jay Okocha found exactly the same spot with a peach of a free kick.

If the first half was fun, the second half was pure drama. The worst fear of all Wanderers' fans for weeks has centred around Michael Ricketts coming back to the Reebok and scoring his first goal for Middlesbrough to send his old club down. His second half substitute appearance was met with a chorus of boos which was repeated at every touch. But, love him or loathe him, he is a quality striker when he sets his mind to it, and he meant business.

Twice he found far too much space in the box to loop headers off target and he made it third time lucky as he steered Stuart Parnaby's cross past Jaaskelainen with no challenge coming in. When news filtered through of Les Ferdinand's breakthrough goal for West Ham minutes later the nerves started jangling on the pitch and in the stands. Eight minutes later the Reebok erupted when everyone seemed to hear at once that Geoff Horsfield had levelled for Birmingham, and it was party time for the last 10 minutes.

Wanderers were in full cry, but still there was no end to the drama as first Birmingham went ahead with four minutes still to play at the Reebok and then lost the lead almost on the stroke of full time.

Teams -
Bolton: Jaaskelainen, N'Gotty, Bergsson, Whitlow, Gardner, Campo, Frandsen, Okocha, Djorkaeff, Pedersen, Mendy.
Subs: Andre for Pedersen (66 mins), Nolan for Mendy (72 mins), Charlton for Djorkaeff (90 mins), Poole, Salva.

Middlesbrough: Schwarzer, Parnaby, Riggott, Southgate, Boateng, Juninho, Greening, Maccarone, Christie, Wilkshire, Queuedrue.
Subs: Downing for Christie (45 mins), Ricketts for Maccarone (45 mins), Doriva for Greening (45 mins), Crossley, Davies.

The final match of the 2002-3 season was also long-serving player Gudni Bergsson's last for the club. After postponing his retirement twice previously, he had made up his mind to hang up his boots and return to his native Iceland to follow his career as a solicitor and spend more time with his family.

Gudni Bergsson admitted the Ice Man almost melted as he took his final bow. His central defensive partner Mike Whitlow hailed him a "dear, dear friend" and a "legend", and Wanderers were delighted to have given their skipper the perfect send-off into retirement. It was enough to make a grown man cry, and Bergsson admitted that it nearly did - even one from Iceland.

The paper said: "He showed on the final day that he remains as quick on his feet and in his brain as he ever has been. Allied to his strength and experience, Bergsson at 38 years old is as good as virtually any centre half in the Premiership. He has finished at the top, on the greatest and most historic occasion of his eight-year Wanderers career and at the peak of his form. How every player would love to do that?"

30 DECEMBER 2003
REEBOK TAKEOVER GO-AHEAD

Bolton Wanderers are now firmly under the control of the Isle of Man based businessman Eddie Davies. The millionaire, born in Little Lever, gained 94.5 per cent control of the parent company, Burnden Leisure plc, when he won a series of votes by overwhelming majorities at Monday's annual meeting - despite protests from some shareholders.

Mr Davies did not attend the four-hour meeting art Reebok's Lion of Vienna Suite, but a set of resolutions which were recommended by his fellow directors and approved in his absence allowed him to treble his shareholding in exchange for a £2.5 million cash injection by way of an exclusive share issue.

The investment, which will be used to settle bank loans due to be paid next month, takes his financial commitment to the club to £14 million since he became a Burnden director four years ago, making him by far the biggest single investor in the club's history. Chairman Phil Gartside insisted the move was necessary to ease the pressure of a £38 million debt burnden.

But there were protests from shareholders who were angry that their own holdings were being drastically diluted and were worried that the football club should be at the mercy of just once man.

However, Mr Gartside said: "We've left no stone unturned in our effort to raise long term finance, but the only person who has come along and put substantial sums in this club over the past four and a half years, or even 10 years, is Eddie Davies.

"There are 92 clubs in this country who would love an Eddie Davies, and the thing is he's a Boltonian, not a Russian or an Arab, but a lifelong Wanderers' fan. Because of his support we are watching Okocha, Djorkaeff and Campo, and I find it strange that people want to question his integrity. Fans and shareholders should consider where we would be without his support."

Answering criticism of Mr Davies' non-appearance for such an historic meeting, the chairman added`: "I am not his keeper. I can't tell him to be here or not to be here. He doesn't want the publicity and I can't force him to have it."

Eddie Davies.

In February, 2004, Wanderers got to the final of the Carling (League) Cup, and it was expected that the trophy would be brought home to Bolton in glory. The Cardiff Millennium Stadium was packed with excited fans from Bolton and Middlesbrough, but two goals for the North East team within the first few minutes meant an uphill battle for the Trotters to get back into the game, as Gordon Sharrock reported.

1 MARCH 2004

WANDERERS' BIG GUNS FAIL TO DELIVER

Wanderers 1 Middlesbrough 2

When so-called small clubs play on the big stage, they rely on their big players to produce top performances.

Sadly, when the anger over Mike Riley's handling of the 44th League Cup Final subsides, Wanderers will know precisely why it was Middlesbrough who took the season's first major prize in Cardiff. They will see how a strangely-subdued Jay-Jay Okocha failed to rise to the occasion and how a rare spate of squandering by Youri Djorkaeff left Boro celebrating their first trophy success in 128 years, while Allardyce's men trooped home thinking of what might have been - Carling Cup glory and a first-ever venture into European competition.

They will see how Kevin Davies, who bullied the Boro defence into submission when Wanderers recorded their first Premiership win of the season back in September, found Gareth Southgate and Ugo Ehiogu - one of the best centre-back pairings in the business - an altogether different proposition when the chips were down. And they will have to admit that, for all their experience, their thorough preparation and their pre-match confidence, they were caught cold.

They were 2-0 down before some of their fans had managed to find their seats and at this level and against a defence as resilient as Steve McClaren's, chances of a revival were slim. That they managed to pull a goal back and have Boro reeling for a spell was down to Davies getting lucky when Mark Schwarzer let his hit-and-hope daisy-cutter of a shot bobble through his hands.

The packed Bolton end of the Millennium stadium.

For a split second the stadium went deathly quiet . . . then the ripple of the net had the Bolton fans off their seats in celebration. Suddenly, from the depths of despair, they had flashbacks of Wembley, 1995, when Bruce Rioch's team came back from 2-0 down to beat Reading in the Play-off Final to reach the Premiership for the first time.

Miracles do happen and, if Djorkaeff had been at his lethal best, this one could have been an altogether different story. Schwarzer, to his credit, did atone for his awful blunder with some excellent saves but, by his own high standards, the Frenchman knows he could not have asked for more than three clear scoring chances in the space of four minutes.

Even Boro's millionaire chairman Steve Gibson admitted: "At 2-1 I thought we were fortunate to hang on."

With nothing to show for their best spell of the match, Wanderers became more anxious and, subsequently, more desperate as the game wore on. Ivan Campo plugged away, and Djorkaeff tried to inspire with a couple of penetrating dashes that promised so much but had no end product.

Okocha, the man who did so much to book Wanderers into the final with his performance in the first leg of the semi-final against Aston Villa, carried the hopes of every Bolton fan. But, in his first start since he returned from Tunisia where he was the most outstanding performer in the African Nations Cup, the Nigerian could not raise his game - for all his determination to win his first-ever domestic trophy.

The Carling Cup was never top of Sam Allardyce's priority list, of course. But that doesn't lessen the sense of disappointment. The nearer Wanderers got to the Millennium Stadium, the greater the commitment to the competition; and not for the financial rewards - for they are miniscule compared to the earnings to be made from the Premiership - but for the glory and the spin-offs.

And as Kevin Davies made abundantly clear in advance, getting to the final would be a waste of time and effort if they didn't win it.

Middlesbrough's Joseph-Desire Job goes down after a challenge by Wanderers' defender Emerson Thome, right, to win a seven minute spot kick which pout Middlesbrough two up.

Who knows what might have happened had Mr Riley decided there was as much merit in Wanderers' appeal for a penalty in the 89th minute when Ehiogu stopped a Stelios shot with his hand as he did with Boro's successful claim when Emerson Thome brought down Joseph Job with seven minutes on the clock? Job had already put Boro a goal up when Gaizka Mendieta and Bolo Zenden combined to catch the Bolton defence cold and their own manager with his pants down. McClaren was still in the dressing room changing out of his designer suit and into his tracksuit when the first goal went in, and surfaced just in time to see Zenden shaping up to take the spot kick.

How lucky can you get? Zenden slips as he strikes the ball, gets a double-hit and wrong-foots Jussi Jaaskelainen, just enough for the ball to strike the keeper's leg and fly into the roof of the net.

The rule book states that the goal should be disallowed and a free kick awarded to Wanderers, but Mr Riley did not see it that way - or that is what we must assume since he left the ground refusing to comment on that or any of his other contentious decisions.

Allardyce had to be careful, of course, not to leave himself open to "sour grape" accusations. So he first acknowledged that his team had not done themselves justice, conceding that Boro were the better side overall and congratulating McClaren - the first English manager to lift a major trophy for eight years. Then he rounded on Mr Riley, England's appointed referee for the European Championship Finals in Portugal this summer and a man with whom he has, let's say, some history.

Playing for such high stakes, it is understandable that managers and players will look to contentious decisions when they count the cost of failure. But the performance of the man in green and black might have been irrelevant had the big players in white lived up to their high reputations.

Teams -
Bolton: Jaaskelainen, Hunt, Thome, N'Gotty, Charlton, Campo, Frandsen, Okocha, Nolan, Davies, Djorkaeff. Subs: Pedersen for Frandsen (64 mins), Moreno for Nolan (78 mins), Stelios for Hunt (87 mins), Barness, Poole.

Middlesbrough: Schwarzer, Mills, Ehiogu, Southgate, Queuedrue, Mendieta, Boateng, Doriva, Zenden, Job. Subs: Ricketts for Job (65 mins), Massimo, Maccarone, Donning, Riggott, Jones.

Sam Allardyce consoles Jay Jay Okocha after the final whistle.

That result wasn't only a great disappointment for club and supporters, but seemed to affect the performance of the players for a while, and fears began to grow that they may be dragged for yet another season into the scrap for Premiership survival. But a win against Wolves on Easter Monday, followed by victories over Spurs, Southampton and Leeds (equalling their best top-flight sequence since 1927-28) put them on the road to consolidation in the Premiership, and they ended the season in eighth place, the best top division finish for 44 years.

So 130 years after the Christ Church team which became Bolton Wanderers had been formed in 1874, the club retained its rightful place near the peak of English football, with the hope that it will stay there for at least the next 130 years. . .

But let the last word go to Gordon Sharrock, with his round-up report of the season from the Evening News:

24 MAY 2004
GLORY DAYS ARE HERE AGAIN

There were times in the dark days of the 1980s when not even the most optimistic of fans would have dared suggest Bolton Wanderers could ever regain their position as a respected force in English football.

The darkest day of all was Saturday, April 4, 1987. The venue, Somerton Park, Newport; the occasion, a relegation battle in the old Third Division; the result, a 2-1 win for Newport County in front of 1,193 spectators - the lowest crowd on record for a competitive match involving the Wanderers. It was a pivotal result that helped condemn the club to its one and only season in the Fourth Division.

At such times in the course of following the team's fortunes - mostly misfortunes in those days - you could not help but envy your predecessors, in particularly Haydn Berry, the grand old man who reported for this newspaper during the glory days of the 1950s, when Nat Lofthouse and Co. had an unbroken run in Division One, frequently in the top half of the table. What a joy it must have been in 1958 to have the satisfaction of

seeing Wanderers return to Wembley, the scene of their dramatic defeat by Blackpool five years earlier, and beat Manchester United to win the FA Cup.

Unfortunately, there has been no trophy to parade at the end of the season that has just drawn to a close, and it must be acknowledged that, in the days before the abolition of the maximum wage, it would not have been considered worthy of celebration to finish as the eighth best team in England - but if any of the old timers ever saw a more entertaining team than the one led with such distinction by Jay-Jay Okocha, then they were well-blessed indeed.

Bolton Wanderers' fans have been privileged over the last nine months to see some of the most gifted footballers ever to pull on the famous white shirt, and they responded in their droves, taking the average attendance to a 44-year high, with the Reebok almost filled to capacity for every league game.

They have had the pleasure of seeing players such as Okocha, Youri Djorkaeff and Ivan Campo when, less than five years ago, the extent of the club's ambition was to keep the financial wolf from the door and avoid relegation to Division Two! Since then, with Phil Gartside leading the board and Sam Allardyce managing the team, Wanderers' fans have not only had their sense of pride restored but also had the joy of witnessing the club's re-emergence and a year-on-year improvement to become established as a force in the top half of the Premiership. That they have done it on a tight budget makes the achievement all the more impressive; that they have done it in style makes it extra special.

They have had their problems along the way, of course. Alarm bells were ringing when they managed to win just one of their first 10 games, and there was no question that reaching the Carling Cup Final knocked them right out of their Premiership stride and caused a few hearts to flutter.

But there is now a genuine and ever-growing respect for Big Sam and his Wanderers. A record-equalling eight away wins and five successive victories at the back end were major contributions to a record Premiership points haul, but 2003-2004 was about more than just keeping the statisticians busy.

It was about Djorkaeff rolling back the years with some vintage performances, Campo answering his critics with some immense displays in midfield, Bruno N'Gotty living up to his impressive pedigree as one of the coolest of defenders, Jussi Jaaskelainen emerging as one of the best goalkeepers in the land; it was about Kevin Nolan proving himself as one of the game's finest young players and Nicky Hunt following him out of the academy ranks to enjoy a stunning first Premiership season that brought the bonus of England U21 honours.

It was about unsung heroes - Simon Charlton, a revelation as an emergency centre-back; Henrik Pedersen coming out of the shadows to run defences ragged; Kevin Davies, ditched by Southampton last summer, but who swept the board in the player of the year polls after some some titanic displays that would have delighted any of the old centre-forwards.

Yet, measured in newspaper column inches and headlines, it seemed it was mostly about Okocha. The gifted Nigerian might not have lived up to the breathtaking standards he set towards the end of last season; he could not even muster a single Premiership goal. But he bore the responsibilities of captaincy with dignity and dedication, all under the constant pressure of speculation concerning his future and, at times, his personal finances. And he did it all with a smile on his face.

Oh yes, those dark days of 1987 are now just a dim and distant memory of a different life, a different Bolton Wanderers.

Ivan Campo says an emotional goodbye after the last game of the season to Per Frandsen, whose last game it was for the club. He was on his way to Wigan Athletic.

Manager Sam Allardyce in turn applauds the fans at the end of the 2003-2004 season.

Among facilities open to the public are a museum of Bolton Wanderers' history, and tours of the stadium. Here, Tom Hall, Stadium Tours Manager, takes a group of schoolchildren round the Reebok in 2001.

The Wanderers' squad in 2001/02. Back row: Mike Forde (Sports psychologist), Leam Richardson, Jeff Smith, Ricardo Gardner, Nicky Southall, Michael Ricketts, Wayne Buchanan, Dean Holdsworth, Henrik Pederson, Per Frandsen, Bo Hansen, Craig White (Senior strength and conditioning coach). Middle: Mark Howard (Assistant strength and conditioning coach), Jussi Jaaskelainen, Anthony Barness, Dean Holden, Mike Whitlow, Paul Warhurst, Colin Hendry, Dibrell Diawara, Gudni Bergsson, Kevin Nolan, Emanuele Morini, Akinori Nishizawa, Steve Banks, Fred Barber (Goalkeeping coach). Front: Jack Chapman (Chief Scout), Mark Taylor (Physiotherapist), Ryan Baldacchino, Simon Charlton, Ian Marshall, Neil McDonald (First team coach), Sam Allardyce (manager), Phil Brown (Assistant manager), Paul Wheatcroft, David Norris, Gareth Farrelly, Faz Page (Assistant physiotherapist), Russell Byrne-Fraser (Kit manager).

A piece of Bolton Wanderers' history went on sale in 2002 with the sale of England caps won by Joe Smith, one of the club's pre-war heroes. They were from matches played against Ireland, Wales and Scotland between 1913 and 1919.

In January, 2003, to celebrate 125 years of the Wanderers (a slightly late celebration!) the team played in special shirts which dated back to their formation in 1877. Here, in the game against Fulham, Ivan Campo, wearing one of the shirts, battles with Facundo Sava.

In January, 2004, more than 800 people attended a tribute night for Sam Allardyce organised by the Bolton branch of the Variety Club of Great Britain, for which £22,000 was raised. Glowing personal tributes were made by fellow professionals in the football world, including Sir Alex Ferguson (seen here with Sam and Lady Ferguson), Gordon Taylor of the PFA, and former Bolton player (and manager, but not for Bolton!) Peter Reid.

........and this is only the beginning.

ADVANCED SUBSCRIBERS

William Hugh Ramsden
To Vinny, all our love Sarah and Joe
To Jeff.M.liffe from Mum and Dad
To Graham Potter - Thank you x
To David Gwilliam from his No.1 fan
The Goldston Family
Terry Smyth - 50 years a fan!
Stewart Ogden
Ryan John Crompton
Robin Linday, Bradshaw
Robin Cooper
Ray O'Donnell
Peter Southern
Norman Vickers
Nathaniel Campion youngest fan 2004
Myles John Harris
Michael Downs - Forever Bolton
Martin Nisbet, South Woodford
Martin McMulkin and Sam McMulkin
Mark Heys, Bolton
Mark Fernside born a Wanderer
Lynda W Rands, Sheffield White
Kenneth John Cottam
Ken Horrocks, Valley, Anglesey
Karl Michael C J Phillips
John and Jeremy Crawford
John and Michael Davidson
Harold and Michael Small
Gerald Barnes
Geocities.com/nigelsheppard/bwfc
Fryer-Fam, Tom, Alex, Ste, Val and Carol
For Judy Watson, a true fan
For James Jarvis and Thomas Bayne MW
David Wallwork (Ramsey, Cambs.)
David Eastham
David and Margaret Baker
David and Daniel Croughton
Darren John Howarth
Christopher Almond
Chris Wilkinson
Canada

Bill Pye, long time Trotters fan
Audrey Helena Miller
Arthur Wallwork
Andrew Pearce
Alan Richard Bolton, Telford
Alan Dorey
Alan Cremins - Happy Christmas
Alan and Gill Kay, Lostock, Bolton
Alan Jermyn, Daventry
Neil Simmons, Bolton
Ian Watson, Sleaford.Lincs
Andrew James King, Bolton.
Martin Timothy Steward
Stephen D Holden, Bolton.
Ian Barnes, Westhoughton
Duncan & Brandon Topp, Bolton
Charley Wood, Bolton
Graham Compton, Manchester
Ray Briggs, Penrith
To: Thomas, Robert, Bethan and Jack
Andrew Knowles, Bolton
Mike Singleton, Bolton
Graham Edge, Bolton
Ron Stockton, Skipton
Steve Ashcroft, Bolton
Roy Glover, Westhoughton
Chris Evans, Bristol
Mark Swift, London
Geoff Swift
Steven Denham, Manchester
P.J. Leatham, Darwen
David, Kaye, Bolton. October 2004
To Paul Happy Xmas 2004 love Dad
To Stephen Happy Xmas 2004 love Dad
Chris Barber-Lomax, Isle of Man
James Arthur House, Leigh Common.
Westhoughton
Glynn Jones
Andrew Hulme
Ken Horrocks, Valley. Anglesey
Neil Leach. Bolton

Alex Hyland.
Erika Hyland
W. Harrison
J.A Dodd
Peter Gilmore.
John Walsh O.B.E.
Mr Daniel Lewis
In memory of Bob Winrow
John, Denise, Catherine & Andrew Pietralski
Phil Rostron
Anthony A. Shepherd
Brian Holden
Royston Briley
Alex Coward
Albert Coward
Alan G. Gorton
Michael and Charlotte Walsh
Trevor Peacock
Viv Brown
Andrew Morris
Terry Herrity
Julian, Simon & Peter Hewitt
Stephen Shannon
Malcolm Dean
Ian Andrew Browne
John Dutton
Stephen Walmsley
Mr and Mrs Sterling. Bury
Mr J Fishwick.
Michael Ackers
Eileen H Owen
Hilary Hodgkinson
Geoffrey Culshaw
Lee Owen
Wilson Clough
Norman Lewis
Mr David Hobson
Mr Andrew Hobson
Alex Machell
Andy Wyatt
Matthew Whittle

Clifford Dougill
Peter Rushton
Denis Pomfret
Philip Massey
Rob Rainford
John Cubbage
Peter Chandler
Peter E Morris
Arnold Wood
Florence and David Brandwood
Danny Mageean
Barry Taylor
Jim Furey, Worsley
Keith Robert Nuttall
Paul and Catherine Smith
Phil Eccles
Paul Dingsdale
B W Heeley
Norman Fort
Mr R A Wilcock
Don Cole
Mr Fred Ratcliffe
Andy Childs
Iorwerth Williams
Bernard Slater
Richard Slater
Louise Harvey
Tim Greenhalgh
The Howcroft Family. Farnworth
Mel and Neil Woodcock.
Christine Ann Isherwood
David G Bailey
In loving memory of Peter Bromilow
Mr R O'Donnell
Mrs Llissse
Mr J Taylor
Jay Preston
Mr E G Brown, Leicester
Mr Nuttall. Leigh
Mr T Woods. Bolton